C000091914

9-

THE CONTEMPORARY NARRATIVE POEM

THE CONTEMPORARY
NARRATIVE POEM

Critical Crosscurrents

EDITED BY STEVEN P. SCHNEIDER

University of Iowa Press | Iowa City

University of Iowa Press, Iowa City 52242
Copyright © 2012 by the University of Iowa Press
www.uiowapress.org
Printed in the United States of America

Design by Ashley Muehlbauer

No part of this book may be reproduced or used in any form
or by any means without permission in writing from the
publisher. All reasonable steps have been taken to contact
copyright holders of material used in this book. The publisher would be pleased to make suitable arrangements
with any whom it has not been possible to reach.

The University of Iowa Press is a member of the Green Press
Initiative and is committed to preserving natural resources.

Printed on acid-free paper

Library of Congress Cataloging-in-Publication Data

The contemporary narrative poem: critical crosscurrents
/ edited by Steven P. Schneider.
p. cm.
Includes bibliographical references and index.
ISBN-13: 978-1-60938-125-7; ISBN-10: 1-60938-125-4 (pbk)
1. Narrative poetry, American—History and criticism.
I. Schneider, Steven P.
PS309.N37C66 2012
811'.0309—dc23 2012005964

To Ed Folsom
Mentor, Scholar, Friend

CONTENTS

ACKNOWLEDGMENTS

The Contemporary Narrative Poem: Critical Crosscurrents had its genesis in the annual Exploring Form and Narrative West Chester University Poetry Conference. Many thanks to the founders and organizers of the conference, Michael Peich and Dana Gioia, who invited me to lead several of the annual critical seminars. Thanks also to all those who participated in the seminars on the contemporary narrative poem and shared their ideas, which helped inform this book. Special thanks go to Robert B. Shaw, Gregory Dowling, April Lindner, and Daniel Tobin, who were regular participants in our ongoing discussions of contemporary narrative poems. Stephen Paul Miller and Christine Casson also participated in the West Chester critical seminar, and I am grateful for their contributions.

I am equally grateful to Alfred Bendixen and Jacqueline Brogan for their dedication to organizing the American Literature Association Symposium on American Poetry, held in Puerto Vallarta, Mexico. It was there that I met several of the other contributors to this book, who broadened its scope and range of critical concerns. Heartfelt gratitude goes as well to Ed Folsom, who has been a pillar of support of my critical work.

I am deeply appreciative of the work of my editors at the University of Iowa Press, Joe Parsons, Catherine Cocks, and Charlotte Wright. Joe's vision, commitment, and enthusiasm helped make this book possible, and Catherine's and Charlotte's meticulous attention to detail and steadfast encouragement shepherded the book to publication.

Finally, and most important, *abrazos* to my wife, Reefka, who has been an abiding source of love and support during the years of my work on this collection.

Permission to reprint from the following sources is hereby acknowledged:

"Belongings: 1" and other excerpts from *Belongings*, by Sandra M. Gilbert. Copyright © 2005 by Sandra M. Gilbert. Used by permission of W. W. Norton and Company.

"Out for the Elements," "Shore Lines," and "Millennium Letter" from *Collected Poems*, by Andrew Waterman. Copyright © 2000 by Andrew Waterman. Used by permission of Carcanet.

Excerpts from *The Golden Gate*, by Vikram Seth. Copyright © 1986 by Vikram Seth. Used by permission of Random House.

"Rifle, Colorado" and "Silt, Colorado" from *Capitalism*, by Campbell McGrath. Copyright © 1990 by Campbell McGrath. Used by permission of the author.

"A City in the Clouds," from *Florida Poems*, by Campbell McGrath. Copyright © 2002 by Campbell McGrath. Used by permission of the author.

"A Letter to James Wright," "A Map of Dodge County, Wisconsin," "Campbell McGrath," "Plums," and "The Prose Poem" from *Road Atlas: Prose and Other Poems*, by Campbell McGrath. Copyright © 1999 by Campbell McGrath. Used by permission of the author.

"March 10 (Barbarians): In Flight, Chicago to Miami" from *Seven Notebooks: Poems*, by Campbell McGrath. Copyright © 2008 by Campbell McGrath. Used by permission of the author.

"Sunset, Route 90, Brewster County, Texas" from *American Noise*, by Campbell McGrath. Copyright © 1993 by Campbell McGrath. Used by permission of the author.

"The Bob Hope Poem" from *Spring Comes to Chicago*, by Campbell McGrath. Copyright © 1996 by Campbell McGrath. Used by permission of the author.

"About Campbell McGrath" from *Ploughshares*, by Joel Brouwer. Copyright © by Joel Brouwer. Used by permission of the author.

"Accordion Music and Raw Profusion" from *Parnassus*, by Joel Brouwer. Copyright © by Joel Brouwer. Used by permission of the author.

"My People," "Chemistry 101," "The Penol Cures," "Out of Slave's Ransom," "The Prayer of Miss Budd," "Watkins Laundry and Apothecary," "The Perceiving Self," "From an Alabama Farmer," and "The Sweet-Hearts" from *Carver: A Life in Poems*, by Marilyn Nelson. Copyright © 2001 by Marilyn Nelson. Published by Front Street Books, an imprint of Boyds Mills Press. Reprinted by permission.

"Colonel Charles Russell Lowell 1835–64" from *Collected Poems*, by Robert Lowell. Copyright © 2003 by Harriet Lowell and Sheridan Lowell. Reprinted by permission of Farrar, Straus and Giroux.

Excerpts from *The Red Virgin* by Stephanie Strickland. Copyright © 1993 by the Board of Regents of the University of Wisconsin System. Reprinted by permission of the University of Wisconsin Press.

Excerpts from *Thomas and Beulah* by Rita Dove. Copyright © 1986 by Rita Dove. Used by permission of the author.

"Parting" and "Sweetened Change" from *A Coast of Trees*, by A. R. Ammons. Copyright © 1981 by A. R. Ammons. Used by permission of W. W. Norton and Company.

"Mountain Talk," from *Collected Poems 1951–1971*, by A. R. Ammons. Copyright © 1965 by A. R. Ammons. Used by permission of W. W. Norton and Company.

"Ballad" from *Diversifications*, by A. R. Ammons. Copyright © 1975 by A. R. Ammons. Used by permission of W. W. Norton and Company.

Excerpts from *Tape for the Turn of the Year*, by A. R. Ammons. Copyright © 1965 by A. R. Ammons. Used by permission of W. W. Norton and Company.

"The Waleboat Struck," "At Dawn in 1098," and "Turning" from *Ommateum: With Doxology*, by A. R Ammons. Copyright © 1955 by A. R. Ammons. Copyright renewed 1983 by A. R. Ammons. Used by permission of W. W. Norton and Company.

"The Double Dream of Spring" and "The Skaters" from *The Mooring of Starting Out*, by John Ashbery. Copyright © 1986 by John Ashbery. Used by permission of the author.

"Self-Portrait in a Convex Mirror" from *Selected Poems*, by John Ashbery. Copyright © 1986 by John Ashbery. Used by permission of the author.

"View of Delft" from *Chinese Whispers*, by John Ashbery. Copyright © 2002 by John Ashbery. Used by permission of the author.

Excerpts and image from "Writing," in *Tabula Rosa*, by Rachel Blau DuPlessis. Copyright © 1997, 2012 by Rachel Blau DuPlessis. Used by permission of the author, with thanks to Potes and Poets Press.

Excerpts and image from "Etruscan Pages," in *when new time folds up*, by Kathleen Fraser. Copyright © 1993 by Kathleen Fraser. Used by permission of the author.

Excerpts and image from *Crowd and not evening or light*, by Leslie Scalapino. Copyright © 1992, Estate of Leslie Scalapino. All rights reserved.

ter, Pennsylvania. From its inception in 1994, the West Chester conference, Exploring Form and Narrative, has provided a forum in which poets and critics devoted to poetic form and contemporary narrative poetry can pursue critical engagement with the topic and each other. Founded by Dana Gioia, former chairman of the National Endowment for the Arts, and Michael Peich, founder and publisher of Aralia Press, the conference offers a variety of workshops on poetic form taught by poets, as well as several critical seminars that foster conversation between poets and scholars.

I had the pleasure of leading five of these critical seminars from 2001 to 2005. Several were devoted to the book-length narrative poem and the narrative lyric sequence. My goal in leading these seminars was to look closely at the claims being made for New Narrative, or "Expansive Poetry," which heralded a return to linear storytelling in the narrative poem, an engagement with history, and the lofty aspiration of moving poetry and verse narrative to the center of American culture. These objectives for the Expansive Poetry movement were touted in the journal *The Reaper*, edited by Mark Jarman and Robert McDowell, and in essays such as Dana Gioia's "The Poet in an Age of Prose."[2] Whether one agreed or disagreed with Gioia's claim that "narrative poetry helped fill the void left by the diminishment of the common cultural context,"[3] the critic of contemporary poetry could not help but be fascinated by the phenomenon of contemporary poets turning back to the narrative poems of Robert Frost and Robinson Jeffers to write a new body of narrative poetry that notably included many book-length works.

In the West Chester seminars, we discussed a wide variety of contemporary narrative poems, including Andrew Hudgins's *After the Lost War*, Rita Dove's *Thomas and Beulah*, Marilyn Nelson's *Carver: A Life in Poems*, Brad Leithauser's *Darlington's Fall*, and David Mason's *The Country I Remember*, along with *The Cherokee Lottery*, by William Jay Smith, and Mark Jarman's *Iris*. The seminars attracted several prominent poets and critics, among them Gregory Dowling, Willard Gingerich, April Lindner, Stephen Paul Miller, Daniel Morris, Meg Schoerke, Robert B. Shaw, Christine Casson, Daniel Tobin, and William Wenthe. Three of these critics, Shaw, Lindner, and Dowling, have contributed essays to this book that grew directly out of the West Chester seminars.

The West Chester critical seminar, with its focus on New Narrative, has provided one among diverse lenses to view contemporary narrative poetry of the last thirty years. One year I slipped onto the seminar reading list the book-length poem *Garbage,* by A. R. Ammons—a subversive gesture, as *Garbage* is neither a verse narrative nor a linear story, but I wanted to see how it would fare in the atmosphere there. I was surprised to discover that the poet-critic Robert B. Shaw, who was associated with the New Formalist movement, liked the nonlinear, jazzy quality of *Garbage.* This led me to believe that while the New Narrative movement had gathered a head of steam in the 1980s and 1990s in American poetry, it was not the only story. In fact, there are many different "tellings" of narrative in contemporary American poetry, and this essay collection attempts to trace and illuminate the rich tapestry of narrative threaded through American poetry of the last thirty years.

My critical journey led me next to Puerto Vallarta, Mexico, where the American Literature Association held a poetry conference in December 2007.[4] The scholars who attended the ALA poetry meeting were a very different group from those who attended the West Chester seminar. Among those presenting papers were Robert von Hallberg, Ed Folsom, and Paul Christensen, critics whose major interests include respectively Charles Olson, Walt Whitman, and Clayton Eshleman.

Alfred Bendixen of Texas A&M University, the conference director, had invited me to put together a panel to explore narrative poetry from different critical perspectives. The essays by Christine Casson, Daniel Tobin, and Roger Gilbert grew out of this panel on narrative. In Puerto Vallarta I also heard insightful papers by Robert Miltner on the prose poems of Campbell McGrath, Jacqueline Vaught Brogan on Sandra Gilbert's narrative poem "Belongings," and Elisabeth Frost on experimental narrative poetry by women. All these critics added analytical depth and detail in revising their work for publication in this book.

The first section of essays is primarily concerned with formal strategies in contemporary narrative poetry. The opening essay by Jacqueline Vaught Brogan, "Narrative Strata in the Sonnet Sequence: Sandra M. Gilbert's 'Belongings,'" establishes the foundational theme for much of the discussion that follows in the other essays: the tension between lyric and narrative elements. The integration of lyrical intensity into narrative poetry was a challenge for writers like Virgil and Milton, just as it continues to be for writers of contemporary narrative poetry.

Brogan's essay reminds us that behind much modern and contemporary narrative poetry is "an appeal to the most canonical narrative poetic form, the epic." In Gilbert's "Belongings," Brogan discovers the incorporation of several epic conventions as well as a story—the onset of disease and debilitation, and ultimately the death of the poet's mother—consistent with the epic pattern in its chronology.

Brogan bristles at what she perceives to be the tensions between "adamant lyricists" and New Narrative poets, and praises Gilbert for combining "heightened moments of emotional intensity with straightforward narration." The intertextual literary dialogue Gilbert engages in "Belongings" by mobilizing a plethora of literary allusions primarily appeals to readers with academic training in the discipline, and so may disqualify the work from inclusion in the populist Expansive Poetry movement, which has staked a major claim to narrative poetry of the last three decades. Nevertheless, Brogan makes a compelling case for Gilbert's sonnet sequence as a powerful narrative of personal loss in a time bereft of traditional consolations.

Dana Gioia in his 1994 essay "The Poet in an Age of Prose" argues that various schools and "camps" within contemporary poetry have responded to the loss of a wide readership for poetry by creating their own audiences, often through some meaningful coalition outside the university. He sees African American poets, protest poets of the Vietnam War, and feminist poets as having in this way successfully created readerships for their work. For Gioia, the New Formalists' embrace of narrative poetry is one of their strategies to resist "poetry's cultural marginality." "Formalists," he writes, "chose to embrace rather than repudiate the broader cultural trends of their era. Rather than be bards of the poetry subculture, they aspired to become the poets for an age of prose." Thus, they turned to narrative poetry as "an inclusive literary mode that . . . had immediate appeal to the non-specialist reader of novels and short stories."[5]

The most ambitious account of this effort by formalist poets to write narrative poetry in an age of prose is Gregory Dowling's essay, "The Fascination of What's Difficult: Narrative Poetry in Strict Forms." Dowling begins his essay with an account of the negative reviews of Michael Lind's 1997 verse epic, *The Alamo*, and muses that Lind's failing is not so much one of subject matter, the Alamo's defenders, but rather form. Dowling observes that "the historical matter of the poem was at times awkwardly squeezed into the verse." Lind, however, is far from being alone in adopting such forms today. According to Dowling, "over the last two or three decades a number of long poems have been published that use such stanza forms as rhyme royal, ottava rima, the Spenserian stanza, or the Onegin stanza." His erudite essay, which moves everywhere, from Bryon to Chaucer, from Spenser to James Fenton and Pushkin, proposes and then, remarkably, offers answers to the question, "Is it possible for an extended narrative in complex rhyming stanzas to work successfully today?"

Part I concludes with Robert Miltner's excellent essay on the prose poem and the work in this genre by Campbell McGrath. McGrath established his reputation early as a writer of long poems in the tradition of Walt Whitman and Allen Ginsberg, garnering recognition and major awards, such as a Guggenheim Fellowship and a MacArthur Foundation grant. Yet, as Miltner points out, McGrath has also proved himself to be a master of the contemporary prose poem. Miltner's essay sheds light on how this hybrid, or "double-helix" form, may be used effectively to create "a fusion of 'literary' travelogues and the pop culture road trip narrative."

The essays in part 2 are concerned with how contemporary narrative poetry has incorporated historical and biographical elements. Poets such as Rita Dove, Daniel Hoffman, Andrew Hudgins, David Mason, Campbell McGrath, Marilyn Nelson, Robert Penn Warren, C. D. Wright, and Kevin Young, among many others, have all written narrative poems that carry the burden of conveying a story rooted in history, often focused through the life of a single character. Mason in his essay "Other Voices, Other Lives" places this work in a compelling critical context. "Fiction's advantage has usually been considered its interest in society as well as the lives of specific individuals, and poets can envy this, particularly when the lyric 'I' has become repetitious, nearly automatic."[6] Like Gioia, Mason sees narrative poetry as a way to recapture some of the ground lost to fiction, especially in an era when the first-person lyric poem has been so dominant. "By involving us in the nuances of social and individual problems," Mason argues, "narrative poetry can address issues beyond the narrow confines of the poet's life, or it can focus emotions too painfully personal to be revealed directly in a lyric."[7]

In his contribution to this book, "Contrived Corridors: History and Postmodern Poetry," Robert B. Shaw draws sharp distinctions between the practice of the modernist poets, such as Ezra Pound, T. S. Eliot, Hart Crane, and William Carlos Williams, and that of contemporary narrative poets who similarly look to history as a muse. April Lindner in "Eloquent Silences," a reading of Marilyn Nelson's *Carver: A Life in Poems*, Stephanie Strickland's *The Red Virgin*, and Rita Dove's *Thomas and Beulah*, argues that the lyric sequence effectively carries the burden of both history and narrative in these book-length poems. Christine Casson in her extended examination of Robert Penn Warren's *Audubon: A Vision* draws on the work of Paul Ricoeur in *Time and Narrative* to explore the ways in which human experience "takes on resonance through narrative constructions" that the narrative poet must wrest into form. Although the publication date of Robert Penn Warren's poem, 1969, is earlier than that of the other poems discussed in these essays, it is considered one of the most interesting narrative poems of the post–World War II era. Casson's theoretical insights into it are essential to our understanding of the contemporary narrative poem. She is concerned with "how, in the orchestration of the sequence, the poet creates a 'hierarchy of levels of temporalization,' each one determined by the significance of events."

The essays in part 3 argue for a primary role of consciousness in the contemporary narrative poem and explore how contemporary and experimental poets have redefined narrative in the context of their work. The essays by Daniel Tobin and Roger Gilbert explore new ways of viewing the relationship between consciousness and narrative poetry. Tobin draws on the pioneering work of the modernist fiction writer Virginia Woolf to reexamine the treatment of plot and consciousness in the work of modernist writers. Tobin then considers how these key elements intertwine in Hart Crane's *The Bridge*, a poem that incorporates multiple perspectives, and compares it with more recent narrative poems, such as Andrew Hudgins's *After the Lost War*. Roger Gilbert, who acknowledges that Ammons is best known for his lyric poems, such as "Corsons Inlet," also points out that in a 1980 interview, Ammons suggested that narrative is one of his greatest interests. Gilbert's essay focuses on three strains of narrative in Ammons's work, the mythic, the procedural, and the anecdotal. In taking this tack, Gilbert asks us to consider a different definition of narrative, one that includes any qualitative progression. In reading Ammons's work from a new critical perspective, Gilbert provides us with a fresh way of thinking about narrative poetry.

Both Stephen Paul Miller's and Elisabeth A. Frost's essays push the concept of narrative poetry to the edge and in this way contribute to the critical crosscurrents examined in this book. If the New Narrative poet-critics Gioia and Mason call for a return to linear narrative structures, and if Dowling questions how this can be done within strict verse forms, Miller and Frost examine poets who intentionally dispense with linearity and traditional form. Nevertheless, a thread (or "shred") of narrative persists in their work. In his essay on John Ashbery, Miller suggests that in a typical "narrative" poem by Ashbery, the stylistic play, "the poem's telling," becomes its true story. Thus, the impulse to tell a story is subverted by Ashbery, whose work dodges linear storytelling and closure "in favor of a perpetual abeyance."

The subject of Elisabeth Frost's essay is the serial poems of the avant-garde feminist poets Rachel Blau DuPlessis, Leslie Scalapino, and Kathleen Fraser. In their work we discover an interesting conjunction of art and poetry, handwriting and image. These poets embrace language not for its symbolic function but as material. They highlight the concrete aspects of words so that the words might function precisely as objects within the poem. While the linkage between poetry and artworks has historically often embodied a narrative impulse—to tell a story within or about the work of art—the materiality that surfaces in the works of these poets resists narrative. Nevertheless, as Frost points out, their work offers a radical perspective on narrative poetry. All three poets challenge and disrupt the notion of linear narrative, yet the threads of connection in their work—between handwriting and the human body, between margin and center, between writing and drawing—challenge us to rethink the concept of narrative poetry.

This book, then, is the result of almost a decade of critical thinking about contemporary narrative poetry and represents a kaleidoscope of critical views and responses. The collection transcends narrow conceptions of narrative, antinarrative, or metanarrative by embracing poets of widely differing persuasion and ideology. The resurgence of narrative poetry is evidence, as Roland Barthes has suggested, that narrative "is present in every age, in every place, in every society; it begins with the very history of mankind and there nowhere is nor has been a people without narrative."[8]

Notes

1. For a selection of critical articles on contemporary narrative poetry, see Alan Shapiro, "In Praise of the Impure: Narrative Consciousness in Poetry," *Triquarterly* 81 (Spring–Summer 1991): 5–31; Jonathan Holden, "Contemporary Verse Storytelling," *Southern Review* 30.4 (Spring 1991): 376–399; Thomas B. Byers, "The Closing of the American Line: Expansive Poetry and Ideology," *Contemporary Literature* 33.2 (1992): 396–413; Ellen Bryant Voight, "Narrative and Lyric: Structural Corruption," *Southern Review* 30.4 (Autumn 1994): 725–741; Mark Jarman, "Robinson, Frost,

and Jeffers and the New Narrative Poetry," in *New Expansive Poetry*, ed. R. S. Gwynn (Ashland, OR: Story Line Press, 1999), 188–198; Brian McHale, "Weak Narrativity: The Case of Avant-Garde Narrative Poetry," *Narrative* 9.2 (May 2001): 161–167; Tony Hoagland, "Fear of Narrative and the Skittery Poem of Our Moment," *Poetry* 187.6 (March 2006): 508–519; and Natasha Sajé, "Narrative and Poetry," *Writer's Chronicle* 41.1 (September 2008): 62–72. The most comprehensive anthology of narrative poems that reflects a resurgence of interest in story is titled *Story Hour: Contemporary American Narrative Poems* and is edited by Sonny Williams (Ashland, OR: Story Line Press, 2004). For book-length studies of contemporary narrative poetry, see Kevin Walzer's *The Ghost of Tradition: Expansive Poetry and Postmodernism* (Ashland, OR: Story Line Press (1998) and Gregory Dowling's *Someone's Road Home: Questions of Home and Exile in American Narrative Poetry* (Pasian, Italy: Campanotto, 2002).

2. Dana Gioia, "The Poet in an Age of Prose," in *After New Formalism: Poets on Form, Narrative, and Tradition*, ed. Annie Finch (Ashland, OR: Story Line Press, 1999), 31–41. First published in *Can Poetry Matter* (Saint Paul, MN: Graywolf Press, 1992), 221–231. For a selection of pertinent writings, see *The Reaper Essays*, ed. Mark Jarman and Robert McDowell (Ashland, OR: Story Line Press, 1996).

3. Gioia, "The Poet in an Age of Prose," 39.

4. The American Literature Association Symposium on American Poetry, Puerto Vallarta, Mexico, December 13–15, 2007. Conference director, Professor Alfred Bendixen, Texas A&M University.

5. Gioia, "The Poet in an Age of Prose," 34, 39.

6. David Mason, "Other Voices, Other Lives," in *After New Formalism: Poets on Form, Narrative, and Tradition*, ed. Annie Finch (Ashland, OR: Story Line Press, 1999), 107.

7. Ibid., 107–108.

8. Roland Barthes, "Introduction to the Structural Analysis of Narrative," in "On Narrative and Narratives," special issue, *New Literary History* 6.2 (Winter 1975): 237–272.

PART I

Formal Strategies in Contemporary Narrative Poems

NARRATIVE STRATA IN THE SONNET SEQUENCE

Sandra M. Gilbert's "Belongings"

JACQUELINE VAUGHT BROGAN

Whatever tensions or disagreements there may be between what we might call the "adamant lyricists" and the New Narrative poets described elsewhere in this book, the opening suite of sonnets called "Belongings" (in a volume of the same name) by Sandra M. Gilbert[1] unabashedly combines exquisite lyric poems and heightened moments of emotional intensity with the straightforward narration of the decline and eventual death of the poet's mother over the latter stages of a deteriorating condition very similar to Alzheimer's disease called Lewy body disease. Without question, we find ourselves reading a story in these poems, and a very personal one at that. With a dedication to the poet's mother, "in memory of Angela Maria Incoronata Caruso Mortola, May 21, 1903–January 14, 2001," "Belongings" traces with great tenderness and felt pain but also with unexpected humor the gradual loss of what the poet calls "the light of her mind," the "In-and-out sun" that "knows / and doesn't feels and forgets,"[2] concluding with a rage attributed to how her mother would have reacted to the priest's words at her funeral (a rage that would have satisfied Dylan Thomas's wish for his father). In between, the paranoia and pathos of dementia are unflinchingly recorded, along with both the embarrassment and humor spectators and family inevitably feel in the presence of this ravaging disease.

"Belongings" is, for all of its heartfelt longings and loss, brutally honest. And yet, with Gilbert's exquisite artistry, the sonnet sequence emerges with a complexity and, yes, a universality (to use an older term) that belie the short plot summary given above and that perhaps can best be understood neither from the plot nor from its exquisite lyrical moments but rather through the multiple and sophisticated narrative strategies that Gilbert employs. They are, in ascending order of importance: an appeal to the most canonical narrative poetic form, the epic; an intense internal narrative tension that is best understood in relation to the narrative theory of fiction (rather than of poetry); and, finally, a complicated invocation of past literary history, an invocation that itself comes to tell a much larger story than the personal narrative alone.

Unexpected Epic Conventions

As a sonnet sequence, "Belongings" might recall most immediately the sonnet sequences of Spenser or Shakespeare, or any number of other such famous collections (particularly previous coronas, a point to which I return later). Certainly, the expectation of love as the possible subject of a sonnet sequence is partially confirmed in this corona, dedicated as it is to the memory of the poet's mother. But even if this suite of poems tells a highly personal story, at the level of narrative structure "Belongings" most clearly if rather surprisingly follows the epic pattern, not only in terms of sheer chronological development but also by incorporating several epic conventions—among these, that an epic

— begins in medias res,
— treats a single heroic figure in a historic event,
— incorporates stylized descriptive devices, such as detailed descriptions of arms or armor,
— includes lesser characters who serve as foils to the hero (or, as here, heroine),
— incorporates panegyric and lament,
— follows to its conclusion the action set in motion at the beginning, and
— is concerned with the traditions and beliefs of its culture.[3]

The epic structure of "Belongings" is immediately signaled by the poem's beginning in medias res. With no explanation of the prior events that have led up to the situation, we are immediately confronted with a woman (the heroine of the sequence, who will turn out to be the poet's mother) who does not "want to die,"[4] though she is already in a hospital or institution, deep in the mental and physical decline accompanying Lewy body disease, all the while fighting for her life, her independence, and her dignity. Using the traditional epic technique of flashbacks, Gilbert then moves the scene within a couple of subsequent sonnets from a hospital (located in California, as we later find out) back to the mother's home in New York, incorporating references to friends and family from Brooklyn, and Sicily from even earlier years, along the way. In sonnet 5, the scene abruptly shifts back to the present, as Gilbert describes the horrors and indignities of "soiled bed pads," the "wheelchair," and "bruises stains and spills" in the hospital, while the mother fights, "flails and shrieks" "*Tuono di Dio!*"[5] In a subsequent flashback within a flashback, sonnet 9 recounts earlier memories of Jackson Heights, "one of the better blocks in New York City," when the "mother father daughter"—the poet—were quite young: "my father's face blade-thin in sepia / my baby self in flounces or undressed / from times when she was poor but happier."[6]

It is in this sonnet that the poet first identifies herself as the daughter, a crucial point to be elaborated in the next section. Thereafter, starting from this deepest personal memory, Gilbert makes the events from sonnet 11 move rapidly forward—from the first moments of the mother's mind's unraveling to her being forced to give up her home on the East Coast and give away all her belongings, to being put on a plane to the West Coast, where she will be institutionalized (all this in one sonnet)—continuing in subsequent sonnets with several grim and also humorous experiences, culminating in the conclusion that the opening action of the sequence has set in motion—the mother's death in sonnet 13, the penultimate one, and her subsequent burial back on the East Coast in the final sonnet 14.

In terms of the chronology of events, the epic pattern is clearly the overarching narrative structure controlling the sonnet sequence, even if the heroine of this sequence is a much-deflated figure when compared with the heroes of traditional epics. And that alteration acts as a critical commentary about our contemporary culture, a culture that seems largely to have lost belief in the possibility of heroic actions, even to have lost belief in belief itself. Gilbert incorporates several other traditional elements of the epic, all to similar effect. For example, as in most of the major epics, the heroine (caught in medias res) has indeed left her home, has gone beyond the confines of normal society to engage in her struggle, and will eventually return home, accompanied by a muted requiem, as it were, in the form of the priest's blessing in the final sonnet (however ironically it is presented):

> the priest says the words she scorned she didn't believe
> (she has to be blessed to belong to holy ground)
> and O she would scold us if she were still alive![7]

In addition to this clearly deflated but still epic plotline and its predictable but necessary panegyric and lament, Gilbert includes other epic elements, such as the details of her mother's "arms and armor" with which she defends her identity—her "belongings"—pearls, bookcases, rugs, silver, bracelets, mahogany, the television, vacuum cleaner—all those things that the mother ironically says "must go on / . . . must / survive outlast her."[8] As in a traditional epic, Gilbert also employs minor characters who serve as foils to her mother (though this relation becomes more complicated in following sections of this essay since one of these characters, in contrast to traditional epics, is the poet herself, who appears within the narrative as a persona, the actual daughter). As opposed to the elevated nature of most traditional minor characters (such as Patroclus in *The Iliad*), the minor characters in "Belongings" are largely reduced to the ghosts of family members that the mother hallucinates and feels compelled to speak with, or imagined thieves that the mother projects in paranoid delusions, or lascivious couples "*screwing* / coarse as goats in corners" of her hospital room and "back home," "behind her lovely bookcase."[9] In contrast, there are some anonymous, well-meaning but also irritating nurses, and, of course, the actual doctor, who suddenly appears in the opening sonnet, mocking the mother's desire not to die:

> and the doctor laughing "Cute old lady said
> she doesn't care about the why and wherefore
> she just doesn't want to die . . ."[10]

Seen as foils, all of these characters, imagined or real, serve not to heighten the mother's potentially heroic capacities but rather to underscore her enforced and increasing decline in a battle impossible to win.

Of the epic elements listed above, however, there is one in particular that deserves more discussion, the expectation that the work will be concerned with the traditions and beliefs of a given culture. Although at the level of plot, Gilbert's sonnet sequence seems exclusively devoted to describing a personal narrative, ultimately "Belongings" is a finely wrought examination and exposé of our larger culture and the diminished ways in which we experience death and mourning in modern times. Thus, "Belongings" does offer a cultural commentary, but one that the poet herself both records and resists. To examine this final point, it is especially helpful to consider a particular narrative theory—of fiction, not poetry—elaborated by Peter Rabinowitz in *Before Reading: Narrative Conventions and the Politics of Interpretation.*[11]

An Unexpected Application of Theory

While the theoretical turn in literary studies may well have had its heyday, one of its most lasting consequences was to break down, permanently, many artificial, even arbitrary boundaries between certain kinds of writing. (In this regard, I find the current stand-off between the new lyricists and New Narrative poets with which I began this chapter a curiously reactionary disagreement.) In any case, the central tenet of Rabinowitz's theory of fiction in *Before Reading* proves especially revealing in understanding the internal tension in Gilbert's "Belongings" and the ways in which that tension is exploited in the sequence form to tell a larger cultural narrative.

Significantly, the whole volume *Belongings* is dedicated to Gilbert's parents, "to whom," Gilbert says, "I first belonged." "Belongings," then, is a word with many strata, one of which is clearly self-referential. In fact, the entire volume, which begins with her mother's death and concludes with another sonnet sequence devoted to her husband's unexpected death more than a decade before, is very much the story of the poet, who is also daughter and wife, trying to negotiate the possibility of meaning, especially the meaning of death and mourning, in a culture that wants to ostracize death itself and muffle any sustained expressions of grief.[12] Consequently, as readers, we encounter emptiness, despair, and the irreducible finality of death, and simultaneously the ordering presence of the poet herself, attempting to give dignity and even a kind of transcendence to the many bleak events and feelings she records. This is not to say that the volume is monolithic in either subject or mood. There are many humorous moments, both in the sequence "Belongings" and in the volume as a whole. Consider, for example, the humorous exposure of family dynamics in which the poet's mother-in-law has uttered, in the title of the poem, this dismissive pronouncement: "No thank you, I don't care for artichokes."[13]

The humor in the poems, despite their frequently grim subjects, signals the internal tension that is characteristic throughout. Here, Rabinowitz's distinction between a narrator in a fictional work and the author of a given fictional work—as well as his distinction between the differing audiences for each—is especially useful. As summarized by James Phelan, Rabinowitz argues that in fiction, "The narrative audience is the one implicitly addressed by the narrator; it takes on the beliefs and values that the narrator ascribes to it. . . . The authorial audience takes on the beliefs and the knowledge that the author assumes it has, including the knowledge that it is reading a constructed text."[14] The latter sentence is remarkable for two insights, especially when applied to "Belongings." First, it suggests that the author (in this case Gilbert) assumes that we as readers have a certain set of beliefs and values with which we readily align ourselves, and second, it suggests that in that alignment, we will simultaneously recognize that we are reading a constructed text. I should stress that a constructed text is not to be confused with "fiction" in the reductive sense of that word, that is, the "facts" are not real, are not true, or are wrong. The "facts" of the sonnet sequence we are attending are altogether too painfully true. Instead, I would argue that when it comes to this particular poetry, attention to the fact that the sequence is a constructed text allows us to pay attention to the poet (the *scop*, as it were) shaping the presentation of the story and to the fabrication (in the etymological sense of "making a fabric") that the poet is weaving—a kind of tapestry that offers a story larger than the obvious plot and one that is at times both distressing and triumphant.

Rabinowitz's larger thesis also allows us to see that the various audiences of the whole volume, but of "Belongings" in particular, may well divide into a narrative audience, one that responds to the diminished beliefs and traditions in our modern, largely mechanistic culture within which the woman Sandra (the narrator) has experienced the events described, and an authorial audience that, whether by accident or education, has access to a literary tradition or culture the poet Gilbert is drawing on to shape—and give meaning to—this story. In this way, "Belongings" is deeply concerned with our culture's diminishing traditions and beliefs in recent times, even as Gilbert is simultaneously recording and resisting that very diminishment.

If Rabinowitz's theory of reading fiction is truly applicable to this poetic sequence, we should expect to find within the text a schism between narrator and author, persona and poet, or between the woman, whom we might call "Sandra," and the poet, whom we might call "Gilbert." And indeed, that schism is made overt in sonnet 9 of the sequence, at the moment of deepest memory, in which the psychic disjunction that the actual person Sandra felt at the time of looking at (or remembering looking at) a picture of herself and family when much younger is matched by the ironic conjunction Gilbert creates between the persona's and the mother's disjointed sense of time. That is to say, it is deeply distressing at the personal level, but curiously satisfying at the aesthetic level, that the very temporal disjunction of *self* Gilbert records in this scene mimics the disjunction evidenced in the mother's loss of the present and her entrapment in past memories (perhaps the most horrible effect of Lewy body disease):

> Yet O it's nice that all her things are pretty
> her smile blazes back in Jackson Heights
> (on one of the better blocks in New York City)
> her beautiful apartment basks and waits
> a hush of rugs a drawn Venetian blind
> keeping the silence keeping the bars of shadow
> gathered like silent guardians around
> the hanging shelf the Wedgewood the piano
> and there the family photographs are massed
> my father's face blade-thin in sepia
> my baby self in flounces or undressed
> from times when she was poor but happier
> belongings blurry as if underwater
> bearing the prints of mother father daughter[15]

Here we see the narrator "looking" at a memory of looking at photographs in a place remembered by the mother while the author, the one who is shaping the remembrance of this ironic moment, creates a textual mise en abyme (a phrase appropriately popularized during the theory movement decades ago)[16] that parodies in a very painful and personal way the temporal disjunction caused by the disease itself. The horrible irony here is that the mother's memories have also triggered and become the narrator's memories, creating an intensely unsettling conjunction that the poet describes as a kind of death, "underwater." (It is quite fitting that in a section called "Haunting Photographs" in *Death's Door*, a concurrently written prose volume, Gilbert describes the ghostly life-in-death, death-in-life phenomenon experience we have when looking at any picture, whether of ourselves, loved ones, or strangers.)[17] That "Sandra" is, at some level, reduced to an object within the poem is signaled by the fact that Gilbert only calls "herself" "baby" or "daughter" in this poem, eschewing the subject pronoun "I" altogether. (In fact, the pronoun "I" is rarely used in the entire sequence, which comes as something of a surprise, given the deeply personal nature of the corona.) In addition, in this sonnet, the loss of the mother's "memory" (that is, the loss of awareness of the present) is experienced by "Sandra" as a kind of death, even before the mother dies, of both mother and self—an awful moment, which then comes to be recorded by Gilbert only after the mother has died. We see, therefore, in this sonnet, and with acute clarity, the personal pain and loss Sandra has experienced for herself and her mother and simultaneously the poetic expertise of Gilbert, who is able, self-reflectively, to render in words and with great dignity what is, finally, beyond words altogether.

Literary Tradition as Narrative History

Rabinowitz's distinction between the author and narrator in fiction and between their respective, distinct audiences goes a long way toward explaining the power of this sonnet sequence. For in a way distinct from but complementary to the way she incorporates the epic temporal structure into "Belongings," Gilbert the poet incorporates numerous textual allusions in this sonnet sequence, engaging in an intertextual dialogue that ultimately comes to record a much larger story than the narrower one that the daughter or narrator within the narrative line finally tells. That is to say, while the narrator may experience death as something inconsolable and without meaning (that is, in the way that Gilbert would argue our modern culture does),[18] the poet nonetheless appeals to a literary tradition that suggests the possibility of a kind of consolation, even communion. In this way, Gilbert at least partially inverts the place and function of narrative and lyric expectations that critic Bonnie Costello has elsewhere attributed to Wallace Stevens and Elizabeth Bishop. As Costello writes in "Narrative

Secrets, Lyric Openings," "For both poets, narrative is a way of expressing their sense that we live in time and wish to give shape to that passage, that we long to bring our pursuits to fruition and conclusion, to consummate our desires. Poetry, on the other hand, is a way of resisting the end, a way of continuing or imaginatively staying in place, and also a way of releasing the world from the distortions of causal logic, back into its secrets."[19] In contrast, for Gilbert, the narrative line, experienced by "Sandra" as a participant in the drama, is without closure, without consummation, whereas the poetic dimension shaped by the poet offers closure, even a tentative consolation.

For example, when approached formally rather than either chronologically or theoretically, the most striking aspect of "Belongings" is that it is deeply concatenated: the last line of each sonnet becomes (with only minor alterations at times) the first line of the next sonnet. This concatenation achieves formal closure as the final lines of the entire sequence, uttered as requiem for the mother's death—"no *Tuono di dio* no bolt so fierce and true / as the light of her mind that felt that thought that knew"[20]—return to the opening lines of the first sonnet, in which the mother is described as experiencing the "In-and-out sun like the light of her mind that knows / and doesn't feels and forgets."[21] The circle, as it were, is complete, though one could argue that the chain created by this formal arrangement also ensures that the grief is never-ending, going on and on, ad infinitum.

As a concatenated sequence rather than as a chronological sequence, "Belongings" emerges as a corona, quite possibly recalling the famous prologue to John Donne's *Holy Sonnets,* the formal structure of which reflects an older and particular way of telling the rosary.[22] But to my mind, both the concatenated structure and the larger theme of "Belongings" most clearly invoke "The Pearl" and the Pearl Poet, who was himself recording his own mourning (in his case, the death of his daughter instead of his mother). But whereas the Pearl Poet is persuaded that his grief is unnecessary and even wrong in the face of the fact of eternal life, Gilbert finds no consolation for death in this sequence, nor does she give any to her readers. As in *Death's Door*, we are living in a spiritually diminished culture whose forces have constructed what she calls, citing Wallace Stevens, "the mythology of modern death."[23] As Stevens says elsewhere of a person living "in a bad time," "Without understanding, he *belongs to it*" (emphasis mine)[24]—a remark that could well apply to the narrator in the sonnet sequence and to us, the narrative audience, identifying with apparently inconsolable loss.

Gilbert does give us two consolations in "Belongings." First, she manages to create, often through the unexpected humor, the full embodiment of a woman who was incredibly strong in spirit (even with Lewy body disease) when alive. Second, against the stark pain of the subject, the mother's decline and death, she produces a work of such fine intertextual play that it is almost a perverse delight to read it—and that, I think, is part of the point. Such delight is matched, at the level of plot or narrative, precisely by the humor, including the mother's first words in the first sonnet—"I just don't want to die not scared not that / I just don't want to and I told the doctor!"—a humor that is characteristically offset by the "shadows on the walls / that gather where the light collects and falls."[25] The next sonnet begins, "They gather where the light collects and falls,"[26] the pronoun "they" now referring to the imagined ghosts of her family whom the mother sees and with whom she speaks in her bedroom. And so the real saga of the mother's decline begins, and ends, with her death and funeral.

On the way from its irruptive beginning to its logical conclusion, the sequence incorporates countless other texts and authors, ultimately creating a different story, at least in part, from that told in the obvious plotline. Appropriately, the "prologue" to the whole volume, "Afternoon Walk: The Sea Ranch," sets the tone for this alternative story by invoking a literary knowledge, and a love for it, that Gilbert and her deceased husband Elliot once shared:

Late light, uneven mole-gnawed meadow,
gullies, freshets, falls, whose start and speckle
Hopkins would have loved—and you—you too,
who loved the sheen and shade, the forest dapple
where grass meets cypress just beyond the house—[27]

Addressing "you" (Elliot), Gilbert speaks intimately, implying the possibility of communication between herself and Elliot's spirit (if only a memory) after death. Yet what may be equally important here is that Gilbert also creates a kind of shared intimacy between herself and her readers—us, now the authorial audience—as we recognize in the lines above the kind of alliteration, sprung rhythm, and vocabulary characteristic of Hopkins even before he is named. We are invited to share, therefore, in a private intimacy and in a larger public and literary history, the words of which (in the latter case) are precisely what make such intimacy possible. In this regard, I find it not accidental that the particular words of this opening sonnet recall most immediately Hopkins's "Of Pied Beauty," a sonnet that begins "Glory be to God for dappled things—" and concludes "He fathers-forth whose beauty is past change: Praise him."[28] In this sonnet, written in 1877, Hopkins is able to rest firmly in that consolation that traditional faith had provided for centuries, a consolation neither the poet of nor the persona in "Belongings" finally experiences or shares.

Immediately after the allusion to Hopkins, Gilbert opens the concluding sestet of that same sonnet with the phrase, "This time of year," clearly invoking Shakespeare's most famous sonnet on love and the way that the passage of time and the ultimate terminus of death make that love so precious. The sonnet concludes with lines that allude to the ending of Wallace Stevens's "Sunday Morning," though (as with Shakespeare) neither the poet nor the poem is named, thus making the shared knowledge that Gilbert creates between herself and her audience all the more intimate:

> light seems to slow
> and sorrow as the meadow turns its face
> into your unlived season, the winter hollow
> where only a steep sky, in quarter inches,
> adjusts descending sun, ascending branches.[29]

I am reminded here of a very similar movement in the final lines of "Sunday Morning": "And, in the isolation of the sky, / At evening, casual flocks of pigeons make / Ambiguous undulations as they sink, / Downward to darkness, on extended wings."[30] But whereas Stevens, who was also questioning traditional faith in this famous poem, finds consolation in the delights of this earth, delights possible only with temporality—which necessitates death (so that he can finally call "Death" the "mother of beauty"[31])—Gilbert subtly rejects even that consolation with the subjunctive verb "seems" above, thereby undercutting the pathetic fallacy of nature to which Stevens appeals. Clearly, the dialogues, even disagreements, with other poets that Gilbert is having in this sonnet are myriad, as they are throughout the following sonnet sequence for her mother. But even as she undermines the traditional faith of many of the works to which she alludes in her sonnet sequence, Gilbert makes her own grief all the more potent and present in this shared literary story. At the same time, without ever stating it directly, Gilbert manages in her deft use of both past and contemporary texts to tell the story of that very loss of traditional faith that has come to mark our spiritually impoverished modern world.

For example, in addition to the Pearl Poet, Shakespeare, and Stevens, "Belongings" incorporates a wide array of poems and poets, including (among others) "The Seafarer," Sylvia Plath, Dylan Thomas, W. B. Yeats, John Keats, Andrew Marvel, Percy Bysshe Shelley, Elizabeth Bishop, and even one of Ezra Pound's cantos where (as he says of his daughter) "What thou lovest well remains."[32] Yet in reference to the latter, once again in Gilbert's hands, we are left only with the mother's "remains"[33]—her body—as well as such other remains as her "belongings," which the mother has said "must go on / [. . .] must / survive outlast her."[34] The continued existence of her material possessions after her death is presented in the sequence as something of a horrible truth, as it were, but without either Hopkins's or Keats's attendant "beauty." In a nearly ruthless exposure of human folly, in the seventh sonnet of the sequence Gilbert records how her mother, while delusionally imagining thieves, begs of the family, "don't let my *belongings* go astray."[35]

A full iteration of the textual interplay of "Belongings" is beyond the scope of this essay. But I would like to demonstrate, with attention to a few more references to anterior texts that Gilbert incorporates into the body of this sequence, that the accumulation of these allusions and the intertextual play and dialogue that emerge over the course of the sequence create a narrative of their own, one that is at once the author's and one that we are invited to witness and retell. Before doing so, however, I would like to note one unexpected aspect of her use of, or recourse to, the sonnet genre itself that is crucial to understanding the tone, purpose, and power of this work.

As is reasonably well known, the majority of accomplished American sonneteers of the twentieth century employed the sonnet form in highly subversive ways, to undermine variously the class, gendered, or racial norms that had come to be associated with sonnets in the nineteenth century. (That Petrarch's and Shakespeare's sonnets are deeply subversive is beside the point. By the nineteenth century, the sonnet was associated so fixedly with a conservative and narrow ideology that William Carlos Williams would come to declare sonnets "fascistic.") For example, as Gillian Huang-Tiller carefully argues throughout "The Power of the Meta-Genre,"[36] e. e. cummings undermined the expectation that the province of the sonneteer was that of the educated gentile; Edna St. Vincent Millet, that of educated males; and Countee Cullen, that of the white establishment. All three used what had come to be regarded as a rigid, fixed form to undermine precisely the imposition of form (in whatever ideological guise). For a woman who, when wearing her critical hat, is so clearly a feminist and so clearly alert to subversive expressions in the hands and pens of women poets, it may come as something of a shock that Gilbert's sonnets are not, finally, subversive of the actual genre *as genre*. While Gilbert does play with form, by adding unusual spaces in the place of traditional punctuation as ironic "breathing points" in the sonnets and by frequently writing lines of twelve syllables instead of the expected ten (a strategy that I think is intended to invoke Jewish instead of Christian numerology at times),[37] these sonnets seem to honor tradition or, shall we say, our canon, without irony or intrusion at all. The overarching tone of the sequence is in keeping with the epigraph of the entire volume:

> For the ones to whom
> I first belonged:
> Alexis Joseph Mortola
> and
> Angela Maria Caruso[38]

Here, respect for genre and for generation actually merge.

However, if Gilbert's sonnets are not tonally subversive or subversive of the genre itself, they are nonetheless thematically so—meaning that over and over, Gilbert denies our traditional recourse to faith in the face of death, even as she alludes to many previous poems that have promised consolation (as well as to a few others, largely contemporary, that do not). Of the many possibilities to explore, I have chosen five particularly strong allusions for the larger story they collectively tell to the author's "authorial audience."

First, in much the same way that the formal structure invokes "The Pearl," only to deflate its spiritual message, the imagery in sonnet 12 recalls that of "The Seafarer," another famously complex poem about metaphysical meaning, only to undermine the final, traditional Christian consolation found there. I cite the full opening octet of Gilbert's sonnet, with special attention to the last two lines:

> At sundown tantrums shake the sunset west
> the nurses turn her toward the flashing window
> "See the flowers? See the pretty bird's nest?"

bushes tug in tubs on the patio
where a night wind rises over Astroturf
batters the waiting tables chairs and wheelchairs
as if they stood in a swirl of Pacific surf
whose icy water glitters darkens clears[39]

Those imagined and therefore entirely unnecessary waters are imagined precisely by the poet (and not by the mother in some paranoid projection), recalling the archetypal story of a man who, on a physical journey alone over "ice-cold" seas and with nothing but its wrenching sounds, also makes a spiritual journey of self-alienation from this world in order to understand and eventually arrive at an eternal home. As awful as the actual seafaring section is in its dark imagery and intense isolation, the seafarer himself in that famous Anglo-Saxon poem is autonomous and self-motivating, seeking and finding spiritual satisfaction. The irony here is obvious: the mother, who is clearly not alone, has no autonomy as a direct consequence of Lewy body disease and is therefore incapable of making any kind of decision or journey, whether physical or spiritual. Nor, the sonnet seems to suggest, is there any spiritual dimension to be had to begin with. At its end, life may be reduced to nothing more than "lukewarm grown-up mush."[40]

While "The Seafarer" offers the most compelling points of comparison with this particular point in the sonnet sequence, the imagery here also recalls Elizabeth Bishop's "At the Fishhouses" (and Bishop may well have had "The Seafarer" in mind herself when she wrote that poem). While describing an "old man . . . netting" in "the gloaming almost invisible," Bishop turns again and again to the "Cold dark deep and absolutely clear, / the clear gray icy water. . . ."[41]

Certainly, the imagery is very similar to the poetic intrusion Gilbert makes in the lines above. In addition, once again in "At the Fishhouses" we have a persona asking metaphysical questions as she faces a harsh physical landscape, but without the Seafarer's consolation in an immutable absolute. (Actually, Bishop clearly undercuts Christianity in this poem with these lines: "Bluish, associating with their shadows, / a million Christmas trees stand / waiting for Christmas.")[42] Instead, in a tone highly resonant with Gilbert's overall sequence, Bishop concludes her own famous poem with the devastating remark that all "our knowledge is historical, flowing, and flown"—as is already the case, in Gilbert's sonnet, of the mother's memory. In this way the mother's condition comes to encapsulate our whole human condition—one in which our very consciousness, aware of its own impending ending, is aware of the possibility of ending as nothing. No afterlife. Nothing.

Aside from the intriguing reference to those dark, glittering, icy waters in sonnet 12, the actual scene (the hospital room) repeats an earlier scene described in sonnet 5, in which the physical indignities many of us may be forced to endure with age are intensified by the presence of grotesque and mechanical objects in an increasingly institutionalized and depersonalized world:

> The curses learned in childhood have their uses
> *Tuono di Dio!* she swears when they strip her bare
> to bathe her *Tuono di Dio!* when the nurses
> slide the soiled bed pads to the floor
> or prop her in the wheelchair to be fed
> thunder of God echoes along the halls
> when she tries to fight the husky nurse's aide
> come to sponge her bruises stains and spills[43]

In imagery, tone, and strategy, these lines (and those from sonnet 12 as well) sound very similar to Sylvia Plath's "Berck-Plage," a relatively contemporary elegy that Gilbert herself has described as offering "crucial, if disquieting, insights not just into its author's life and her often death-drenched work but more generally into our contemporary poetry of mourning."[44]

"Berck-Plage," set by the sea, juxtaposes the natural world with a hospital—what Gilbert calls "the ubiquitous medicalization of the place"—which both Plath and Gilbert see as becoming an increasingly nightmarish modern reality[45]:

> *Tubular steel wheelchairs, aluminum crutches.*
> *Such salt-sweetness. Why should I walk*
>
> *Beyond the breakwater, spotty with barnacles?*
> *I am not a nurse, white and attendant,*
> *[. . .]*
> *On a striped mattress in one room*
>
> *An old man is vanishing.*[46]

As Gilbert says of this poem, in a summary that well applies to her own sonnet here, "Wheelchairs, crutches, even a surgeon with a clinical 'mirrory eye': all have been assembled to stave off death, but nonetheless a representative old man is 'vanishing.' "[47]

And yet the parallels between Plath and Gilbert noted here may be all the more important for pointing us to something else Gilbert says of Plath's poetry: "All the works on which I've been meditating here are of course *poems*, which is to say they are in some sense *fictions*. . . . They needn't necessarily predict any particular life course or, more specifically, any pull toward death. What they do show, however, is that Plath's career as a poet, an elegist, and a metaphysician was shaped by the same tide of existential despair that has engulfed many other late twentieth-century elegies, although it sounds with an unusually 'long hiss of distress' in 'Berck-Plage.' "[48] The same can be said of the narrator "Sandra" in "Belongings" and of ourselves when we occupy the place of the narrative audience. And yet the poet Gilbert is still resisting this existential despair in her construction of her own larger "fiction." For example, in terms of Plath's elegy, Gilbert finds the eerie "estrangement" Plath creates in her poem from the deceased person (Percy Key) whom she is supposedly eulogizing to be even more "unnerving" and even more "nightmarish" than the scene described.[49] In contrast, in "Belongings" there is no estrangement from the mother, who, for all her faults, foibles, and weaknesses, emerges over the course of the sequence as a woman of tremendous spirit. In that sense, "Belongings" eventually makes a powerful poetic commentary on the turn of a larger modern culture that has abandoned the kind of faith and attendant satisfactions articulated in "The Seafarer," "The Pearl," and "Of Pied Beauty" to embrace instead bleak expressions of nihilism.

We should be careful to note, however, that Gilbert is not facilely returning to an earlier poetic tradition of privileging art over nature (or the world of aesthetic permanence over the natural world of temporality, fruition, and decay). For example, in sonnet 10, which alludes to Keats's "Ode on a Grecian Urn," Gilbert undercuts even that poetic consolation with the literal and literary collapse of that elegant urn to this tattered object:

> [. . .] the gray hooked rug where silent bluebirds sang
> and a rabbit ran away among the trees
> but never vanished never could escape

whatever chased him from the knitted haze
a scary thing[50]

While the authorial audience may share something of an intellectual community with the author, Sandra Gilbert, as a real woman in this contemporary world, is not letting herself or ourselves off so easily. And that, too, is
part of the point. Just as Gilbert offers absolutely no assurance that there
is an afterlife, no ready-made consolation in the face of death, the sonnet
sequence and the entire volume in which it appears are intensely ambivalent
about the final value of art and literature, even as they embrace an entire
literary tradition without which that ambivalence could not be expressed.

If this threatens to become too abstract, Gilbert continues to make such
complicated thoughts and questions deeply personal in the complicated figure of her mother. Here I would like to turn to the final sestet of Sonnet 5,
discussed in part above:

embarrassed we shiver in the corridor
while she flails and shrieks for the police
"*Tuono di Dio!* Call the police!" God's thunder
will scorch us if we leave her in this place
away from her apartment calm and peace
away from her belongings purse and keys[51]

Although the mother's rage is horribly futile in the enforced conditions
surrounding her affliction with this horrible disease, her spirit remains
indomitable, especially when contrasted with the seeming passivity of
Dylan Thomas's father in his own elegy, "Do Not Go Gentle into That
Good Night," in which Thomas urges his father to "Rage, rage against
the dying of the light"[52] (implying, therefore, a modern metaphysics of
existential despair in which rage is a final gesture, doomed to obliteration
and meaningless itself).

Even if the mother's rage in sonnet 5 appears, at least initially, not only
impotent and futile but even ridiculous to the "embarrassed" narrator Sandra, Gilbert the poet changes both the meaning of rage and of the dying
light in Thomas's poem, by changing the very lines just cited into the final
ones, which crown her whole sequence (lines that repeat and also revise
the opening lines of the very first sonnet). Picking up from lines I've cited
before, in which the mother would have decried the traditional consolations

uttered at her funeral (an imagined gesture that ironically empowers the mother), Gilbert concludes the whole corona this way:

> the priest says the words she scorned she didn't believe
> (she has to be blessed to belong to holy ground)
> and O she would scold us if she were still alive!
> no *Tuono di dio* no bolt so fierce and true
> as the light of her mind that felt that thought that knew[53]

Seen, at times, in the sequence as someone struggling pathetically, ineffectively, even ridiculously, in the end, the mother and her spirit convey something of that heroic, epic valor implicit in the chronological trajectory of the epic. Although Gilbert has produced a sonnet sequence that relentlessly reminds us of our own impending death and the impossibility of resting on traditional consolations now largely gone from our collective cultural experience, she has also succeeded in conveying her own genuine, personal grief—and the person she is mourning—in a powerful and unforgettable way. This is her own victory, one that parallels the tenuous yet still realized victory of her mother's spirit.

And yet from our own perspective, as actual readers of these remarkable sonnets, the most important legacy of these poems is that even as they lament and expose the loss in our modern culture of traditional faith and its concurrent consolations, they demand of us, who (like Gilbert herself) know and love a *literary* tradition, a certain collective knowledge that allows us to understand and appreciate—and even participate in—Sandra's grief. This is perhaps an ironic communion but a real and important one for all that.

Postscript: Auto-exegesis, or, The Story Never Ends

I have prescinded one other narrative strategy that Gilbert employs in *Belongings*, though it may well have been implied in my discussion of Plath and Gilbert above. As with her earlier pairing of poetic and prose volumes (specifically, *Ghost Volcano: Poems* and *Wrongful Death: A Memoir*),[54] Gilbert's *Belongings* and her concurrently written *Death's Door* are most fruitfully read in conjunction with one another, the latter offering something of an exegesis of the other—a venerable tradition extending from Dante through Yeats and beyond. Ranging from a section on the author's personal experiences of mourning the death of her husband years earlier to a second section that engages in cultural criticism as it explores the way the twentieth century has reshaped dying and mourning, and concluding with a section of more traditional literary analysis of certain seminal elegiac poets over the nineteenth and twentieth centuries, *Death's Door* neatly comprises what Alicia Ostriker has called an "integration of plurality,"[55] in which different kinds of writing are put into interplay. Even more is true when the mixed personal and scholarly prose of *Death's Door* is coupled with the exquisite poetry of *Belongings* and the personal and cultural story that it tells.

By itself, *Death's Door* is a wide-ranging, highly detailed work that examines how modern times construct and respond to death, all the while employing personal narrative, especially in the first section, called "Arranging My Mourning," cultural studies in the second section, "History Makes Death," and close literary analysis in the final section, "The Handbook of Heartbreak: Contemporary Elegy and Lamentation." Toward the end of the first section Gilbert disturbingly writes of her (and others') attempts to record grief, and that our larger culture regards such writing as *wrong*: "writing wrong is wrong, or at least problematic, because it's not only painful but *writing pain*—pain, that, as I've just claimed, can't really be righted or sedated."[56] Perhaps the most chilling aspect of the second section is the detailed documentation of the increased mechanization modern culture has foisted on human bodies, whether alive or dead. Gilbert's reading of the Holocaust, in particular, as the logical culmination of a modern perspective that would result in a literal factory in which the workers (stripped and subjected to grotesque filth) were forced to manufacture the means of their own deaths in a parody of modern industrial factories is profoundly disturbing.[57] And, according to the author, subsequent decades have fared little better as we have come increasingly to view death, once regarded spiritually as "expiration," as mere "termination."[58] Of the myriad poets and poems I have raised in connection with my discussion of "Belongings," Gilbert's meditation on Sylvia Plath's "Berck-Plage" proves the most provocative. *Death's Door* is also profoundly philosophical, facing squarely the inscrutability of death itself.

As auto-exegesis, however, an old literary tradition that I am invoking here, *Death's Door* obviously offers many insights and details into the personal tragedies of Sandra Gilbert's lived experience, as well as into specific ritualistic traditions or larger cultural practices of our contemporary world. The first section recounts, among other things, the death of her husband, her reactions to that shock, the subsequent writing of *Wrongful Death* and

Ghost Volcano, all of which bear on *Belongings*. For example, the chapter titled "Yahrzeit," which describes the yearlong mourning of a close family member, culminating in the placement of a tombstone or marker on the grave, is especially important in understanding "A Year and a Day," the final sonnet sequence of *Belongings*, which mimics, in its own chronological construction, that very ritual—as Gilbert eulogizes her husband in the final thirteen sonnets that conclude the volume *Belongings*. Or again, at one point, when discussing the contemporary metaphysical angst any of us might feel in these modern times when confronting death, Gilbert describes the eruption of an anguished primal scream—which she reveals was not only her own reaction to her husband's death but also that of her mother when her own husband (the poet's father) died many years before.[59] This is important to *Belongings* as well, for that particular moment is described in the sonnet titled "March Moon" (which appears in the sequence dedicated to Elliot, Gilbert's husband), in which the narrator (in contrast to the author writing the sonnet) seems incapable of understanding what was happening: "these / were the times my real-life mom would scream and shriek / in nightmares whose wild echoes made me freeze / in my little-girl bed in my silver little-girl room. / What was scaring her, what did she know just then?"[60] Everything, we might answer, that the adult poet knows in writing these works: the unending power and pain of the nothingness that is death.

Elsewhere in *Death's Door*, Gilbert explores our tendency to project *human* (not spiritual) attributes onto nature, specifically that of human sexuality, which then, in the throes of grief, appears almost disgustingly lascivious—an insight that goes far in explaining certain poems of *Belongings* in other sections of the volume I have not discussed here. In addition, Gilbert's critical analysis in *Death's Door* of the ways in which grief has come to be regarded in modern times as both a psychological illness and an embarrassment clarifies the steely resistance to that very diminishment she has exhibited in her multiple tellings, whether in prose or in poetry, of the tremendous grief and losses she has endured. Obviously, the final section, in which she surveys and analyzes other elegiac poets, contributes greatly to seeing both what Gilbert is doing and what she is not doing in her own elegies.

Despite the numerous narrative intersections to be found between *Death's Door* and *Belongings*, I would like to conclude with the following, more abstract intersections between the two works, precisely for a deeper and perhaps ultimately more important resonance between the two and the larger story they, collectively, tell. In *Death's Door*, referring to the reactions to Whitman's "Crossing Brooklyn Ferry," in which the poet speaks to us as if from the dead, Gilbert says, "Fantastic as it is, this tentative textual resurrection has a power that even the most unpoetic (often, indeed, *antipoetic*) undergraduates tend to acknowledge."[61] *This tentative textual resurrection has a power.* Elsewhere she writes, and insists, "that every theme has its degraded and degrading variations doesn't mean that we should abandon art."[62] *We should not abandon art.* With reference to the famous painting *La Victoire* by Magritte of an opened door—a door she equates with death—Gilbert concludes the whole book with this statement: "To focus on such a mysterious blank is a struggle. So perhaps Magritte meant to tell us that looking, just *looking*, at this perpetually open door is in itself a victory."[63] *Looking at the inscrutability of death is itself a victory.* The book is filled with such provocative insights and pronouncements. All of them, and more, well apply to *Belongings* in general, and to "Belongings" in particular, and help to explain Gilbert's power in producing a poetry that fully animates in words that which is finally beyond words—*the* story, as it were, that we, as poets and critics alike, are compelled to tell and retell.

Notes

1. Sandra M. Gilbert, "Belongings," in *Belongings: Poems* (New York: W. W. Norton, 2005).

2. Ibid., 17.

3. I am roughly paraphrasing what I regard as the most salient characteristics of the epic (at least as they apply to this particular sonnet sequence) to be found in the "Epic" entry (by J. K. Newman) in *The New Princeton Encyclopedia of Poetry and Poetics*, ed. Alex Preminger and T. V. F. Brogan (Princeton, NJ: Princeton University Press, 1993), 362. Of the epic conventions not included here, we should consider the epic simile. While there are none in "Belongings," at first glance the entire sequence could be read as elaborating one long epic simile. The first sonnet opens with a description of the fading light, which then is compared to the mother's fading memory. Thus, the real subject—the mother's mind and its decline—is made secondary to the nominal subject. But the last sonnet, revising the opening sonnet's first line and comparison, says there is no force "so fierce and true / as the light of her mind that felt that thought that knew" ("Belongings," 30), thereby inverting the position of the opening subject and its simile to end with the real subject—the honoring of the mother. It should be noted, in addition, that the majority of the

most famous epic similes from Homer through Milton deal with "temporality and mortality" (see my own discussion of epic similes in the entry "Simile," *The New Princeton Encyclopedia of Poetry and Poetics*, 1150).

4. Gilbert, "Belongings," 17.

5. Ibid., 21. In-text poetry quotes do not preserve original spacing.

6. Ibid., 25.

7. Ibid., 30.

8. Ibid., 22.

9. Ibid., 19.

10. Ibid., 17.

11. Peter Rabinowitz, *Before Reading: Narrative Conventions and the Politics of Interpretation* (Ithaca, NY: Cornell University Press, 1987).

12. I am summarizing here and elsewhere in the text the central vision of how death and mourning have come to be regarded in a culture that has largely lost faith in traditional belief (and its attendant consolations, such as a belief in God and a belief in an afterlife) as summarized throughout Gilbert's own book, *Death's Door: Modern Dying and the Ways We Grieve* (New York: W. W. Norton, 2006).

13. Gilbert, "No thank you, I don't care for artichokes," in *Belongings*, 37.

14. James Phelan, "What Hemingway and a Rhetorical Theory of Narrative Can Do for Each Other: The Example of 'My Old Man,' " *Hemingway Review* 12.2 (1993): 5.

15. Gilbert, "Belongings," 25.

16. The mise en abyme, a figure for infinite regress in which closure is forever forestalled (thus frustrating the possibility of any definite meaning), can be readily understood by the phenomenon of the old Morton's salt shakers, in which a little girl carrying an umbrella was also carrying a Morton's salt shaker which in turn had the picture of the little girl carrying the umbrella, who was also carrying a Morton's salt shaker. . . .

17. See *Death's Door*, 230–241, as well as the other particularly germane section, "Death and the Camera," 218–222.

18. Again, I am summarizing Gilbert's position in *Death's Door*.

19. Bonnie Costello, "Narrative Secrets, Lyric Openings: Stevens and Bishop," in "Stevens and Elizabeth Bishop," ed. Jacqueline Vaught Brogan, special issue, *Wallace Stevens Journal* 19.2 (1995): 198.

20. Gilbert, "Belongings," 30.

21. Ibid., 17.

22. The possibility that Donne was imitating in his corona an older, Italian way of telling the rosary is suggested in the entry "*Corona*," by Elias L. Rivers and T. V. F. Brogan, in *The New Princeton Encyclopedia of Poetry and Poetics*, 242. Fittingly, in an

email the author sent to me, Gilbert explained how this sonnet sequence developed: "I was myself surprised when I found I was writing this—the first corona I'd ever produced—& realized that it was an unconscious tribute to my mother's confirmation name, Incoronata!" (June 10, 2008). This is highly suggestive of the way that an unconscious source can become part of the conscious craft of writing.

23. Gilbert uses this phrase, taken from Wallace Stevens's "The Owl in the Sarcophagus," as a point of particular focus in *Death's Door* for understanding the ways in which modern culture has come to construct a very different idea about death from that which was the norm for most previous cultures and centuries; first cited in *Death's Door*, xviii.

24. Wallace Stevens, "In a Bad Time," in *Wallace Stevens: Collected Poetry and Prose*, ed. Frank Kermode and Joan Richardson (New York: Library of America, 1997), 367–368.

25. Gilbert, "Belongings," 17.

26. Ibid., 18.

27. Ibid., 26.

28. Gerard Manley Hopkins, "Pied Beauty," in *The Poetical Works of Gerard Manley Hopkins*, ed. Norman H. Mackenzie (Oxford: Clarendon Press, 1990), 144.

29. Gilbert, "Belongings," 13.

30. Stevens, "Sunday Morning," 56.

31. Ibid., 55.

32. Ezra Pound, "Canto LXXXI," in *The Cantos* (London: Faber and Faber, 1987), 534.

33. Gilbert, "Belongings," 29.

34. Ibid., 22.

35. Ibid., 23.

36. Gillian Huang-Tiller, "The Power of the Meta-Genre: Cultural, Sexual, and Racial Politics in the American Modernist Sequence," PhD diss., University of Notre Dame, 2000.

37. While Gilbert, like her mother, was raised a Catholic, her husband of many years was Jewish. Questions of faith, from many different perspectives, permeate the total experience of the entire volume. While the number 12 has important connotations for any number of religions and cultures, it is particularly important in Judaism. Recalling the twelve tribes of Israel, Jewish priests wore twelve precious stones in their breast plates, with twelve loaves of bread on the table in the tabernacle. In addition, the number 12 was considered to symbolize the union of the people with God, by being the product of 3 (which in Judaism designates holiness) and 4 (which signifies "heaven," as "the throne of God"). In Orthodox and Conservative Jewish communities, a bat mitzvah is celebrated when a girl reaches the age of twelve.

38. Gilbert, "Belongings," 5.

39. Ibid., 28.

40. Ibid.

41. Elizabeth Bishop, "At the Fishhouses," in *Elizabeth Bishop: Poems, Prose, and Letters*, ed. Robert Giroux and Lloyd Schwartz (New York: Library of America, 2008), 52.

42. Ibid.

43. Gilbert, "Belongings," 21.

44. Gilbert, *Death's Door*, 295.

45. Ibid., 297.

46. Sylvia Plath, "Berck-Plage," in *Collected Poems of Sylvia Plath*, ed. Ted Hughes (New York: Harper and Row, 1981), 196–201, cited in Gilbert, *Death's Door*, 302.

47. Gilbert, *Death's Door*, 302.

48. Ibid., 327.

49. Ibid., 306.

50. Gilbert, "Belongings," 26.

51. Ibid., 21.

52. Dylan Thomas, "Do Not Go Gentle into That Good Night," in *The Poems of Dylan Thomas*, ed. Daniel Jones (New York: New Directions, 1957), 207.

53. Gilbert, "Belongings," 30.

54. Sandra M. Gilbert, *Ghost Volcano: Poems* (New York: W. W. Norton, 1995), and *Wrongful Death: A Memoir* (New York: W. W. Norton, 1995). In another instance of pairing poetry and prose, Gilbert wrote *Ghost Volcano*, a collection of poems recounting her experience and grief as a widow following the unexpected death of her husband, Elliot Gilbert, on February 11, 1991, as well as a powerful memoir that details the botched surgery and treatment Elliot received for what should have been a routine surgical procedure, which led to his death only hours later.

55. Alicia Ostriker, *Feminist Revision and the Bible* (Cambridge: Blackwell, 1993), 30.

56. Gilbert, *Death's Door*, 92.

57. Ibid., 153.

58. Ibid., 106ff.

59. Ibid., 20.

60. Gilbert, "March Moon," in *Belongings*, 113.

61. Gilbert, *Death's Door*, 73.

62. Ibid., 162.

63. Ibid., 463.

THE FASCINATION
OF WHAT'S DIFFICULT
Narrative Poetry in Strict Forms

GREGORY DOWLING

In 1997, Michael Lind published a long narrative in rhyme royal stanzas with the title *The Alamo*, and—on the cover itself—the ambitious subtitle *An Epic*. The dust jacket bore glowing testimonials from Larry McMurtry and Dan Rather of CBS News, but on the whole, the book was not well received by the literary world. With crushing charitableness, William Logan wrote, "Michael Lind's *The Alamo* isn't as awful as you'd think—not nearly as awful as it might have been."[1] Garry Wills was more blatantly drastic: "Things not worth doing can sometimes be done well. But here is something not worth doing that is done ill, a classical epic poem on the Alamo's defenders."[2]

A number of other negative reviews took as their basic premise the notion that the whole enterprise was ill-conceived. Perhaps Michael Lind was asking for it with his long essay-appendix "On Epic," in which he appeared to be demanding that his work be considered alongside the great poems of Homer, Virgil, and Milton. In fact, his argument was not quite as brash as that, and he gave a closely considered appraisal of previous American attempts at the epic, from Joel Barlow to Stephen Vincent Benét, assessing the faults and virtues of such attempts with some discernment. However, faced with the apparent presumptuousness of his claims, the reviewers were not going to let him get away with anything. Almost every aspect of the enterprise was called into question, with special emphasis on the clumsiness of his rhymes and versification.

Some of these complaints were certainly exaggerated, and there is no doubt that almost any long poem in a strict stanzaic form is likely to contain moments of awkwardness; Byron's *Don Juan* and *Beppo* contain frequent inversions of the sort, "Meantime the goddess I'll no more importune, / Unless to thank her when she's made my fortune."[3] We seem to have a lower tolerance level for such expedients nowadays, considering "natural" word order as something that must never be sacrificed for the sake of meter or rhyme.[4]

Nonetheless, it is undeniable that the historical matter of the poem was at times awkwardly squeezed into the verse:

> To Bonham's words, the flames began to snap.
>   "Let Texas be annexed unto the South
> and we can leave a Union grown a trap.
>   Just think of the potential for our growth—
>   there's Cuba, Haiti, the isthmus, and the mouth
> of the Amazon. Our cotton and our cane
> could ring a Gulf renamed the Dixie Main."[5]

The syntax is not actually contorted, and Lind has conceded himself a half-rhyme. However, the overall impression is of an awkward match of content and form. Indeed, there seems little reason for the form at all here. The problem, perhaps, lies precisely in the ponderous earnestness of the subject matter. The qualities of technical adroitness required by such a rhyme scheme seem more suitable—at least to modern sensibilities—in poetry that takes itself less solemnly. We cannot help but be aware of the poet's role as virtuoso, and we are more inclined today to accept such displays of dexterity in lighthearted or even frankly comic poetry.

There are moments when the narrator does step forward and refer to his own role as recorder of events (as Byron, for example, constantly does in *Don Juan*), but here, too, the general tone of solemnity prevails, even while the poet professes the "modesty" of his aim:

> The last to sink within that ringing hall
>   was William Lewis. Visiting a friend

in Carolina, he had heard the call
  of glory, not dreaming that his life would end
  in tomblike darkness where a blade would rend
his collarbone. His mother, Mary, four
years later, published letters, begging for

some relic, some memento of the son
  she raised for Santa Anna's scythes to reap.
Moved by her plea, Bexar's citizens, from one
  corroded stone in the Alamo's heap,
  commissioned a mason to carve a keep-
sake they then sent the proud and grieving mother,
a modest monument. These stanzas are another.[6]

These are undeniably worthy sentiments. The problem is, they remain sentiments, relying strongly on certain loaded terms ("call / of glory," "proud and grieving") to which a perhaps overly skeptical age is disinclined to grant the weight they are clearly supposed to bear.

Does this mean we have to accept Wills's premise, that the whole enterprise was not worth the effort? And is it the very idea of a classical epic that is manifestly absurd today, or more specifically the idea of a classical epic on such a theme? Is it the specific form of this classical epic? Would it have been possible to take the work more seriously had Lind adopted blank verse, or even some kind of loosely free verse? There are clear precedents for such a practice in twentieth-century poetry: the historical narratives of Robert Penn Warren, for example, or more recent ones by such writers as Daniel Hoffman, David Mason, Mary Jo Salter, William Jay Smith, Marilyn Nelson, and Andrew Hudgins, many of which have won critical acclaim. So the question arises, is it possible for an extended narrative in complex rhyming stanzas to work successfully today?

That is the question I address in this essay, and the main reason for posing it is that Lind is far from alone in adopting such forms today. Over the last two or three decades a number of long poems have been published that use such stanza forms as rhyme royal, ottava rima, the Spenserian stanza, or the Onegin stanza. I will try to answer the question of just why and how such forms have been revived (or, in the case of the Onegin stanza, first used in English) in an age in which free verse has come to be the dominant mode. And I will try to see whether such poetry is likely to offer any challenge to the norm or whether it is destined to remain a kind of private circus for metrical acrobats to display their technical proficiency to a dwindling audience of enthusiastic antiquarians.

It hardly seems necessary to point out that, while free verse may remain the prevailing mode, there has been a general revival of interest in form. The idea that such an interest is reactionary or nostalgic can no longer be taken seriously; if anything, as David Caplan has shown in his book, *Questions of Possibility*, writers can demonstrate their cultural and social openness by exploring such "new" forms as the ghazal. Recent (or fairly recent) publications, such as the essay collection *An Exaltation of Forms*, edited by Annie Finch and Kathrine Varnes, suggest that the great range of poetic forms available to writers today is a clear testimony to the vitality of a multicultural society. In this context one can understand how such stanza forms as those listed above have been adopted by important poets. The question remains whether they can be successfully used at length in narrative, in light of our greater familiarity with the forms of prose narrative and our consequently diminished tolerance for certain verse conventions once considered almost indispensable for long poems in tight forms, such as inverted sentences ("the goddess I'll no more importune") or the pleonastic use of auxiliary verbs ("Thus conscience doth make cowards of us all").

Since the discussion in this essay is necessarily a somewhat technical one, it makes some sense to proceed by taking each form in turn and briefly considering its history before examining its current uses. I will confine myself to the ones already listed; a case could be made for including terza rima as well,[7] but the most important long poems of recent years in that form, Walcott's *Omeros* and Glyn Maxwell's *Time's Fool*, rely on the almost constant use of half-rhyme or pararhyme, and I am specifically concerned here with poems that accept the conventions of strict form, in both meter and rhyme.[8]

Rhyme Royal: A Form That's Large Enough to Swim In

It seems best to begin with rhyme royal, as it has already appeared as a point of discussion in this essay and was arguably the first of these forms to enter English-language poetry. Rhyme royal was used by Chaucer in *Troilus and Criseyde, Parlement of Foules,* and four of the *Canterbury Tales.* King James I of Scotland adopted the stanza form for his poem *The King Is Quair* (according to some, this explains the name), and Robert Henryson used it in *The Testament of Cresseid*. Shakespeare's poem *The Rape of Lucrece* is in rhyme royal, but after this the form seems to have fallen into disuse until it was adopted by Wordsworth in "Resolution and Independence."

Rhyme royal was used at length (perhaps excessive length) by William Morris in *The Earthly Paradise*, which is a deliberately Chaucerian work. At the beginning of the twentieth century, John Masefield wrote three long narrative poems in the form, *The Widow in the Bye-Street, Dauber,* and *King Cole*; in the first of these poems, a story of jealous passion and murder, the debt to *Troilus and Criseyde* is clear. These poems were all very popular at the time and remain highly readable. Masefield avoids the risks of pomposity or overstraining that some reviewers attributed to Lind's work by adopting a language of deliberate simplicity and narrative directness; at the time, he was even accused of sensationalism. In 1926, C. S. Lewis published an allegorical narrative, *Dymer*, in the form, a work that is intriguing but not entirely satisfactory; the debt to Morris is clear, although Lewis himself in his introduction to a later edition talks more of Yeats (even while explaining that the poem allegorizes his rejection of Yeats's occult beliefs).

Undeniably the most significant and influential use of the stanza form in the twentieth century was in Auden's "Letter to Lord Byron," a witty and chatty autobiographical poem published as part of his and Louis MacNeice's *Letters from Iceland* (1937). Auden frankly admitted that he adopted rhyme royal as slightly less difficult than the ottava rima used by Byron, since it requires only one rhyme triplet instead of the two required in the octave stanza. Declaring that he wants "a form that's large enough to swim in," in which he can "talk on any subject that I choose," he says, with comic humility,

> Ottava Rima would, I know, be proper,
>   The proper instrument on which to pay
> My compliments, but I should come a cropper [. . .].[9]

Although in subsequent lines he invokes the name of Chaucer, he is clearly aiming for the same airily digressive manner that Byron achieved in his ottava rima poems; even the metaphor he adopts, "large enough to swim in," pays sidelong homage to Byron. He makes it quite clear that one of his aims is to restore the reputation of "light verse," which at present is "under a sad weather; / Except by Milne and persons of that kind / She's treated as *démodé* altogether."[10]

In the "Letter to Lord Byron," Auden quotes Yeats on "the fascination of what's difficult," and it is perhaps precisely this element that has resulted in the greater popularity of ottava rima than of rhyme royal in recent years.[11] It is as if poets have taken the lesson of Auden on the stimulus that strict form can provide for the comic imagination but have decided to increase the odds against themselves. Why, so to speak, limit yourself to juggling on the tightrope with china plates when you can do so with flaming torches? For this reason, I will proceed straightaway to a discussion of what we might consider rhyme royal's sister form, ottava rima.

Ottava Rima: Sometimes They Contain a Deal of Fun

Another possible reason for the popularity of ottava rima is that contemporary poets might have decided to go back beyond Auden to the source himself, Lord Byron. Byron, of course, was not the first poet to use ottava rima in English poetry. There were early translations of Tasso and Ariosto in the Elizabethan Age, but it was rarely used for any original work. It was not until John Hookham Frere's poem of 1817, *Whistlecraft*, that its potential as a form for comic verse was recognized—and it was Byron's recognition that counted. As Auden pointed out, perhaps the only poet since Byron to use the form for serious poetry (as it is often used in Italian) is Yeats—and he only does so by resorting to frequent half-rhymes and, of course, never at length (a famous example is "Sailing to Byzantium").

Other Romantic era poets adopted ottava rima. Shelley used it in his translations of the Homeric Hymns and in his lively narrative, "The Witch of Atlas," and Keats used it in "Isabella," his verse adaptation of a tale by Boccaccio. The form undoubtedly adds to the vivacity of Shelley's narrative, one of his most purely playful pieces, while it seems ill-suited to the more macabre material of Keats's poem, and this perhaps explains why the poet himself came to dislike the work. In any case, it was undoubtedly Byron's use of ottava rima that was to condition almost all later poems written in the form—or those written in closely related forms, such as Auden's "Letter."[12] If the form is used for narrative, the story is likely to take second place to chatty digressions in which the narrator takes the opportunity to be, as Byron put it, "quietly facetious upon everything."[13] The opportunity, of course, is provided by the form itself; this suggestion of the serendipitous seems to be an almost indispensable element in successful works in these forms. In his first work in the form, the Venetian narrative poem *Beppo*, Byron includes a nod to the "improvvisatori," and clearly his own work is supposed to have something of the nonchalance and casualness of improvised art. Part of the fun of the thing, he suggests, is that the poet is not in full control: "This Story slips forever through my fingers, / Because, just as the Stanza likes to make it, / It needs must be, and so it rather lingers."[14]

The serendipitous element is very clear in two of the longest works in ottava rima to be published in the second half of the twentieth century, Kenneth Koch's narrative poem *Ko, or a Season on Earth* (1959), and his later work *The Duplications* (1977); both works were republished with a verse introduction in 1987 under the title *Seasons on Earth*. The narratives are openly comic, not to say frivolous; Koch himself has pointed to the loose narrative structure of the verse romances of Ariosto to explain the almost totally haphazard nature of the story line. The jacket blurb for the first edition of *Ko* gives a fair idea of the gleefully anarchic nature of both narratives: "Among the principal characters are a Japanese baseball star, a neurotic financier who wishes to control all the dogs on earth, an unhappy Cockney, an English Private Eye, and an 'Action Poet.' The main themes are baseball, neurosis, art, and death; travel, weather, self-realization, and power; love, error, prophesy, destruction, and pleasure."[15] The story leaps from Cincinnati to Tucson, Paris, Tahiti, Pompeii, Rome, Kalamazoo, Tibet, and beyond.

Koch has always declared himself to be on the side of the "overproducers" of poetry as opposed to the niggardly perfectionists because, as he puts it, poetry is "esthetecologically harmless and psychodegradable."[16] It is possible to feel that there is something overly facile in his inventiveness, and after a while the arbitrary weirdness of his narrative can become rather wearying; however, the introduction he wrote to the two poems in 1987 does help us understand the spirit in which he wrote them—and makes them in retrospect more attractive; probably the introduction itself, also written in ottava rima, with the occasional indulgence of an extralong stanza, is his best work in the form. He devotes an octave to describing the political and literary climate in which he wrote the work ("the nineteen-fifties, / When Eisenhower was President, I think"), concluding with the rhyming couplet:

The Waste Land gave the time's most accurate data,
It seemed, and Eliot was the Great Dictator [. . .].[17]

In such a climate, "One hardly dared to wink / Or fool around in any way in poems, / And Critics poured out awful jereboams / To *irony, ambiguity, and tension*— / And other things I do not wish to mention."[18] However, he himself was in Florence with his wife and two-year-old daughter, and they were feeling happy—and so the temptation to "fool around" was irresistible:

> and on one airy
> Young day, while gazing at some yellow folders,
> I wrote three stanzas that made me feel dizzy with
> Delight, as if I wrote for Queen Elizabeth—
> In fact it was an Ariostic azimuth
> I tried to trace, of all things on earth vis-à-vis.[19]

This is the first of his stanzas ("paradisal octaves," as he will define them in the very next stanza) to expand beyond its eight lines (those cited are lines 5–10), as if out of pure elation; the final rhyming couplet swells into a quatrain of ingenious and comic rhymes, all centered on the frothing "z" sound, like an overbrimming glass of fizzy champagne. He refers to the recently crowned queen of Great Britain, but with the invocation of Ariosto in the subsequent line we are reminded of the earlier queen, during whose reign Ariosto was first translated into English—a period that has been referred to as the great springtime of English poetry. The word "azimuth" is a term of astronomical measurement and is used paradoxically in combination with the phrase "of all things on earth." Together with the inventive adjective "Ariostic," it serves to indicate the fantastic nature of the narrative (Ariosto's *Orlando Furioso* contains perhaps the first-ever account of a space voyage). The last three syllables of the final line, with the comic placing of "vis-à-vis," hint at a desire both to list and name "all things on earth" (*viz*), and to confront them (*vis-à-vis*). There is an element of sheer nonsense in all this, but it is difficult not to be captivated by the energetic brio of the verse.

In answer to the common criticism that formal verse somehow bestows an artificial order on our experiences, Koch points, like Byron, to the role that fortune plays in such poetry, declaring that the random nature of the rhymes serves as a kind of comic stimulus to mix together past and present "at random." The rhymes "interrupt one's quietly attending to one's intellectual business" and

make one feel one can't entirely
Say what one wants, and profit from this funniness
By mixing things that in states of sobriety
One would not mix, and give the proper airiness
To what is neither chance nor arbitrariness—[20]

"The proper airiness" is perhaps the best description of Koch's two narratives; the stories themselves may lack substance, but there is no denying their power to elate. As with Byron and Auden, Koch enjoys what one might call the "cocktail" aspect of the form, the curious paradoxical freedom that its irrational restrictions seem to bestow on the skillful user to mix otherwise unconnected things. The elation verges, he suggests, on inebriation.

The capaciousness of the form, its natural tendency to celebrate what Louis MacNeice described as "the drunkenness of things being various,"[21] derives from its technical qualities. Paul Fussell has described these shrewdly: "The stanza itself, with its six lines of interlocked, unified preparation followed by its couplet of climax, release, or commentary, constitutes a paradigm of inflation and deflation, or of the heroic which swells and swells until it bursts into the mock-heroic. . . . The very rhyme scheme implies that each stanza will contain two more or less distinct kinds of materials."[22] Of course, there is a risk that the poem may degenerate into mere dispersiveness; in the purely narrative parts of Koch's poem, he occasionally succumbs to this risk. It is where the narrator asserts his presence that the poem holds together best—and succeeds in keeping the reader's attention. It would seem that the engaging personality of the poet-narrator is an essential element in poetry of this sort.

It is interesting that in one of the few poems of recent decades to use ottava rima for serious purposes—James Fenton's poem from the Vietnam War, "In a Notebook"—the narrator's role in organizing the material is the very key to the meaning. Here it is not the ebullient high spirits of the narrator that hold the poem together; rather, we see the poet-journalist at work, whittling down an abundance of "notebook" material gathered in apparent haphazard fashion in the first three stanzas to a single stanza of telling details, which is followed by another octave of bleak narrative desolation. Here are the final two stanzas:

There was a river overhung with trees.
The girls stood waist-deep in the river washing,

And night still lingered underneath the eaves
While on the bank young boys with lines were fishing.
Mothers and daughters bowed beneath their sheaves
While I sat drinking bitter coffee wishing—
And the tide turned and brought me to my senses.
The pleasant war brought the unpleasant answers.

The villages are burnt, the cities void;
The morning light has left the river view;
The distant followers have been dismayed;
And I'm afraid, reading this passage now,
That everything I knew has been destroyed
By those whom I admired but never knew;
The laughing soldiers fought to their defeat
And I'm afraid most of my friends are dead.[23]

For this poem, which combines historical tragedy and bitter personal memories, Fenton avoids the flamboyance of the form. In the last stanza the rhymes are all masculine, and the final couplet deliberately avoids full closure.

Anthony Burgess's *Byrne*, on the other hand, is in full Byronic mode (as the name of its eponymous hero suggests). This was Burgess's last novel, published posthumously in 1995, and it came as a surprise to many readers. As Dana Gioia notes, Burgess's previous poetry, which had made occasional appearances in earlier novels, had never been anywhere nearly as accomplished as his prose, and so few readers could have expected such polished and witty versifying. The form was new, but, as Gioia points out, the themes were familiar ones in Burgess's fiction: "sex, religion, art, and mortality."[24] The novel recounts the story of an imaginary artist and composer, Michael Byrne, and his numerous offspring. Byrne is a man of small talent but a keen eye for the main chance; he will take any road that is likely to further his career, even if it means composing propaganda music for the Nazis. His real skills are purely sexual, and this helps explain the number of his illegitimate children scattered around the globe. The story focuses in its second part on this second generation, now in middle age and surprised to learn their father is still alive. The entire novel is in ottava rima, apart from a Venetian section written in the Spenserian stanza.

The novel provides a darkly comic portrait of artistic failure and moral turpitude. It offers sour reflections on the relations between art and history, and on the role of the artist. Earlier novels by Burgess on such themes had at their center such great artists as Shakespeare, Marlowe, and Keats—but also comic failures like Enderby. Byrne is halfway between such figures; he is a second-rate talent but achieves a legendary status thanks to his involvement in the great events of history. The first section of the novel is perhaps the most accomplished, presenting the figure of Byrne and locating him in history. As in Byron's poetry we are given a sense of the sheer randomness of historical events and the way they affect the individual, a point reinforced by Burgess's outlining of Byrne's ancestry, born in Ireland but ultimately descended from the Spanish survivors of the scattering of the Armada:

> God's wind blew and they scattered, and some scattered
> To Ireland's coast. When they had dried their doublets,
> Survival seemed the only thing that mattered.
> They swilled their buttermilk from peasant goblets
> And, vowing they would never more be battered
> By wind and wave, said, with a Spanish sob, 'Let's
> Resign ourselves to pigshit, peat and mud,
> And tickle these mad Irish with our blood.'[25]

The ingenious rhyming and enjambment are typical of the work, as is the tenor of fatalism. History works in this poem just like God's scattering wind (the word "scatter" recurs in the poem), and the only option open to the characters, it seems, is to adapt themselves to circumstances, just as the narrator, who presents himself in sub-Byronic fashion as a talentless hack, has to accept the constrictions of the "hard stanza" he has chosen.[26] This, at any rate, is the philosophy of Byrne himself; the spirit of the poem is thus not so much mock-heroic as antiheroic. Byrne is a twisted version of the hero, if we accept the definition of hero as a maker of history. At the heart of the novel is a great sense of the futility of things; Byrne is clearly aware of the worthlessness of his talent, and even his sexuality is destined to leave no lasting mark, since all his children are themselves childless.

In the end, the poem is a triumph of technique and verbal wit. While the material of the poem seems calculated to depress, with its emphasis on failure and aridity, the stanzas themselves crackle with high-spirited energy. The characters may worry about their infertility, but the rhymes are spawned with a generous and ingenious fecundity.[27]

The Spenserian Stanza: A Marvelous Ugly Duckling

Byrne includes a section in the Spenserian stanza, which has a different momentum, slower and more stately (or less lively) than the narrative in ottava rima. The narrator himself punningly and alliteratively expresses his relief when the section comes to a conclusion: "My dried-up pen, sir, / Madam, gladly dispenses with that brief spell of Spenser."[28] The Spenserian stanza has always been a curiosity among narrative forms, being apparently designed, with its final dragging alexandrine, to slow things down. It seems to take the fascination of what's difficult to almost absurd extremes. R. S. Gwynn gives a fine description of its potential and its difficulties (even if his arithmetic seems a little wobbly): "I have always considered it a marvelous ugly duckling among the English fixed forms. In skilled hands it is capable of soaring to great heights, but its inherent difficulties seem sufficiently daunting to deter novices from attempting it; ineptly handled, it waddles along awkwardly with its forty-nine webbed iambic feet mired in mud."[29]

After Spenser's great epic, *The Faerie Queene*, the stanza was used by such poets as Shenstone and Thomson in the eighteenth century, but its real revival came with the Romantics, who seemed charmed by what Peter Conrad describes as its power to offer "a resistance to temporal harassment which approached mysticism."[30] Coleridge praised the "charmed sleep" of *The Faerie Queene*. Keats used the stanza form in "The Eve of St. Agnes," fully exploiting its pictorial and sensuous qualities. Shelley used it in his elegy for Keats, *Adonais*, which is essentially a long pastoral meditation. Most famously—and most influentially—Byron adopted it for *Childe Harold's Pilgrimage*, the least dynamic of all travel poems. Peter Conrad again captures the peculiarly lethargic quality of this poem, stating wittily that the "trailing final line drags a lamed foot and declares that this is a halting, morose and introspective journey, not a grand tour, for each stanza returns to the predicament of Harold immured—in a parody of the Keatsian bower—within himself."[31]

Tennyson used to full effect the unenergetic quality of the stanza for the opening of his poem "The Lotos-Eaters" (1833), and James Thomson adopted it for a poem with the telling title "The Lord of the Castle of Indolence" (1859). After that it seems to have fallen, like the rhyme royal stanza, into disuse.[32]

A number of contemporary poets have experimented with the Spenserian stanza, but few at length. There are interesting examples by Daryl Hine ("Bluebeard's Wife," a sensuously descriptive poem reminiscent of Keats's

"Eve of St. Agnes"), John Updike ("The Dance of the Solids"), and R. S. Gwynn himself ("Two Views from a High Window"). Clive James used it for a verse letter to Martin Amis, and the British poet John Whitworth adopted it for part of his narrative sequence, "The Way It Was And The Way It Is And The Way It Will Be," published in 1989 in his fourth volume, *Tennis and Sex and Death*. In Whitworth's hands the stanza is a perfect vehicle for the expression of a mixture of confused and contradictory yearnings and emotions; the rhymes are often irresistibly amusing, and the final alexandrine is frequently used to add a final touch of humorous deflation.

The longest work in Spenserian stanzas in recent years is almost certainly Andrew Waterman's "Millennium Letter," in one hundred stanzas. As he admits in the poem, which is addressed to an imaginary reader in the future, he has modified the stanza:[33]

> Will you still use this sort of old-style stanza?
>   Rhymed, metrical? It's filched from Spenser's fine
> Allegorical extravaganza
>   *The Faerie Queene*, except that this of mine
>   Omits one foot of his long final line
> Which makes his verse move statelier, more solemn
>   Than suits my mix—chats, skits, yarns, in a brine
> Of more astringent flavouring, like alum—
> Or my course, zigzag like a ski-slalom.[34]

"Millennium Letter" is a high-spirited work, with moments of the frankly comic, such as the imaginary tennis game in the future between *Young Brat* (nine years old, who "was inducted into the game before / Birth, his parents having the womb-floor / Wired for sound-tracks"[35]) and *Old Vet* (age twenty-eight, who "droops and shambles"[36] onto the court), and moments of the purely gleeful, such as Waterman's own memory of having driven the "Manchester intercity / To London: every small boy's dream come true, / A fantasy outdoing Walter Mitty."[37] These are mingled with ruminations on the state of poetry and the Balkan conflict. An attempt to justify the variety of subject-matter is offered in one stanza, with the reflection that "From the Greeks on, sport, poetry and war / Show us profoundly who and what we are."[38]

The stanza form, of course, also serves to give some kind of unity to the poem, even though, as we have seen, each stanza can tend to create a discrete picture. Although Waterman refers to the movement of his poem as "zigzag like a ski-slalom," and although he devotes much attention to such sports as tennis, some of the most memorable moments in the poem have a quality of rapt stillness, as if he were interested in what manages to persist amid change. A fine example of this quality can be seen in the penultimate stanza, in which he addresses once again his imagined reader in the future:

> I like to think your time will still have leisure
>   (I know, you have a million different and
> Electronic forms of fun) to know the pleasure
>   Of days at seasides doing things unplanned;
>   Watching (as I've watched mine) your child just stand
> Squirming bare toes at the sea's edge for hours
>   To lose his feet but for the clasp of sand;
> Or roam marsh burnished by rain-waves, sunshowers
> Between grass head-high flecked with purple flowers.[39]

Waterman is fascinated by the quality of resilience, by what survives and remains steadfast amid the upheavals of time and the turmoil of personal and political troubles. His finest tribute to this quality—and probably his most important work—is his long poem in the Onegin stanza, "Out for the Elements," a work published in 1981 that has been described by Neil Powell as "one of the central poems of our time."[40] There is no doubt that it represented something of a breakthrough in Waterman's poetry—and, as with Byron, the breakthrough seems to have been to a great extent a technical one. Waterman has himself said, "What I did not realise when I wrote 'Out for the Elements' was that using a rhymed form for that long poem would trigger my using rhyme (which I had not done before) for the huge preponderance of what I was to write during the next twenty years."[41] In this sense, "Millennium Letter" derives from "Out for the Elements."

The Onegin Stanza: Inner Momentum . . . Infectious Vitality

The *Whistlecraft* in Waterman's case (and in John Fuller's and Vikram Seth's, as we shall see) was Charles Johnston's translation of *Eugene Onegin*.[42] Johnston himself has stated that it was while writing *In Praise of Gusto*, a meditative poem that alternates sections in Spenserian stanzas with sections in Onegin stanzas, that he realized the virtues of the Onegin stanza: "it has an inner momentum, a sort of infectious vitality of its own."[43] It was this experiment that was to lead to his English verse translation of Pushkin's masterpiece, generally acknowledged as one of the great translations of the twentieth century. There had been previous verse translations of the work,[44] and some very competent ones, but it was not until Johnston's highly accomplished work appeared that other poets realized the possibilities of the form. Within less than a decade of the publication of his translation (1977), three fine long poems had been written using the form: John Fuller's *The Illusionists* (1980), Waterman's "Out for the Elements" (1981), and Vikram Seth's *The Golden Gate* (1985). All three poets were inspired directly by Johnston's translation; Waterman has stated that he only heard about Fuller's poem two years after his own had been published, and Seth includes a direct tribute to the translation in his verse novel.[45]

Andrew Waterman's masterpiece, "Out for the Elements," was his first experiment in the form of the long journal-like poem. It undoubtedly looks back to Auden's verse letter and also perhaps to Louis MacNeice's *Autumn Journal* (Waterman would borrow the metrical form of the *Journal* seventeen years later for a poem titled "A Letter from Taormina"). Like Auden and MacNeice, he interweaves personal reflections and memories with contemporary events; Grevel Lindop said of the poem in the *Times Literary Supplement*, "If someone in a century or so would like to know what it was like to live in Britain in the 1980s, he could do worse than turn to 'Out for the Elements.'"[46]

It begins with the poet on the beach in his adopted home of Northern Ireland, and the opening stanza promises reflections on history that will take us back to the beginning of life on earth; however, these dauntingly vast reflections are handled with lightness and humor as the poet broods on the curious caprices of nature that have resulted in the phenomenon of mankind:

> How did it
> come about? How could nature bid it
> we should attain such livings as
> insurance, market research, and jazz,
> mining for coal, or crawling under
> purring metal contraptions, or
> inspecting wickets, or the law?[47]

And this leads gradually to the personal note:

> Which brings me to myself, revolving
> such matters on a starlit beach
> on Ireland's northern rim, and solving
> none of my problems as I reach
> perhaps my own half-way, at forty.
> Pure romanticism, each sortie
> risking its leap before the look
> jells, has run into Life's left-hook
> absurdly often. Once more home is
> dwindled to little more than these
> shoes I stand here in, where the sea's
> belling as wind gets up, and foam is
> whitening now to topple sheer.
> There's plenty of the void round here.[48]

This gives a good idea of the tone and movement of the poem. Waterman presents himself as the deracinated poet, at the Dantean midway point of life's journey, but the tacit comparison is offered with rueful humor, echoing an image from a P. G. Wodehouse novel ("has run into Life's left-hook"). The off-hand humor ("There's plenty of the void round here") does not, on the other hand, detract from the suggestive power of the imagery of the sea, which will return at key points during the narrative. As Johnston pointed out, the stanza form with its nimble tetrameters and its constant alternation between masculine and feminine rhymes has an "infectious vitality of its own," which allows swift changes of mood and imagery and seems to stimulate a kind of mental athleticism, resulting in provocative associations of ideas. Many of the critics who have talked about the qualities of the Onegin stanza have used images that suggest the idea of play. Nabokov compares the stanza to a painted spinning top whose patterns are only visible when moving slowly at the end and beginning of each spin. Clive James compares it to a "self-loading jack-in-the-box,"[49] and Bayley describes Pushkin as "glid[ing] into rhymes and rhythms like an expert skater onto ice."[50]

Waterman takes full advantage of the protean qualities of the form. The poem recounts the course of a year in the poet's life, during which he takes a sabbatical from his teaching job in Northern Ireland. The poem switches from Northern Ireland to Manchester and London; the poet reflects on his unsettled life, his early years in cheap lodging houses, his loves and friend-ships, all intermingled with ruminations on current political problems, such as (inevitably) the Irish troubles. The poem is undeniably very personal, but it is never purely self-centered; Waterman has a wonderful ear for other people's speech patterns, managing even within the tight restrictions of the stanza to give an impression of entirely natural conversations, whether caught on the streets of Belfast or in the pubs of Moss Side:

'In Failsworth at the Cloggers Fred
first downs his pint, then drops down dead . . .'
'Them black clubs, friend, don't take your wallet.
They roll you as you leave the door.
The prozzies there are rough, and sure
a jump would cost you . . .' 'Grabbed her doll, it
broke my Lyn's heart . . .' 'When dark arrives
keep off the Precinct, they use knives.'[51]

He even devotes one stanza to a perfect parody of sociological jargon ("In-terpersonal situations / of conflict most arise, we find, / among those whose accreditations / if societally defined, / extrapolate as, well, inferior . . .").[52]

In this poem Waterman writes less about his own performance than do some of the other practitioners in strict form that we have mentioned so far. However, he does provide one highly suggestive simile for the poet's task, returning to the sea imagery with which the poem began:

Meanwhile, the fishing boats go trawling
winter or summer, for what catch
they can; and still my right hand crawling
on paper waits, then moves, to scratch
ink nets upon unfathomed oceans
of experience, complex emotions
more subtle and vast than words can say.
The poem knows its only way
is trust in craft, collaboration
with elements; some lucky tide
remote from dock-lights, that may guide
and buoy its venture, saturation
in inchoate stuff; that just might
net lustres shoaled beyond its sight.[53]

The poet is both lone explorer and collaborator with the elements; he must dare and trust at the same time. And one of the elements will always be that of pure fortune—or serendipity. But it is no use playing safe; the poet has to expose himself if he wants that lucky catch. In that sense, he has to be out for the elements.

The remarkable thing about the three long poems that were published in the 1980s in this form is their diversity. Each one is highly accomplished and abides by the very strict rules of the form, but each work creates its own world and establishes its own individual tone. John Fuller's *The Illusionists* is essentially a witty satire that exploits to the full the purely ludic qualities of the stanza. The poet himself has described it as "a bit of a romp."[54] The story concerns the London art world, with characters ranging from the innocent "Camford" graduate, Tim, to crooked art dealers, forgers, Middle Eastern oil crooks, and a transvestite socialite. At the center of the plot is a forged painting, allegedly by William Hogarth, depicting a scene from *The Rape of the Lock*; this is clearly suggestive of the satirical intentions of Fuller's own poem. We are undoubtedly meant to see analogies between Pope's and Hogarth's world and Fuller's (which is to say ours). However, although the poet devotes an acrostic stanza to Hogarth, a clearer idea of the true spirit of the work comes in another of the poem's three acrostic stanzas (a third one is devoted to one of the characters in the plot); this stanza comes in chapter five and serves as the dedication of the novel ("I'm sorry that you've had to wait: / It's 1800 lines too late"),[55] being addressed to the poet Matthew Prior:[56]

> To you, clear-headed, lean, sarcastic
> Observer of the Government,
> Master of the hudibrastic
> And self-styled "poet by accident"
> That out of vacant hours not vanity
> Took pen and ink to save your sanity,
> Happily I dedicate
> Each line of this that I relate.
> Were civil servants panegyrists;
> Poets of low-life, diplomats;
> Roisterers, ministers; kings, cats;
> I doubt we'd have lugubrious lyrists

Or such dull politics—instead
Rulers would think, writers be read.[57]

Prior, as Fuller sees him, was not a caustic and vituperative satirist like Hogarth. His verse was intended to amuse rather than to criticize—and he certainly had no intention of indulging in anything so futile as self-analysis: "To keep the mind in a good humour / Just like one's wife, was your advice, / Not to dissect it like a tumour, / Gravely examining each slice / For evidence of everlasting / bliss to come. . . ."[58] Fuller clearly intends that his own poem should have some of the same joyous irresponsibility:

Poets adore a divertissement:
They are the hooligans of wit
Not intellectual policemen,
And all the poems they commit
Make shocking reading. Every sentence
Is met with gleeful unrepentance.
Most of them are doing time
For loitering with intent to rhyme
Or being found in the possession
Of little sense. Since words began,
A close conspiracy to scan
Has led to many a false confession,
When po-faced readers cock an ear
For what's not meant to be sincere.[59]

We may be reminded, in the end, of Auden's pertinent declaration in "A Letter to Lord Byron": "Art, if it doesn't start there, at least ends / Whether aesthetics like the thought or not, / In an attempt to entertain our friends."[60]

The third of these long narratives in the Pushkin stanza was that rarest of phenonemena, a best-selling volume of poetry. *The Golden Gate* came out in 1986 and not only received glowing reviews on both sides of the Atlantic (and in the author's native India) but sold extremely well. To a certain extent, one could say that its success was due to the fact that, of the three works under consideration, it was the most similar to a conventional novel. Indeed, Faber and Faber took care to market the work as a novel rather than as poetry. Nonetheless, as Vikram Seth ironically notes in the book itself, the success was not entirely foreseeable; he tells of how an editor seized his arm at a party:

> "Dear fellow,
> What's your next work?" "A novel . . ." "Great!
> We hope that you, dear Mr. Seth—"
> ". . . In verse," I added. He turned yellow.
> "How marvelously quaint," he said,
> And subsequently cut me dead.[61]

On the whole, the narrator remains rather in the background. Digressions are less frequent than in the poems by Byron or Pushkin (or Fuller). He is not so flamboyant a rhymer as these poets either; even the feminine rhymes call less attention to themselves. Nonetheless, despite his technical skills, he admits at one point to doubts about the whole enterprise:

> How do I justify this stanza?
> These feminine rhymes? My wrinkled muse?
> This whole passé extravaganza?
> How can I (careless of time) use
> The dusty bread molds of Onegin
> In the brave bakery of Reagan?[62]

But this moment of crisis concludes with the down-to-earth couplet: "If it works, good; and if not, well, / A theory won't postpone its knell."

Whereas Pushkin presents himself in his story as a friend of Onegin, Seth plays a more discreetly anagrammatic role as the economist Kim Tarvesh, who gets invited to the parties and weddings; ironically recalling the economics PhD thesis that he never completed, Seth presents himself as "a joyless guest amid the jollity":

> While round him voices rise and fall
> In oral goulash, Occam's call
> Leaches his vision of variety:
> He mumbles, "In all likelihood
> An n-dimensional matrix could
> Succinctly summarize society. . . ."
> (Poor Kim Tarvesh—we must recall
> He's an economist after all.)[63]

The whole point of *The Golden Gate* is that society—and the world as a whole—refuses to be succinctly summarized; the novel remains firmly *un*leached, celebrating the irreducible diversity of life.

Here it is worth pointing out that a number of reviews at the time of publication seemed to take it for granted that a novel about yuppies in California must necessarily be satirical in intention. There are, naturally enough, moments of satire in the book—there are some brilliantly bitter lines on art critics ("These chickenhearted chickenshits / Jerk off their weak and venomous wits . . ."[64])—but on the whole, the novel shows a warm appreciation of Californian life and society. It is, in particular, the sense of the sheer variety of options offered by California that the novel exults in. Like Andrew Waterman, Vikram Seth shows a fondness for lists—lists that celebrate the range of possibilities: these can be the items of food in a restaurant, the books his characters read, the music they listen to, the activities they engage in after Saturday breakfast, even the items of graffiti seen on the freeway.

One chapter of the novel is devoted to the antinuclear protest outside "Lungless Labs," with a long speech given by a Catholic priest. Undoubtedly, this part constitutes something of an artistic risk. If Seth pulls it off, it is because he manages to make the protest part of the same celebration of diversity that characterizes the rest of the novel. The crowd outside the laboratory is described as a "motley medley; / A marching carnival parade [. . .] / Quarreling, waving, wrangling, singing, / The lively unanimous throng. . . ."[65] A "motley medley" could serve as a description of the work as a whole.

Vikram Seth shows a willingness to take risks. The finest quality of the work as a whole is the great range of tones and moods he achieves; he himself has described the work in an interview as "a love story, a comedy of manners and a meditation on death."[66] He has also pointed out that "a verse novel allows greater scope for natural unobtrusive variation of tone and mood . . . the unity, to some extent, is provided by the repeating template of the stanza."[67] Clearly, it is also a question of engaging the reader's sympathies so that he or she accepts the tonal and emotional shifts of the narrative; this depends almost entirely on our belief in the characters he presents to us—which in turn depends on the writer's own belief in them.

This is very different from the postmodern coolness and witty disengagement of John Fuller's narrative. Seth is clearly aiming for something more old-fashioned—aiming, one could say, for the same effects that Pushkin achieved in his work. As already noted, Seth pays direct tribute to *Eugene Onegin* in the course of *The Golden Gate*; elsewhere he has talked more generally of the qualities he admires in Pushkin's works, qualities that he strives for in his own: "lightness of touch, simplicity, clarity, and a direct yet unexaggerated speaking to the heart even on subjects—like love or mortality—that have been written about often enough already."[68] Seth's attitude to his characters is very similar to that of Pushkin in his own verse novel. We have the same sense that Seth enjoys the company of his characters. It is not purely out of postmodern whimsicality that he sets himself—or rather an anagrammatic version of himself—in the poem as one of their friends; in an interview, Seth declared, "I felt buoyant writing it . . . having the chance to be with all those characters."[69]

Seth clearly enjoys the otherness of other people. In all his fiction he has shown a great fascination with what other people do; in particular, he manages to communicate a great interest in the specifics of people's jobs and crafts. For example, in his epic prose novel *A Suitable Boy*, he describes in great detail the making of a pair of shoes and manages to make it one of the most gripping chapters in the novel; in part this is because the fate of one of the main characters depends on the success of those shoes, and we have been made to care about this character, but to a great extent it is also because the author is fascinated by the details of this craft himself and communicates this fascination to the reader. A similar if more concentrated feat of description in *The Golden Gate* is the stanza devoted to the pickling of olives:

The salt's mixed as the water's heated.
An egg's released upon the brine.
It floats! The first stage is completed.
Phase two: In stratified design,
Bands of plump olives and thick slices
Of lemon, dusted well with spices,
Are laid inside each pickling jar.
Now into each packed reservoir
A sluice of cooling brine is pouring.
A seal of olive oil to spare
The olives from the ambient air–
And the jar's set aside for storing.
The lid's screwed tightly; sighs are heaved;
The label's stuck: the task's achieved.[70]

In *Beppo* Byron devotes two stanzas to the Venetian gondola; the tribute he pays to its qualities of swiftness and ductility ("built lightly, but compactly [. . .] sometimes they contain a deal of fun") could apply equally well to his own handling of the ottava rima. Similarly, Seth's description of the various stages of the task and the delicacy of the details could well be seen as reflecting on the precision and neatness of the Onegin stanza. It too has a "stratified design" and in skillful hands can serve as a "packed reservoir," preserving the life it describes in the perfection of art; each stanza ends with its final masculine-rhyming couplet that gives a sense of closure: "the task's achieved." However, the description is clearly not intended simply as an allegory. Seth writes it because he really is interested in how olives are preserved, and he sees no reason not to put this information into his poetry as well.

Indeed, one wouldn't want to push the allegory too far. The comparison with a sealed jar, if taken too literally, could be misleading since the greatest quality of Seth's verse novel is its openness: his poem is open to all kinds of subject matter, all kinds of experience and all kinds of characters—and the characters would have to include the numerous memorable animals in the novel, from Schwarzenegger the iguana to Charlemagne the cat.

Perhaps the truth is that the secret of the Onegin stanza lies in its reconciliation of contradictory qualities: closure and openness, form and freedom, movement and stillness. The plot of the novel is centered on the theme of reconciliation[71] (the title of the novel, referring as it does to a bridge, is certainly significant in this sense), and one could say that the form of the work embodies the theme.

Protesting against Protesting

This final consideration helps us answer that question I posed at the beginning of this essay: Is it possible for an extended narrative in complex rhyming stanzas to work successfully today? Or, given that the general tendency of this essay is probably clear by now, the question can perhaps be rephrased a touch more brutally: Why does Seth's use of the Onegin stanza so manifestly work and Lind's use of rhyme royal not?

To a certain extent, our discomfort with the form in Lind's work may arise from the fact that today there is a greater inclination among readers and critics to question the reason for specific forms. Formal poets can expect to have to justify their metrical choices in a way that poets in earlier ages probably did not have to. I have no doubt that for many contemporary poets this hostility toward, or distrust of, formal schemes can in itself constitute a justification of the form: I rhyme because you don't want me to. After all, it was not for nothing that the most influential anthology of New Formalist poetry was titled *Rebel Angels*. Nonetheless, the reader is left puzzled by the apparently arbitrary nature of Lind's choice; we often have the sense that the form contributes little to the meaning.

This is clearly not the case in most of the other long poems I have discussed. There is probably no doubt that many of the poets did choose to adopt such strict forms in part as a reaction to the dominant "ideology" of free verse, and therefore the demonstration of technical adroitness becomes in itself an essential part of the poem's meaning. But we never have the sense that the showmanship is something entirely separate from the narrative content; it is intrinsically bound up with the vision of life that fuels the story. In this sense it is connected to the specific role that the poet-narrator plays within the narrative itself.

The poet who writes in elaborate stanza forms could be said to be doing one of two things. He or she either is bestowing a pattern on an otherwise muddled world or is revealing the hidden pattern that lies beneath the apparent muddle. Often enough, the successful poet zigzags between the two options, as both supreme wizard of words, celebrating his or her own organizational skill, and the gifted seer, rejoicing in the fortune of discovering serendipitous matches of rhyme words and meanings.

As we have seen, in all cases the poet-narrator has a primary function within the story recounted. It ranges from the highly personal, even confessional, role of Andrew Waterman to the flamboyant display of John Fuller and the exuberant exhibitionism of Kenneth Koch, from the pyrotechnical performance of Anthony Burgess to the discreetly supervisory role of Vikram Seth (or "Kim Tarvesh"), but in all cases the acrobacy is partly a balancing act, as the narrator hovers between demonstrating his own skill ("the fascination of what's difficult") and giving the impression of having fortuitously come across these happy combinations. And the success of this metrical and rhyming funambulism is clearly dependent on lightness of touch.

Lightness is probably the most important quality in poetry of this sort in the present day. Even if the poet touches on serious matters, the reader will give more credit to the poem if its effects are achieved without ponderousness.

And here we can mention a third possible aim (or at least effect) for the poet of elaborate verse forms: as we have seen, one of the impressions produced by such poetry is that at times the poet is not so much in cool control of the verse form as in thrall to it; therefore, in the sheer arbitrariness of the rhymes, the poet reflects the sheer arbitrariness of existence. In this sense the poet is not imposing or revealing order but rather extracting what musical, or at least aural, enjoyment can be obtained from so purely haphazard a world. Excessive solemnity would be out of place in such an endeavour.

It is perhaps worth concluding with an observation made by Auden, probably the key figure of the twentieth century for such poetry; the remark comes in an essay on American poetry: "The prose of Emerson and Thoreau is superior to their verse, because verse in its formal nature protests against protesting; it demands that to some degree we accept things as they are, not for any rational or moral reason, but simply because they happen to be that way; it implies an element of frivolity in the creation."[72]

Notes

1. William Logan, "Hardscrabble Country," *New Criterion* 15.10 (June 1997), http://www.newcriterion.com/archive/15/jun97/logan.htm.

2. Garry Wills, "Remember the Alamo?," *New York Times*, March 9, 1997, http://query.nytimes.com/gst/fullpage.html?res=9807E4DA1331F93AA35750C0A961958260.

3. George Gordon, Lord Byron, *Beppo*, in *Byron's Poems*, vol. 1 (London: J. M. Dent, 1963), 385.

4. Of course, put so simply, this begs the question. The whole issue of nature and artifice in art is one that can hardly be dealt with in a footnote, but I think it worth recalling a cogent statement by William Logan, when discussing remarks by various contemporary poets on the "artifice" of rhyme and meter (for example, this statement by John Ashbery: "[Iambic pentameter] somehow seems to falsify poetry for me. It has an order of its own that is foreign to nature"): "The natural is only what we are accustomed to and perhaps has little to do with whether the sonnet can be found in nature or if flowers are metrical" (*All the Rage* [Ann Arbor: University of Michigan Press, 1998], 9).

5. Michael Lind, *The Alamo: An Epic* (New York: Houghton Mifflin, 1997), 54.

6. Ibid., 242.

7. Terza rima was first adopted in English poetry by Chaucer in his *Complaint to His Lady*. Like other forms it really came into its own in English poetry with the

Romantics, when they discovered Dante. It was used in such consciously Dantesque poems as Byron's *Prophecy of Dante* and Shelley's *Triumph of Life* (as well as his "Ode to the West Wind"). Leaving aside translations of *The Divine Comedy*, we can point to a number of twentieth-century poets who have used it, including Thomas Hardy, Robert Frost, W. H. Auden, James Merrill, Seamus Heaney, Elizabeth Jennings, Vikram Seth, and Greg Williamson, mostly for short lyrics or meditative works; the most successful recent work of a certain length (thirty-nine tercets) is Charles Martin's meditative poem, "After 9/11" (*Hudson Review* 48.3 [Autumn 2005]: 367–371). Poets who have used it at greater length in narrative fashion are Louis MacNeice, Derek Walcott, and Glyn Maxwell. However, Walcott and Maxwell understandably enough use a modified form, with abundant (almost regular) use of half-rhyme or slant-rhyme, and Louis MacNeice's work in the form is one of his least successful long poems. I have only recently read the long poem *Flight into Reality* (1989), by the Irish poet Rosemarie Rowley, which is the most ambitious attempt in modern times to use the form with strict rhymes at length; it is an intriguing work and deserves closer attention than I can give it here.

8. Andrew Waterman has pointed out to me that "another long rhymed form which has been powerfully revived in the twentieth century is the sonnet sequence: used by Auden, Heaney, Hill etc for their own highly original purposes very different from those of our Elizabethan sonneteers" (email to author, June 28, 2006).

9. W. H. Auden, "A Letter to Lord Byron," in *Collected Longer Poems* (London: Faber and Faber, 1974), 42.

10. Ibid. Auden used rhyme royal again in later years, most memorably and effectively in "The Shield of Achilles." This poem, which is entirely serious, alternates two different stanza forms, which basically contrast expectations with reality. The rhyme royal stanzas present the scenes of bleak reality; it is possibly a deliberate ploy on the poet's part to use this stanza form, previously associated with light humor, to convey such unremittingly bleak messages. It is noticeable that no feminine rhymes are used throughout.

11. Two twenty-first-century poets have used rhyme royal in direct homage to Auden, both using the title "Letter to Auden." A. M. Juster did so in a short poem in his volume *The Secret Language of Women* (2002) and N. S. Thompson in a highly enjoyable book-length work (2010), in which he updates Auden on literary and political events since his death.

12. In a collective enterprise under the editorship of Andy Croft and N. S. Thompson, sixteen poets are currently creating a modern version of Byron's *Don Juan*, contributing a canto each of adventures and mishaps in ottava rima for the new character, who—as his initials suggest—is now a "DJ."

13. Cited in Leslie A. Marchand, ed., *The Flesh Is Frail: Byron's Letters and Journals*,

vol. 6 (London: John Murray, 1976), 67.

14. George Gordon, Lord Byron, *Byron's Poems* (London: J. M. Dent, 1963), 385.

15. Kenneth Koch, *Ko, or A Season on Earth* (New York: Grove Press, 1959), jacket copy.

16. Kenneth Koch, *The Art of Poetry* (Ann Arbor: University of Michigan Press, 1996), 5.

17. Kenneth Koch, *On the Edge: Collected Long Poems* (New York: Knopf, 2007), 402.

18. Ibid., 402.

19. Ibid., 401.

20. Ibid., 409, 410.

21. Louis MacNeice, *Collected Poems* (London: Faber and Faber, 1979), 30.

22. Paul Fussell, *Poetic Meter and Poetic Form* (New York: McGraw-Hill, 1979), 146.

23. James Fenton, "In a Notebook," in *The Memory of War and Children in Exile: Poems 1968–1983* (Harmondsworth: Penguin, 1983), 25.

24. Dana Gioia, *Barrier of a Common Language: An American Looks at Contemporary British Poetry* (Ann Arbor: University of Michigan Press, 2003), 91.

25. Anthony Burgess, *Byrne* (London: Vintage, 1996), 7.

26. Ibid., 47.

27. Two other twentieth-century poems in ottava rima, both by Australian poets, should be mentioned: A. D. Hope's brilliant "Letter from Italy," written around the same time as Koch's poem, indicates its debt to Byron throughout, and in 1982 Clive James published his witty and technically assured "Poem of the Year." James admitted that the lightness of ottava rima was not always suited to the material. The twenty-first century has already seen *Huncke* (2010), a lively narrative by the New York poet Rick Mullin, and a short sequence, "The Poet's Zodiac" (2011), by Mary Meriam. All these works deserve much greater consideration than can be given in a footnote.

28. Burgess, *Byrne*, 101.

29. R. S. Gwynn, "Spenser's Eponymous," in *An Exaltation of Forms*, ed. Annie Finch and Kathrine Varnes (Ann Arbor: University of Michigan Press, 2002), 148.

30. Peter Conrad, *The Everyman History of English Literature* (London: J. M. Dent, 1985), 62.

31. Ibid.

32. In the mid-twentieth century the poet and diplomat Charles Johnston used it in a meditative poem of fifty stanzas titled "Towards Mozambique." In a later poem titled "In Praise of Gusto," he alternated between the Spenserian and the Onegin stanza.

33. Waterman had already used the Spenserian stanza in its unaltered form in a shorter poem titled "Shore Lines." In this poem the dragging motion of the final

line was well-suited to the subject matter since the poem was a darkly humorous meditation on his severely damaged eyesight, and on a new life full of "days slowed to tortoise speed" (259).

34. Andrew Waterman, "Millennium Letter," in *Collected Poems 1959–1999* (Manchester: Carcanet, 2000), 358.

35. Ibid., 372–373.

36. Ibid., 373.

37. Ibid., 376.

38. Ibid., 371.

39. Ibid., 381.

40. Found on the website www.andrewwaterman.co.uk.

41. Andrew Waterman to author, email, January, 25, 2006.

42. It is a curious coincidence that both John Hookham Frere and Charles Johnston were diplomats.

43. Charles Johnston, *Poems and Journeys* (London: Bodley Head, 1979), 7.

44. In 1935 Babette Deutsch published a translation, maintaining the stanza form; this was followed, in 1963, by a translation by Walter Arndt, also respecting the original form. Since Johnston's version, there have been four more translations, all preserving the stanza form (by James E. Falen, Douglas Hofstadter, Tom Beck, and Stanley Mitchell).

45. Shorter works in the form were written by William Scammell, Clive James (both simplifying the form by avoiding the alternation between masculine and feminine rhymes), and Jon Stallworthy, who exploited the Russian associations and the terpsichorean lightness of the form to tell the story of a love affair between an English diplomat and a Russian ballerina. There was even an enjoyable detective story in the form, *Jack the Lady-Killer*, by the crime writer H. R. F. Keating.

46. Found on the website www.andrewwaterman.co.uk.

47. Andrew Waterman, "Out for the Elements," in *Collected Poems 1959–1999* (Manchester: Carcanet, 2000), 117.

48. Ibid., 118.

49. Clive James, *From the Land of Shadows* (London: Picador, 1983), 160.

50. John Bayley, *Selected Essays* (Cambridge: Cambridge University Press, 1984), 108.

51. Waterman, "Out for the Elements," 136.

52. Ibid., 137.

53. Ibid., 149.

54. Quoted by Nicholas Wroe, "Building Bridges," *Guardian*, March 18, 2006.

55. John Fuller, *The Illusionists* (London: Secker and Warburg, 1980), 80.

56. Oddly enough, another diplomat-poet.

57. Fuller, *The Illusionists*, 81.

58. Ibid., 82.

59. Ibid.

60. Auden, "A Letter to Lord Byron," 61.

61. Vikram Seth, *The Golden Gate* (London: Faber and Faber, 1986), 100.

62. Ibid., 101.

63. Ibid., 239.

64. Ibid., 10.

65. Ibid., 152.

66. Kate Kellaway, "Kate Kellaway Meets Vikram Seth," *Literary Review*, August 1986, 14–15.

67. Vikram Seth, "Forms and Inspirations," *London Review of Books*, September 29, 1988, 20.

68. Vikram Seth, "The Summer Choice: Vikram Seth on His New Book *All You Who Sleep Tonight*," *Poetry Book Society Bulletin* (Autumn 1990): 2.

69. Kellaway, "Kate Kellaway Meets Vikram Seth," 15.

70. Seth, *Golden Gate*, 121.

71. Interestingly, there is only one line in the poem consisting of a single word, and that word is "Irreconcilability" (116). For what it's worth, *The Illusionists* has three such lines: "Individualization" (32), "Inconsequentiality" (84), and "Overdifferentiated" (87).

72. W. H. Auden, *The Dyer's Hand* (London: Faber and Faber, 1963), 364.

IMAGINING GEOGRAPHY
Campbell McGrath's Road Trips, Travelogues, and the Narrative Prose Poem

ROBERT MILTNER

When Campbell McGrath published his first book, *Capitalism,* in 1990, Daniel Halpern located him "in the tradition of Whitman and Ginsberg,"[1] that is, as a writer of "large poems" with long lines that swept across the page, like highways. The seventy-page "The Bob Hope Poem" in McGrath's 1996 book, *Spring Comes to Chicago,* confirmed his status as a poet of the large poem. McGrath subsequently received a Kingsley Tufts Poetry Award, a Guggenheim Fellowship, a MacArthur Foundation grant, and a teaching position at Florida International University, all endorsing perceptions such as Halpern's. Yet the 2005 publication of *Heart of Anthracite,* by Stride Books in England, confirmed what avid readers of McGrath's work already knew: he was also a master of the prose poem, and, as Joel Brouwer noted in *Parnassus* concerning McGrath's poetry, "the method is the catalogue, the means is the road trip."[2]

Because Campbell McGrath's range across the landscape of the contemporary American prose poem is so extensive, it seems best to concentrate on a small number of his more notable narrative forms: the travelogue prose poem, which is a combination of the road trip poem and the landscape sketch, and the catalogue prose poem, which is both part of and a variation on the travelogue prose poem. A brief survey of McGrath's travelogues and catalogues argues for greater recognition of his prowess with the narrative prose poem.

The Prose Poem

The creation of the prose poem has been credited to Charles Baudelaire, whose landmark collection *Le splen de Paris* (*Paris Spleen*), influenced by Aloysius Bertrand's *Gaspard de la nuit* (*Gaspard of the Night*), certainly launched the European prose poem. In considering McGrath's position as a contemporary American prose poet, however, it is important to recall that it was Walt Whitman who wrote, "In my opinion, the time has arrived to essentially break down the barriers of form between prose and poetry."[3]

The prose poem operates as a sort of double-helix form in which prose and poetry combine and intertwine. The resulting fusion is often a negotiation between the impulse of prose to narrate, to tell, and the impulse of poetry to experience, to show. As a result, prose poetry must negotiate registers of language; develop sentence rhythms that both retain the music of poetry and project the suppleness of prose; respond to the insistence on brevity; consider fugitive subjects that resist falling easily into the category of either prose or poetry; choose between fictional and poetic closure techniques; and determine when to break the prose block into stanzagraphs, a choice that must consider the operations of both the prose paragraph and the poetic stanza.

What Robert Alexander stated in "Prose/Poetry," his introductory essay to the important 1996 anthology *The Party Train: A Collection of North American Prose Poetry,* is worth considering: "The ability of the prose poem to . . . masquerade as different sorts of literary or non-literary prose, is one of its distinguishing characteristics—what Margueritte Murphy calls (after Mikhail Bakhtin) its *heteroglossia.* Some of the poems in this anthology seem therefore like brief memoirs, or travelogues."[4] Alexander's suggestion that the prose poem can be a literary travelogue bears on how we read Campbell McGrath's prose poems.

Campbell McGrath and the Prose Poem

Joel Brouwer's observation that McGrath's first book, *Capitalism,* "garnered attention for its irreverent variety of forms, which included . . . expansive prose poems,"[5] suggests that while many saw McGrath working in the shadow of Whitman's long lines, readers of prose poetry were drawn to *Capitalism*'s other Whitmanesque influences: travelogues of the open road and encyclopedic listings and repetitions, or catalogues.

Heart of Anthracite: Prose Poems 1980–2005 contains just over forty prose poems, yet each of his seven collections contains some prose poems: *Pax Atomica* (2004) contains only three, and *Florida Poems* (2002) includes prose poem sections within longer poems, as in "A City in the Clouds," McGrath's homage to Aristophanes. The collections *Capitalism* (1990) and *Road Atlas: Prose & Other Poems* (1999) are filled predominantly with prose poems, while *American Noise* (1994), which has only a few prose poems, is filled with travel poems in verse. *Seven Notebooks* (2008) has the largest number of prose poems, more than thirty, but it is McGrath's biggest book to date, at 223 pages more than twice the length of his other books.

Brouwer reports that, in the late 1990s, McGrath became "ever more attracted to the prose poem's capacity for digression and essayistic techniques," so much so that he called *Road Atlas: Prose & Other Poems* a "free book."[6] Reflecting on the demands of working in the poetic long form, McGrath recalls that during a particularly stressful period in writing "The Bob Hope Poem," something would "show up that was really clear and simple. 'I'm just going to write a prose poem about sitting on that hill in Nebraska.' And it would seem like a huge relief."[7] What is clear and simple is "Plums," from *Road Atlas*, which begins: "I'm sitting on a hill in Nebraska, in morning sunlight, looking out across the valley of the Platte River. My car is parked far below, in the lot behind the rest stop wigwam, beyond which runs the highway."[8] Beyond the river, in a sort of Hemingwayesque landscape panorama, is the inevitable highway, the road trip calling, the security of the homey "wigwam" ready for leaving. And thus the poem launches its travelers. But the poem also launches McGrath into an homage to William Carlos Williams: "For lunch, in a paper bag: three ripe plums and a cold piece of chicken. . . . My senses are alive to the warmth of the sun, the smell of the blood of the grass, the euphoria of the journey, the taste of fruit, fresh plums, succulent and juicy, especially the plums. // So much depends upon the image: chickens, asphodel, a numeral, a seashell; // one white peony flanged with crimson."[9]

Here are the plums from William Carlos Williams's "This Is Just to Say,"[10] succulent and juicy instead of "so sweet / and so cold," the asphodel, the chicken (cold as Williams's plums), the "So much depends / upon" lines from "The Red Wheelbarrow,"[11] and the crimson flanging the white peony (not chickens), evoking the red wheelbarrow from the poem of the same name. In a moment of connection, Williams and McGrath merge like prose and poetry, and the discovery of the road with its "promise of open space, the joy of setting out, the unmistakable goodness of the land and the people, the first hint of connection" becomes synonymous with the discovery of self through the act of writing the poem, of what is "entirely personal, associative, magical significance," and born from his being "witness to that moment. I heard it pass, touched it, tasted its mysterious essence"[12] and found it to be as tempting and satisfying as Williams's plums. "Sometimes," writes C. W. Truesdale, "a prose poem will just record an incident rather than a full-blown story and the effect of it will come through the details of what is observed."[13] McGrath's "Plums" records such an incident.

The Travelogue Prose Poem

The travelogue prose poem is related to and extends what Truesdale labels the "Landscape or Place Poem," which is "one of the most common forms of prose poetry, whether familiar landscapes are being described . . . or unique and even exotic ones (as in the travel poems of James Wright)," though it could be argued that the travelogue prose poem borrows from what Truesdale labels the "Hyperbolic" or "Exaggerated" prose poem, often noted for its "verbal play."[14] If we take that play to include sound patterns and the startling copresence of odd objects yoked together by placement within the prose poem, then what Truesdale proposes holds true. How interesting that, for the intention of presenting readers with a sense of place, either visited or imagined, prose poems have often used travel metaphors to try to describe the prose poem itself. David Young calls prose poems "maps on postage stamps" and "essays the size of postcards,"[15] while Louis Jenkins asks us to "Think of a prose poem as a small suitcase. One must pack carefully, only the essentials, too much and the reader won't get off the ground."[16]

In the development of the American prose poem during the twentieth century, the popularity of the travelogue prose poem is relatively recent. Two writers associated with the post–World War II generation and with the influential poet Robert Bly and his circle, Russell Edson and James Wright, have made important contributions to the development of the contemporary American prose poem, with Wright contributing particularly to the travelogue prose poem.

Russell Edson, who was a student at the experimental Black Mountain College, writes fabulist prose poems that take readers on surreal journeys through the ordinary. He is notable, as Michel Delville claims, for "his personal contribution to the history of the narrative prose poem in English: the neo-Surrealists, absurdist 'fable.'"[17] Because his hyperbolic tales and surreal narratives offered models for aesthetic and intellectual journeys, he prepared the way for later prose poets to add metaphoric and surreal layers of narrative that occur concurrently with the development of the place poem; in essence, the narrator, who is located in an actual locale and in real, mimetic time, can simultaneously travel in fabulist time, both expanding and enhancing the narrative. While Edson's work tends to foreground the prose, the poetry is always important in shaping the sentence rhythms and narrative style. Still, like microfiction, the "so-called narrative prose poem," notes Michel Delville, "generally appears as a further reduction of the thematic and narrative scope of the traditional short story, either in the form of an internal narrative or of a 'plot' restricted to a single anecdote of incident,"[18] and this focus on the single anecdote or incident is characteristic of Edson's narrative prose poems. Factors that distinguish the surreal nature of Edson's narrative prose poems, notes Lee Upton, are his "disruptions of time and space" and his "willingness . . . to conflate reference areas"[19]; they also include, as Gerrit Henry observes, Edson's ability to take his metaphors "to their wildly illogical conclusions."[20]

An example of a surreal narrative prose poem is Edson's "The Canoeing." Using a trope of physical inversion, the poem is a present-tense, first-person narrative of a man who canoes up the staircase to the second floor of a house. Here the inversion operates on two levels: first, the canoe goes up the stairs similar to the way salmon go upstream since, of course, it is physically impossible for a human to paddle up a waterfall, and second, Edson offers a playful variation on the way in which children sometimes imaginatively "sled" down the stairs. The poem thus moves from the real (stairs are for people to walk up and down) to the surreal (children who "sled" down staircases and fish that swim upstream). The surreality is acknowledged by Edson in his description of the "salmon passing us" on the stairs "like the slippered feet of someone falling down the stairs, played backward as in a movie." Once in the "quiet waters of the upstairs hall," the narrator "glides for days" in a heavenly upstairs Eden, "glid[ing] for days by family bedrooms under a stillness of trees,"[21] as if the humans who paddled up the staircase were very like the salmon, completing Edson's fabulist tale told through the vehicle of a surreal narrative prose poem.

James Wright, on another hand, eschews the surreal in his travelogue prose poems, seeking instead to engage the real world as a means of encountering the historical and cultural past. Having moved from traditional to free verse as a result of the influence of his friend Robert Bly, Wright next expanded his writing repertoire to include the prose poem. Influenced by his own translations of European poetic traditions, including its prose poetry, Bly had developed his own nature-centered, deep-image prose poems to express his relationship with the natural world to which he felt so close, exemplified by his collection *What Have I Ever Lost by Dying?* No wonder, then, that James Wright embraced the prose poem when he toured Europe—it must have appeared an appropriate genre for the wonder he felt as he considered the difference between his life in the American Midwest and the Italian landscapes that challenged his lexical and syntactic abilities. The results, seen in *The Shape of Light*, which Christopher Merrill calls "a pivotal book in James Wright's body of work,"[22] helped shape the contemporary travelogue prose poem.

When he went to Italy on a sabbatical in 1973, Wright needed a means to express the new experience of the Old World. As his wife, Annie, recalls, "This new form [the prose poem] blossomed during the long tranquil days of a sabbatical leave. We spent most of our time in Italy, and, among other places, visited Lake Garda and Verona, both of which were new to James."[23] Since he was writing of his own experiences, in a manner akin to memoir, Wright's realist narratives with a lyrical level of observation are examples of what Tess Gallagher identifies as lyric-narrative poems, that is, those in which the poet becomes the hero of his own narrative, as well as the poet's imagination itself as hero,[24] "in the sense that the poetic *persona* and the poet's autobiography are . . . closely engaged."[25] What emerges is the lyrical "intimacy of voice" of the speaker which is "dependent upon narrative, anecdotal strategies,"[26] and what engages readers is that "the poet's voice here is in the same relation to the reader as it is to itself—that is, confessionally open."[27] As Wright traveled to Europe regularly between 1973 and 1979, "he embarked on a different sort of journey, inward and outward, discovering new angles of vision, new ways of writing,"[28] and, through the prose poem, Wright is intimate and confessionally open, anecdotal, and heroic.

Time and place are often important considerations in Wright's prose poems. Despite the changing locales—France, Italy, or his hometown of Martin's Ferry, Ohio—time is often fixed. Annie Wright: "In these prose pieces it might seem to always be summer: summer where blissful afternoons were spent in Italy or France under clear, blue skies and brilliant sunlight, interrupted only by a gentle breeze or the sound of water. But there is a haunting undercurrent of pain or trouble in some of the work."[29] No wonder Wright basked in the light of his writing, reinvigorated by his turn to prose poetry, for it was the stimulus of Italian travel that drew him on and drew him out, for, as Christopher Merrill notes, "like Keats and Goethe, Wright traveled south in search of another way of life, and what he found in the land of his beloved Horace and Catullus, in the realm of eternal verities, was a language informed by the speech rhythms of his native land and inflected through an array of literary traditions—a language adequate to the demands of the moment."[30]

"The Language of the Present Moment," written in three brief stanza-graphs, tells of Wright drifting in a boat on Lake Garda, while the "tall and short mountains" are said to "look barren" in the summer mist as they reflect on the lake's surface, "throw[ing] their own flowers on the water."[31] Might this be the effect of that brilliant sunlight that attracted Wright, its ability to make the commonplace seem magical, almost surreal? But the "haunting undercurrent" is developed in the second stanzagraph as Wright considers how the town of Limone, which "long ago gave up hope of surviving" when it lost its economic base to "the lemons of Sicily, quicker and more numerous,"[32] now casts a shadow, both literally and figuratively, over the lake. What could be sadder, one asks, than a ghost town? Wright's answer arrives in the third stanzagraph: "the stone villa of Catullus [that] still stands at the far southern end of the lake,"[33] for even though the Roman poet is gone, his villa still receives visitors, despite competition from contemporary poets, some of whom might be his poetic inferior, as one uses *lemons* in the American vernacular. Wright's direct address to the villa, "I hope you are in blossom when his ghost comes home,"[34] resonates beyond the visual level, for Catullus or his ghost may magically return to blossom, which is similar to the flowerlike images of the mountains' reflection on Lake Garda's surface, yet unlike the unblossoming lemon trees in Limone. For Wright, blossoming is always symbolic of growth, of progress, of enhancement, as he states at the ending of his often anthologized "A Blessing": after petting a horse, he says, "if I stepped out of my body I would break / Into blossom."[35] Yet in the instant of the present moment of the poem, he has stepped outside the moment of his American present with its lyric verse and into the moment of the Italian past through the prose poem.

Since McGrath has readily admitted to his admiration for and the influence of James Wright on his own work, what applies to any discussion of Wright's lyric narrative prose poems may be equally applied to McGrath's poems. In his poem "A Letter to James Wright," which echoes Wright's own poem to his son, "A Letter to Franz Wright," McGrath writes of his admiration for the travelogue prose poems of James Wright:

> [. . .] my mind is adrift among clouds and boats and poems, and it seems to me that the finest of these vessels may be "A Letter to Franz Wright." At least it is the loveliest to which I give anchorage on this day, the dearest-held poem harbored within me. There's so much I admire in it, so much to be learned—the sense of humility and awe, the wonder of its Italian landscape, its voice, its range, its texture, the charm and formal daring, the perfect pitch of its emotion, the love and respect of a father for his son.

> Italy, prose poems, fathers and sons—well, obviously

> I'm prejudiced.

> Still I return to that work again and again. I love so many of those last poems, treasure them like sacral beings[36]

To pay homage to one's literary mentors is a way to give thanks not only for the pleasures of the text but also for the craft taught, as a writer learns by reading the mentor-writer. McGrath's inventory of skills that advance the craft of poetry he has learned from Wright—voice, range, texture, formal daring, emotional pitch, wonder of landscape—are the same skills McGrath brings to his own landscape and travelogue prose poems.

McGrath's Travelogue Prose Poems

Of the various subgenres of twentieth-century writing, the travel narrative, that semi-autobiographical account of personal travels, is popular "with travelers and the general reading public."[37] One closely linked to it is the contemporary travelogue, especially the road-trip narrative, a pop culture term for what in the United States is rooted in Whitman's sweeping ramblings and which locates its contemporary tradition in Jack Kerouac's Beat classic, *On the Road.* While "travel-writing theory tends to focus mostly on 'literary' travelogues . . . defining them as a separate genre that is both literary and an art form,"[38] Campbell McGrath draws from and is wrapped in pop culture, so that his travelogues create a fusion of "literary" travelogues and the pop culture road trip narrative with its elements of adventure narratives, travel diaries, and semi-autobiographical accounts of personal travel. As a result, McGrath participates in exploring "the important role played by cultural and social factors in a genre [prose poem] too often conceived in terms of its strictly textual characteristics."[39]

Sara Dickinson defines literary travelogues as a "highly stylized literary genre" that provide readers and travelers with "not only metaphors but also fundamental ideas about time, space and culture"[40] that are used to construct "imaginary geographies"[41] that "emphasize issues of 'identity.' "[42] Discussing Russian travelogues written in the eighteenth century and early nineteenth century, Dickinson observes that

> provincial landscapes provided the writer/narrator with an individual origin rather than with a dynamic social or special identity. Only after having transcended the limitations of "the restrictive travelogue format for the broader range of possibilities offered by fiction" . . . were the Russian writers able to mold a new and dynamic relationship to imperial space.[43]

If we consider that the prose poem is located within the parameters of fiction, then perhaps the prose *poem* transcends the limits of the "restrictive travelogue format" and moreover provides Campbell McGrath with an opportunity to establish a new and dynamic relationship to the space of both American empire and American pop culture. Thus, while the travelogue can be seen as an expression of a country's "anxieties about . . . national identity,"[44] it can also be seen as an expression of the writer's shaping his or her personal identity. Because contemporary travel literature focuses on the traveler's experiences and personal point of view, critic Stephan Kohl draws "a parallel between aspects of travel writing and autobiography."[45]

McGrath's travelogues "make remarkable use of geographical places as mirrors (by looking deeply at a place, [he] discovers new territory inside himself) but also stages, even soapboxes, from which McGrath delivers his barbed and witty commentary on contemporary culture," as Joel Brouwer notes, adding that his travelogue [prose] poems are "often driven by awe . . . [by] a sense that certain things can only be discovered through the thrilling alienation of travel."[46]

McGrath acknowledges the importance of travel in his work, both verse poems and prose poems:

> I'm a kind of documentarian, and just seeing new things to document gets me going. . . . It's like turning on the camera to record new landscapes, new cultural observations.[47]

McGrath "has always used geography to channel his imagination,"[48] and Brouwer opines that McGrath "frequently uses past travel experiences to make sense of his present concerns and circumstances."[49]

Readers of MaGrath's work know that travelogues have always been his forte. His first book, *Capitalism,* takes readers from Memphis, Los Angeles, and small Colorado mountain towns like Silt and Rifle to Berlin, Yellowknife, and Negril Beach in Jamaica. *Road Atlas,* however, contains McGrath's rich collection of prose poems, as readers visit Baker, California; Mountainair, New Mexico; Tabernacle, New Jersey; Las Vegas, Nevada; then on to Amsterdam, Manitoba and the Florida Gulf. Readers of *Seven Notebooks* find place poems about Philadelphia, Miami, Phoenix, Chicago, and the New Jersey shore. In addition to sense observations of each locale, McGrath includes wry observations of consumer culture by demonstrating how what we have seems to state who we are.

Of his landscape sketches—a form of travelogue, or maybe a subcategory—none seems more powerful than "The Prose Poem" that opens *Road Atlas.* As McGrath considers how a small gulley without a fence between a corn field and a wheat field goes unnoticed by the two farmers, he notes that the wildest flora grows in the gulley between them, for where corn and wheat, prose and poetry merge, readers find the rich life of the prose poem. Of course, "fusion" in the space between two discrete crops, corn and wheat, is akin to the merging of two forms into prose poetry, each, if the pun holds, in the American grain, a phrase from William Carlos Williams, whose prose poetry in *Kora in Hell* stands beside Gertrude Stein's *Tender Buttons* as some of the earliest *intentional* prose poems collected in book form. Yet McGrath is clear that what exists between the two distinct crops is not "some jackalopian hybrid of the two" but rather is "possessed of a beauty all its own."[50] The poem's movement, on the one hand, is physical, from what "on the map is precise and rectilinear as a chessboard" at the start, to farmers who "grow crops by pattern, by acre, by foresight, by habit," ending with the divergent closure we know as prose: "tell me, if you would, do the formal fields end where the valley begins, or does everything that surrounds us emerge from its embrace?"[51] The poem's movement is also framed within the travel narrative frame, moving from "though driving past you would hardly notice it, this boundary line or ragged margin, a shallow swale "[52] to McGrath's prodding us with the final open-ended question by reminding us, "You've passed this way yourself many times."[53] While some elements of the catalogue are evident in this poem—all the animals and birds that visit the in-between gully—the poem offers an example of a travelogue that is developed through the poetic device of extended metaphor.

Two companion prose poems describe traveling through the small Colorado towns of Rifle and Silt. "Rifle, Colorado" is divided into two stanza-graphs. The first is a series of six sentences showing the traveler trying to determine what he knows of the people in this town: not much, for two of the sentences begin with "I doubt," three begin with "I don't know," and one offers a speculation: "I think." Here readers see the uncertainty and questioning engagement, the thrilling alienation of travel, that is at the heart of the road trip narrative. The second stanzagraph is one sentence of certain knowledge, beginning, in contrast, with "I do know" and offering a catalogue of sights and objects that define the town, or at least the traveler's understanding of the town: "I do know that there were cowboy hats and dirty orange workmen's gloves, the coffee was strong, the pancakes were good, Main Street was gravel, the river ran by" as the traveler moves out of the night's darkness into the illumination (of knowledge) and "the mountains emerged slowly with the dawn—high country in winter is beautiful and lonely,"[54] an aesthetic and emotional awareness, respectively.

"Silt, Colorado" is as much a catalogue as it is a travelogue. Crossing the Rockies by night, the traveler struggles to talk about the new landscape he sees: "To describe Silt would require a tactile vocabulary to match the roiling high country," then attempts to catalogue what he sees: "high country, purple and dusk fading down the peaks: long grazing plateaus above the river, savage dun-pale pastels, the cliffs, gulch and guyot, each shadow, each stone itself."[55] This inventory moves from the high mountain peaks in the distance and draws cinematically in toward the narrator until he can see shadows and stones right at his feet. This cataloguing technique is repeated in the second stanzagraph beginning with the trip's itinerary, "the long pull—Martian Utah, sad Las Vegas, the ponderous, mesquite-crazed Mojave, Baker, Barstow, Los Angeles," and concluding at the end of the country in the great city of lights; he finishes his cataloguing with a quick inventory of the pies in a rack at a local restaurant in Barstow: "apple, cherry, coconut cream, lemon meringue,"[56] as generic an inventory as one associates with old-style diners, the fast-food eateries of an earlier generation. Perhaps it is the silt of the past that McGrath discovers in this prose poem.

What readers observe in these travelogue prose poems is the growing sense of space, of national and personal identity. In the space through which he travels, McGrath observes both the residue of traditional Americana as found in its isolated provincial towns and the pop culture simulacra that pass today for the trappings and wrapping of what this nation has become; moreover, he concurrently develops his own growing personal identity, changing as he is moving, experiencing self-expansion as the road atlas—the title of his book of "prose & other poems"—creates "imaginary geographies" that become the contexts of his poems. No wonder that, in a versed travelogue from the same volume, self- and national identity merge in the poem "Campbell McGrath,"[57] in which he describes roving across a U.S. atlas in search of towns named Campbell or McGrath, and his road trip takes him from Campbell, Florida, to McGrath, Alaska—with Campbells in Ohio, Missouri, Arkansas, and California—offering a perfect metaphor for how, as Brouwer writes, he "use[s] geography to channel his imagination."[58]

Seven Notebooks, McGrath's longest work, is comprised of seven "notebook" sections that divide the year from January 8 to December 30 and vary in form, including prose poems, memoir, verse, haiku, and ode, along with short excerpts from Whitman, Freud, Miłosz, and Coetzee. McGrath includes a travelogue prose poem that uses a sort of topographical trace in which the airplane flight offers an upgrade from the road trip. "March 10 (Barbarians): In Flight, Chicago to Miami" uses an eye-in-the-sky camera effect to relate the changing landscapes he sees from the airplane window as the road trip is replaced by air flight. Looking down over the Midwest where he grew up, he observes "the pitched huts of ice fisherman, sometimes a pickup truck out on the ice, small dark circles carved in the frozen skin of the water,"[59] hallmarks of the traditional sport of ice fishing in upper Midwest winters. This is followed by his consideration of the "blocks of bungalows" that keep neighbors "walled and apart," as emphasized by one of his trademark inventories, which includes "black trees, white snow, bare fields, farms, industrial zones, open lots bereft of significance, hotels, taverns,"[60] as the poet's eye moves from the rural to the urban, from separation and silence to community and American noise. Squares and lines, as he aerially observes, divide people; he'd rather "a giant hive" of communication that offers a tentative though metaphorical answer to his previously raised questions: "Which way do those portals open? What form of transit, what commerce between the realms?"[61]

Passing later over Florida—Tallahassee, Big Bend, Cedar Key, Tampa, the Gulf—McGrath considers the continuing commercial development as golf courses and marinas cut into the Everglades. The contrasts between Lake Michigan and the Gulf, winter ice and endless summer, are obvious, but it is the more subtle parallels—"the northern extremities of Tampa," echoing the north coast of the United States as defined by the Great Lakes; the "dark woods in the organic vertiginous ridges and hollows," which generally define the central part of the country; and the "last swamp forests" and "distant scrubland" of central Florida heading south, that ultimately draw the eye: in this close-up, in the zoom lens focus, is the important terrain, the transitional place where one sees "salt water merging with the land, emerging from the silk of its eminence to crawl, bellywise, into the undergrowth, and burrow into the sandy soil, and wait."[62] The passage evokes both the sea turtle coming ashore to lay its eggs in the sand and the image of creatures leaving the sea to evolve on the shore into creatures of the land; and in this pseudo-estuary, at this point of contact, a question surfaces: "What shall be born of that union—."[63] To answer, McGrath splits the prose block and offers a question in a couplet:

creature with seashell ears and vines for hair,
mermaids fed on manatee milk?[64]

Such fusion between the worlds of land and water evokes Ezra Pound's "Canto II," in which Acœtes watches the kidnapped boy with "a god in him" produce "Fish-scales on the oarsmen" while "The swimmer's arms turned to branches."[65] This is not sailors passing "to the left of the Naxos passage"[66] but Campbell McGrath flying from Chicago to Miami, yet the similarities between water, journeys, transformations, and considerations of worlds in transition are noteworthy. Still, McGrath's response to his query is but a riddle, a Romantic, magical, and anthropomorphic transformation offering an image "as lush as [Florida's] saltwater flats and everglades"[67] no more definitive than a mirage.

The Catalogue Travelogue Prose Poem

Because the prose poem often presents itself as a paragraph, it develops ideas, as paragraphs do, through description, comparison and contrast, classification and division, spatial organization, or orders of importance; in doing so, it often relies on catalogues or inventories as means of providing details, and thus the prose poem can be a catalogue poem, either in part or in its entirety. Catalogue poems trace their roots, historically and literarily, back to Old English literature, as in the "geographically organized catalogue" *Fates of the Apostles,* then they "develop within the proliferation of travelogues," evidenced by "travel diaries, recordings of scientific and exploratory missions, adventure narratives,"[68] and various "histories" of colonization or captivity such as the Norman Domesday Book. Since a number of early travelogues, during the English Restoration and Augustan periods for example, focused on trade, they "trace a material history of common items of trade," and those items, sometimes in lists or catalogues, "demonstrate the material and cultural importance"[69] of objects in national identity. In American literature, at least in its poetry, the encyclopedic nature of much of Whitman's poetry falls within the range of the catalogue poem. Because the terms "list" poem and catalogue poem are often used interchangeably, John Drury sees the "list" poem as "modeled on the catalogs Walt Whitman favored,"[70] an interesting connection, given Whitman's interest, discussed earlier, in seeing the barriers between prose and poetry being taken down.

McGrath's catalogue poems are reminiscent of the list poem, yet because he packs them into the prose poem format—with justified margins and of a length that makes the poems square on the page—the content of the poems echoes the shape. "A Map of Dodge County, Wisconsin" has the look of tables set up at yard sales, covered in discarded objects of our consumer culture—salt and pepper shakers and "margarita glasses stolen from Chi-Chi's" and a vintage beer bottle collection:

> White Cap, North Star, Gold Label, Falls City; Ziegler's, Kurth's, Grat's, Jung's; Alps Brau and Fox DeLuxe, Holiday and Munchner; Hauenstein, Pioneer, Chief Oshkosh, Oconto.[71]

The sixteen different beers, set off by semicolons into sets of four to help the reader envision small tables at a yard sale, seem to offer a final toast to the closed local breweries that once displayed the cultural identity of the residents of this part of Wisconsin. Stylistically, McGrath joins numerous sets of objects with these semicolons; as a result, it feels as if the objects both blur into a tableau of pop culture junk and also, given a moment of scrutiny and inventory, stand out as individual pieces of a cultural identity puzzle. Readers encounter animals: "pewter doves and tin lovebirds, plaster polar bears and ceramic moose"; domestic kitchen objects: "potato mashers, rolling pins, canning jars, ladles"; and variations on single objects, as in "Olde Copenhagen candy bowls in cyanine, verbena, sienna, and spruce," and, as in the cultural residue he found in the pies in the pie rack in Barstow, in "Silt, Colorado," he finds "vintage collections of brown glass bottles embossed with the totem and heraldic crests of the local burghers' vanished brews" contrasted with the "margarita glasses stolen from Chi-Chi's"[72] on another table.

"Sunset, Route 90, Brewster County, Texas" offers a vision of American pop culture spiritualism. Supported by Brouwer's observation that it is "always either midnight or just before dawn" in McGrath's travelogues,[73] McGrath waxes on the building dawn light, offering some 30 types of light: metallic (brass, pewter, silver), stellar (moon, cusp), religious (sermon, gospel, clasped hands), and mechanical (windmills, crossroads, flood, harbor), and he concludes with a litany (catalogue) of a Christ, a savior, and eight Jesuses: "Jesus of cottonwood, Jesus of oil, Jesus of jackrabbits, Jesus of quail, Jesus of creosote, Jesus of slate, Jesus of solitude, Jesus of grace."[74] Readers may conclude from this list that, given the solitude of the open spaces one crosses while on a road trip, writing a travelogue, and the constantly changing landscapes and cityscapes one might use as a measure of personal growth, where else could such a poem end except with grace?

Conclusion

"Hunger for experience," notes Joel Brouwer, and "the mixture of high and low diction, keen attention to musicality, and the sudden leap from the personal to the universal—all these have remained consistent features of McGrath's poems over the years."[75] Daniel Halpern's identification of McGrath's Whitmanesque sweep and range, both in subject matter and in the poetic line, may remain true, but a study of McGrath's prose poetry offers a glimpse of Whitman's encyclopedic rendering in McGrath's encounters with the world.

A master of the contemporary narrative prose poem and the travelogue prose poem, McGrath writes in a tradition that includes early narrative prose poets Russell Edson and James Wright and is similar to the work of the contemporary narrative prose poets Amy Bracken Sparks and Peter Johnson.[76] For McGrath, whose work draws from and is wrapped in pop culture, travelogues create a fusion of "literary" travelogues and the pop culture road trip narrative with its elements of adventure narratives, travel diaries, and semi-autobiographical accounts of personal travel. McGrath sees himself as a "documentarian," and his travelogue prose poems are "like turning on the camera to record new landscapes, new cultural observations."[77] Whether extended metaphor, as in "The Prose Poem," epistemological postcards to the world in "Rifle, Colorado" and "Silt, Colorado," catalogue in "A Map of Dodge County, Wisconsin," spiritual incantation in "Sunset, Route 90, Brewster County, Texas," or topographical trace in "March 10 (Barbarians): In Flight, Chicago to Miami," Campbell McGrath's narrative prose poems show that what can be gained through the thrilling alienation of travel is a greater sense of self and of cultural identity.

Notes

1. Campbell McGrath, *Capitalism* (Hanover, NH: University Press of New England/Wesleyan University Press, 1990), jacket copy quoting Daniel Halpern.

2. Joel Brouwer, "Accordion Music and Raw Profusion," *Parnassus: Poetry in Review* 26.2 (2002): 6, http://web.ebscohost.com/ehost/ (accessed November 20, 2007).

3. Quoted in Robert Alexander, "Prose/Poetry," in *The Party Train: A Collection of North American Prose Poetry,* ed. Robert Alexander, Mark Vinz, and C. D. Truesdale (Minneapolis, MN: New Rivers Press, 1996), xxiv–xxxiii.

4. Ibid.

5. Joel Brouwer, "About Campbell McGrath," *Ploughshares* (Spring 2004): 175–180, http://www.pshares.org/issues/article.cfm?prmarticleID=7916 (accessed November 20, 2007).

6. Ibid., 178.

7. Quoted in Brouwer, "About Campbell McGrath," 178–179.

8. Campbell McGrath, "Plums," in *Road Atlas: Prose & Other Poems* (New York: Ecco Press, 1999), 5.

9. Ibid.

10. William Carlos Williams, "This Is Just to Say," in *Selected Poems*, ed. Charles Tomlinson (New York: New Directions, 1985), 74.

11. Williams, "The Red Wheelbarrow," in *Selected Poems*, 56.

12. McGrath, "Plums," 6.

13. C. W. Truesdale, publisher's preface to *The Party Train: A Collection of North American Prose Poetry*, ed. Robert Alexander, Mark Vinz, and C. W. Truesdale (Minneapolis, MN: New Rivers Press, 1996), xix–xxiii.

14. Ibid.

15. Quoted in *Creating Poetry*, ed. John Drury (Cincinnati, OH: Writer's Digest Books, 1991), 71.

16. Quoted in Michel Delville, *The American Prose Poem: Poetic Form and the Boundaries of Genre* (Gainsville: University Press of Florida, 1998), 245.

17. Delville, *The American Prose Poem*, 104.

18. Ibid., 104.

19. Quoted by Robert Miltner in "Russell Edson," *Dictionary of Literary Biography 244: American Short Story Writers since World War II*, 4th ser., ed. Patrick Meanor and Joseph McNicholas (Detroit, MI: Gale, 2001), 83–90.

20. Ibid., 83–90.

21. Ibid.

22. Christopher Merrill, afterword to *The Shape of Light* by James Wright (Buffalo, NY: White Pine Press, 1986), 85–90.

23. Annie Wright, introduction to *The Shape of Light* by James Wright (Buffalo, NY: White Pine Press, 1986), 7–10.

24. Tess Gallagher, "Again: Some Thoughts on the Narrative Impulse in Contemporary Poetry," in *A Concert of Tenses: Essays on Poetry* (Ann Arbor: University of Michigan Press, 1986), 67–82.

25. Ibid., 70.

26. Ibid., 71.

27. Ibid., 74.

28. Merrill, afterword to *The Shape of Light*, 85.

29. A. Wright, introduction to *The Shape of Light*, 9.

30. Merrill, afterword to *The Shape of Light*, 87.

31. Wright, "The Language of the Present Moment," in *The Shape of Light*, 30.

32. Ibid.

33. Ibid.

34. Ibid.

35. James Wright, "A Blessing," in *Above the River: The Complete Poems* (New York: Noonday Press of Farrar, Straus and Giroux; Lebanon, NH: University Press of New

England, 1992), 143.

36. McGrath, "A Letter to James Wright," in *Road Atlas,* 45–50.

37. "Contemporary Travel Narratives," *Enotes,* www.enotes.com/contemporary-literary-criticism/contemporary-travel-narratives (accessed November 21, 2007), 2.

38. Ibid., 1.

39. Sara Dickinson, "The Russian Tour of Europe before Fonvizin: Travel Writing as Literary Endeavor in Eighteenth Century Russian Literature," *Slavic and East European Journal* 45.1 (Spring 2001): 3, www.jstor.org/view/00376752/sp03003/03x0127w/0 (accessed November 20, 2007).

40. Ibid., 1.

41. Christian Noack, review of Sara Dickinson's *Breaking Ground: Travel and National Culture in Russia from Peter I to the Era of Pushkin,* H-Net Reviews in the Humanities & Social Sciences, H-Travel (March 2007), h-net.msu.edu (accessed November 23, 2007), 1.

42. Ibid., 2.

43. Ibid., 3.

44. "The Restoration and the Eighteenth Century: Topics," in *The Norton Anthology of English Literature,* www.wwnorton.com/college/english/nael/18century/topic_4/welcome.htm 3.

45. "Contemporary Travel Narratives," 2.

46. Brouwer, "About Campbell McGrath," 175.

47. Ibid., 175.

48. Brouwer, "Accordion Music and Raw Profusion," 9.

49. Ibid., 11.

50. McGrath, "The Prose Poem," in *Road Atlas,* 1–2.

51. Ibid.

52. Ibid., 1.

53. Ibid., 2.

54. McGrath, "Rifle, Colorado," in *Capitalism,* 7.

55. McGrath, "Silt, Colorado," in *Capitalism,* 6.

56. Ibid., 6.

57. McGrath, "Campbell McGrath," in *Road Atlas,* 71–74.

58. Brouwer, "Accordion Music and Raw Profusion," 9.

59. Campbell McGrath, "March 10 (Barbarians): In Flight, Chicago to Miami," in *Seven Notebooks: Poems* (New York: Ecco Press, 2008), 45–47.

60. Ibid., 45.

61. Ibid., 45.

62. Ibid., 46.

63. Ibid., 46.

64. Ibid., 47.

65. Ezra Pound, "Canto II," in *The Cantos 1–95* (New York: New Directions, 1956), 9.

66. Ibid., 7.

67. Mike Chasar, "Sunshine State," review of *Florida Poems* by Campbell McGrath, *American Book Review* 24:2 (January–February 2003): 19.

68. "Contemporary Travel Narrative," 2.

69. "The Restoration and the Eighteenth Century," 2.

70. John Drury, *Creating Poetry* (Cincinnati, OH: Writer's Digest Books, 1991).

71. McGrath, "A Map of Dodge County, Wisconsin," in *Road Atlas*, 64.

72. Ibid., 64.

73. Brouwer, "Accordion Music and Raw Profusion," 1.

74. Campbell McGrath, "Sunset, Route 90, Brewster County, Texas," in *American Noise* (New York: Ecco Press, 1993), 12.

75. Brouwer, "About Campbell McGrath," 176.

76. Peter Johnson's *Miracles and Mortifications* (Buffalo, NY: White Pine Press, 2001) and Amy Bracken Sparks's *Queen of Cups* (Cleveland, OH: Burning Press, 1993) each offer book-length examples of travelogue prose poems.

77. Brouwer, "About Campbell McGrath," 175.

PART II

The Contemporary Narrative

Poem and History

CONTRIVED CORRIDORS

History and Postmodern Poetry

ROBERT B. SHAW

The long poem has been an imposing challenge for both modern and postmodern poets writing in English. In seeking subject matter for their extended works, the modernists and their successors (by now some three generations of them) have frequently succumbed to the allure of history. Eliot's "Gerontion" offers some earnest counsel to those thus tempted:

> Think now
> History has many cunning passages, contrived corridors
> And issues, deceives with whispering ambitions,
> Guides us by vanities.[1]

Yet this is a warning repeatedly spurned by poets strolling into the labyrinth. Each explorer, of course, enters carrying his own distinctive equipment, and the results of such ventures are anything but uniform. An essay like this can only hope to sketch some of the more notable recent poetic strategies for engaging history. And before doing this, a glance at the theory and practice of Eliot's generation is in order.

History, often accompanied by myth, is a presence in many canonical long poems: *The Waste Land, The Bridge, Paterson, The Anathémata, The Cantos*. Ezra Pound, who was not given to understatement, described *The Cantos* as "a poem including history." The highly influential use of history by Pound and Eliot dispensed with linear narrative, arranging truncated episodes or even briefer allusions to historical sources in a kind of cubist collage. The point for these poets is not to recount past events in detail but to suggest parallels between the past and the present that such selected moments could illuminate. As early as 1912, in a treatise portentously titled "I Gather the Limbs of Osiris," Pound was advocating what amounts to an imagist approach to history, urging his readers to sift the past in search of what he called "the luminous detail"—a recommendation that could serve as the key to understanding an entire epoch or culture:

> A few dozen facts of this nature give us intelligence of a period—a kind of intelligence not to be gathered from a great array of facts of the other sort. These facts are hard to find. They are swift and easy of transmission. They govern knowledge as the switchboard governs an electric circuit.[2]

An impressive theory, but the trouble comes in the practice. Pound's *Cantos* are crammed with fragmented annals, which he presents as instructive:

THE BOOK OF THE COUNCIL MAJOR
1255 be it enacted:
That they mustn't shoot crap in the hall
of the council, nor in the small court under
pain of 20 dinari [. . .][3]

Died KAO TSEU the emperor's father
   635 anno domini
Died the Empress Tchang-sun CHI
   leaving 'Notes for Princesses'
And TAÏ in his law code cut 92 reasons for death sentence
   and 71 for exile
   as they had been under SOUI[4]

These luminous details have left more than a few readers feeling not only unilluminated but wearisomely harassed. Of course, *The Cantos* are harder going (not least by reason of length) than some other modernist works. In *The Waste Land*, Eliot's ironic juxtapositions of past and present—of the Battle of Mylae with the Battle of the Dardanelles, of the courtship of Elizabeth and Leicester with the sordid trysts of the modern "Thames Maidens"—are more engaging examples of the modernist view of history. History is seen as cyclical, manifesting patterns of repetition, and a philosophical view of civilization's evolution through time is of more interest to these poets than any single event or personage they may choose momentarily to spotlight. The fleeting nature of such historical references makes the level of importance of any single one of them a matter for debate. Hart Crane in *The Bridge* uses the New York subway system as a convenient location for his modern equivalent of the catabasis of a classical epic. Here, after establishing an atmosphere of sordidness and corruption ("The phonographs of hades in the brain / Are tunnels that re-wind themselves, and love / A burnt match skating in a urinal"[5]), he has a visionary encounter with an earlier *poète maudit*, Edgar Allan Poe:

> And why do I often meet your visage here,
> Your eyes like agate lanterns—on and on
> Below the toothpaste and the dandruff ads?
> [. . .]
> And Death, aloft,—gigantically down
> Probing through you—toward me, O evermore!
> And when they dragged your retching flesh,
> Your trembling hands that night through Baltimore—
> That last night on the ballot rounds, did you
> Shaking, did you deny the ticket, Poe?[6]

The nightmare image is soon followed by a sentimental apostrophe to a fellow passenger:

> And does the Dæmon take you home, also,
> Wop washerwoman, with the bandaged hair?
> After the corridors are swept, the cuspidors—
> The gaunt sky-barracks cleanly now, and bare,
> O Genoese, do you bring mother eyes and hands
> Back home to children and to golden hair?[7]

She is "Genoese," of course, to recall Christopher Columbus, the idealistic hero invoked by Crane at the beginning of the poem in the section titled "Ave Maria." Crane's use of a type of stream-of-consciousness narrative allows such historically grounded images to impinge on his present perceptions of the scene in an intermittent (even rather jumpy) way. Interestingly, although one of these figures is hallucinatory and the other is sitting across the aisle, the poet renders both, and the reader experiences both, on the same plane of reality. Each is a piece of the collage assembled from bits of the past and the present: history is flattened out before our eyes (or at least before Crane's).

The method tends to subvert chronology. Williams, in book 1 of *Paterson*, shuttles between historical documents and personal observation in a similarly nonlinear fashion. A newspaper account from 1875 of a dead body discovered near the Paterson Falls gives way to an evocation of the twentieth-century despoilment of the river and its surroundings ("Half the river red, half streaming purple / from the factory vents").[8] And this, after a few pages of the narrator's meditation on the imaginative challenge such ugliness offers the poet, concludes:

> Things, things unmentionable,
> the sink with the waste farina in it and
> lumps of rancid meat, milk-bottle tops: have
> here a tranquility and loveliness
> Have here (in his thoughts)
> a complement tranquil and chaste.[9]

This is immediately followed by the punning line, "He shifts his change:"— and the colon introduces a quotation from a historical source about a local earthquake in 1737, in which "happily no great damage ensued." The poet's shifting the change in his pocket symbolizes the fitful movements of the poem back and forth in time, the kaleidoscopic change in outlook from passage to passage. Whether their outlook is predominantly pessimistic (Eliot, Pound) or optimistic (Crane, Williams), the modernists are concerned to be something other than chroniclers. If one could apply rhetorical terms to concepts rather than phrases, they could be said to favor synecdoche in their approach to history: each isolated, privileged fact they select for exposition is meant to gesture toward some larger whole.

It was probably inevitable that poets after modernism would in various ways dilute the rigor of its program. Eschewing narrative can be seen as perverse in regard to history, for very few people think of historical events in isolation. It is more usual to view them as unfolding in sequence or, indeed, in concatenation. For post–*Waste Land* poets tempted to render history with narrative continuity there was, to be sure, the model of Stephen Vincent Benét's *John Brown's Body* (1928). Benét's book-length poem, a huge popular success, tells the story of the American Civil War in a medley of competently handled, undemanding verse forms, intermingling historical figures and events with fictional ones—stereotypical Northern and Southern enlistees with stereotypical romances. The poem has the flavor of an old-fashioned historical novel of its period. Benét's design requires that he move back and forth between the historical big picture of the war and the common experience of his imagined characters. We feel the strain when he attempts to glide from U.S. and Confederate foreign policy issues to the weary unconcern of his representative Northern soldier, Jack Ellyat, trying to get some sleep in camp at Pittsburgh Landing:

If in the foggy streets of Westminster,
The salty streets of Liverpool and Hull,
The same mole-struggle in the dark went on
Between Confederate and Unionist—
The *Times* raved at the North—Mr. Gladstone thought
England might recognize the South next year,
While Palmerston played such a tangled game
It is illegible yet—and Henry Adams
Added one more doubt to his education
By writing propaganda for the North,
It is all mist to Ellyat.[10]

Benét's political outlook is that of a modern Northern liberal, but he presents his characters with a bland evenhandedness that keeps partisan controversy at bay. The shifts, or cuts, between narrative segments may owe something to the technique of cinema, but the reader is never challenged, as she may easily be by the modernists' deliberate fragmentations. The book's stylistic tameness, together with its middlebrow popularity, made it a target for condescension among Eliot's apostles. Allen Tate, comparing his friend Hart Crane with Benét, dismissed the latter as "an amiable and patriotic rhymester."[11] One senses that for poets of Tate's age or younger a huge gap, difficult to bridge, had opened between avant-garde avoidance of narrative and Benét's often simplistic embrace of it. If historical poems were once more to indulge in storytelling, some compromise would have to be effected.

And this seems to be what happened in ensuing decades among poets dealing with historical material. Collage compromised with chronology; story lines once more sidled cautiously into view. With sometimes tortuous effort, poets took on the job of reconciling modernist stylistic sophistication with the emotional appeal of narrative continuity, of action and character viewed over an extended span. Some of the most talented poets of the mid-twentieth century contributed to this project. Two works by Robert Penn Warren are notable in this regard: *Brother to Dragons* (1953; revised edition, 1979) and *Audubon: A Vision* (1969). *Brother to Dragons* blurs formal boundaries in narrating and meditating on the gruesome murder of a slave in 1811 by two of Thomas Jefferson's nephews. Subtitled *A Tale in Verse and Voices*, it introduces the poet himself as a character engaging the long-dead principals in colloquy, from which the story, as well as much psychological analysis and philosophical commentary, emerges. Such spectral dialogue could be viewed as the transcription of a séance, but a more mundane formal model is the radio play, which was still just barely a viable genre when the poem was written. Warren's unsparing view of the ugliness in human nature and specifically in the American character puts the work in a sphere far removed from *John Brown's Body*. At the same time, he structures the "tale" with a novelist's attention to plot and character in continuous development rather than in modernistic glimpses. His use of himself as a speaker debating with the likes of Thomas Jefferson (who does not come off well) suggests a more continuous way of paralleling past and present than is offered by the modernists' mosaics.

Warren's later and much briefer book-length poem, *Audubon: A Vision*, is less tricky in structure but may for that reason be a more accessible model than its baroque predecessor. Here Warren's size and scope are that of the short story. His friend Eudora Welty's story centering on Audubon, "A Still Moment," was one Warren admired, and it may have been among his inspirations for the poem. The second (and longest) section of the poem is a self-contained episode, telling of Audubon's narrow escape from being robbed and murdered by the degenerate backwoods family with whom he was spending a night; it ends with a grotesque description of frontier justice, in which the would-be murderers, a widow and her two sons, are hanged from a tree limb. In the briefer sections preceding and following this one, events in Audubon's life and excerpts from his writings are more grazingly touched on to build up an impressionist sketch of the naturalist and the American wilderness he knew so well. Here, rendered with a sort of entranced precision, is Audubon's view of a bear fattening itself for the winter:

October: and the bear
Daft in the honey-light, yawns.

The bear's tongue, pink as a baby's, out-crisps to the curled tip,
It bleeds the black blood of the blueberry.

The teeth are more importantly white
Than has ever been imagined.
[. . .]
He leans on his gun. Thinks
How thin is the membrane between himself and the world.[12]

The extreme compression of this book (somewhat unusual for Warren) helps to keep it from bogging down in its background data. Its subtitle seems accurate, for it is not so much a portrait of Audubon as an evocation of his vision of natural beauty transcending even such human corruption as his wanderings brought him close to. Warren shows a remarkable tact in his interweavings of narrative and meditative passages, and his language of description is vivid and memorable throughout. This poem's imaginative use of the past and its narrative tactics have established it as one still compelling model for poets concerned with history.

The mid-century produced other works that, like Warren's, expanded the possibilities of historical narrative in verse. Two may be noted briefly. John Berryman's *Homage to Mistress Bradstreet* (1956) is mostly a monologue in Anne Bradstreet's voice, but it, too, becomes a dialogue between the living and the dead, for Berryman converses with his heroine in the middle of the poem. The work is multifaceted, covering the course of Anne Bradstreet's life in the New World while offering glimpses of that early American civilization and probing recurrent themes of gender relations and of the place of the poet in society (unenviable, whether in the seventeenth or the twentieth century). Berryman's remarkable style manages to seem at once innovative and venerable. Here is one stanza, in which Bradstreet recalls the hardships faced by the Puritan settlers in their first months in New England:

How long with nothing in the ruinous heat,
clams & acorns stomaching, distinction perishing,
at which my heart rose,
with brackish water, we would sing.
When whispers knew the Governor's last bread

was browning in his oven, we were discourag'd.
The Lady Arbella dying—
dyings—at which my heart rose, but I did submit.[13]

Berryman's idiosyncratic phrasing, Hopkinsian rhythms, and rococo stanza form are aesthetically imposing and show that the more expectable free verse or blank verse are by no means the only options for the poet as storyteller. Finally, Robert Lowell's *History* (1973) deserves mention as an audacious, sometimes exhausting narrative enterprise. Beginning with Adam and Eve and proceeding chronologically to the 1970s, this collection of hundreds of blank verse "sonnets" attempts an encyclopedic survey of our common past and of the poet's own life. Lowell capitalizes on his own family history to shed light on momentous national events in a poem like "Colonel Charles Russell Lowell 1835–64," with the family motto "Occasionem Cognosce" as epigraph:

Hard to exhume him from our other Union martyrs;
though common now, his long-short, crisping hair,
the wire mustache, and manly, foppish coat—
more and more nearly looking like our sixties student. . . .
Twelve horses killed under him—his nabob cousin
bred and shipped replacements. He had, *gave* . . . everything
at Cedar Creek, his men dismounted, firing
repeating carbines; heading two vicious charges,
a slug collapsing his bad, tubercular lung:
fainting, loss of his voice above a whisper;
his general—any crusader since Moses—shouting:
"I'll sleep in the enemy camp tonight, or hell. . . ."
Charles had himself strapped to the saddle . . . bound to death,
his cavalry that scorned the earth it trod on.[14]

The fourteen-line segments may offer a sharply fixed focus on their subjects, but the effect is more drawn out and ruminative than we find in the snapshot-like allusions of the modernists. There is also the cumulative force, the traditional chronology, the ongoing flow of the sequence. Lowell here is more inclined to prolonged immersions in history than to the quick dips of his modernist precursors. This attitude was one soon to be shared by other poets.

The works I turn to next, and which I discuss for the remainder of this essay, fall within the emergence and growth of the New Narrative movement. In his essay "Other Lives: On Shorter Narrative Poems," David Mason begins by stressing the attraction to poets and their audiences of narratives that are not autobiographical. As a formal matter, such writing involves strategies "to regain literary territory that in modern times has been lost to the novel."[15] As to the impetus for such work, Mason describes it as a reach for "empathy," which he no doubt correctly terms "a civilizing process" that "implies connection, community, releasing the poet—who otherwise seems 'Encased in talent like a uniform'—from isolation."[16] The New Narrative aims to break free of "Romantic subjectivity," including its later manifestations in modernism and confessionalism. This program can easily be seen reflected in the works I am about to discuss, though the degree to which they eschew subjectivity is questionable. Certainly by the 1980s, whether consciously as part of the Expansive Poetry movement or not, poets were behaving more expansively when they took on historical topics. But which topics? The general appeal of history to the poet is that there is such a lot of it. Earlier, the expatriates Pound and Eliot drew topoi from the Old World; for more recent American poets the interest lies in what our politicians now call the homeland. Following the pioneering efforts of Warren and Berryman (and no doubt with glances back at *The Bridge* and *Paterson*), poets of the last few decades have subjected the American past to insistent scrutiny. In their most compelling works the story in question is given an unconventional slant, or enriched with the kind of detail often glossed over or missing in standard accounts. Poets have in a sense become the rivals not, here, of novelists but of the historians who provide them with source material—inevitably, when taking on the burden of this kind of narrative. Their willingness to challenge received versions of the past is in keeping with the general skepticism toward American motives that many intellectuals expressed in the wake of Vietnam and Watergate. The credibility of government in those years was at a low point; and for many writers a revisionist view of the past, of American civilization and its heritage, was a natural concomitant. The aesthetic aims of these poets coexist with an ethical intent to set the record straight, to cast light on dark corners, to fill gaps. If the New Narrative in general seeks to broaden the audience for poetry through the transmission of empathy, that may be even more emphatically an ambition of historical poems, which present a viewpoint readers are meant to sympathize with. These works, often poetically effective, are by no means repositories of "pure poetry." They come with documentary ballast, and they have agendas. In the space I have remaining I shall examine four such volumes that seem more successful than not in achieving their demanding artistic and documentary aims: *Brotherly Love*, by Daniel Hoffman, *The Cherokee Lottery*, by William Jay Smith, *After the Lost War*, by Andrew Hudgins, and *Carver*, by Marilyn Nelson.

A recurrent note in most of these works is that of disillusionment. The failure of the United States to remain true to its founding ideals, to live up to them in practice, is especially apparent in the relations of the colonizers and their descendants with the continent's native inhabitants. This depressing story—of armed conquest, broken treaties, repeated bad faith, and episodes of arguably genocidal conduct on the part of the white invaders—has drawn the attention of a number of accomplished poets.[17] It is a crucial component of Daniel Hoffman's *Brotherly Love* (1981). Hoffman wrote his poem in commemoration of the three-hundredth anniversary of the settling of Pennsylvania by William Penn and his Quaker compatriots. In contrast to the main drift of American history, Penn's fair and honorable dealings with the native tribes have become iconic both in literature and in paintings such as Benjamin West's *Penn's Treaty with the Indians* and Edward Hicks's *A Peaceable Kingdom*. Hoffman is a demythologizer to some extent—writing in the late twentieth century, it would be hard for him not to be one—but he is not a Menckenesque scoffer or debunker. He does not romanticize the Delaware tribes with whom Penn made his famous treaty but evokes their culture with scrupulous detail that inspires respect and sympathy. Similarly, the portrait of William Penn that emerges is genuinely heroic, the more so for being drawn from a wealth of authentic sources. Some of Penn's words, lineated in verse as an epigraph, suggest the moral value knowledge of the past brings to the present, describing history as "a sort of pre-existence // making us / to have always lived / or to have lived // and had knowledge before we were born."[18]

Hoffman's sources, in fact, are inescapably apparent. The famous paintings of West and Hicks are included in the text under their own section numbers (as is the well-known anonymous portrait of the young William Penn in armor) and are provided elaborate commentary. Numerous sections in whole or in part reproduce the words of William Penn. The text of Penn's treaty is given in full, balanced by the text of a later treaty between Penn's heirs and the descendants of the earlier native signatories. Early in the book the Delawares' myth of creation and of their own origins, the *Walam Olum*, is quoted in both the original pictographs and Hoffman's English rendering. This extensive amount of exact quotation is supplemented by numerous instances of paraphrase and allusion: to read the poem is to be steeped in the history it engages. And also in a critique of it: Hoffman frequently questions, supplements, or corrects his sources. On one level, this is not surprising. Hoffman's mastery of American historical and cultural backgrounds is evident in his prose works. Nevertheless, this is a risky procedure. What prevents a work of this kind from devolving to a mere compilation of documents, or a history of history? The expectable (and accurate) answer is poetic artistry, here displayed in multiple facets.

Most writers of long poems in recent years have gone in fear of monotony when choosing their means of expression. Rather than sustaining a single verse form from beginning to end, such as blank verse or an unvarying stanza, they have shifted forms from section to section within the work, which is what Hoffman does adroitly here. Besides providing the reader with a new set of verse sounds every few pages, this practice allows the creative play of fitting out the matter of the poem with forms that bring to each part an expressive resonance or a historically allusive dimension. For example, several sections quote Penn's descriptions of the Indians and their customs; rather than printing these in the original prose, Hoffman has lineated them as free verse, and done so gracefully enough that there is no sense of artificiality. Section 14 of part I begins:

Their Language is lofty, yet narrow, but like the Hebrew;
in Signification full, like Short-hand in writing; one
Word
serveth in the place of three, and the rest are supplied
by the Understanding of the Hearer;[19]

Penn's words, in these configurations, function as what could be called "found poems" rather than prose interpolations. Another and more obvious formal strategy is in play in several sections that treat their late seventeenth-century subjects in forms borrowed from their epoch. Thus, a naval battle in which Penn's admiral father took part is narrated in heroic couplets, and Charles II's bestowal of the proprietorship of Pennsylvania on William Penn is cast in a Cavalier ballad. Such elements of pastiche can easily get out of control. The poet walks a tightrope here, and it is not only technical adroitness but what might be called taste or tact that keeps him from plummeting into kitsch.

Hoffman excels not only in the interest his poem generates line by line but in his ability to give it an effective structure. In dealing with history a writer must decide when to accept and when to resist the demands of chronology. Rather than proceeding linearly from beginning to end, Hoffman ranges back and forth over his chain of events, producing a work that is more contemplation than chronicle. The book's individual sections are grouped in three large segments. The first of these focuses on the native inhabitants and their culture at the time of Penn's arrival, and on his treaty and continued friendship with them. The second interestingly subverts chronology by moving back in time. It tells of the persecution of the early Quakers in England, of the conversion (or as Quakers would put it, the convincement) of William Penn to the Society of Friends. The third segment tells of the king's grant of land to Penn as payment of a debt to his dead father and sketches the history of the colony as it lapsed from the vision of its founder following his death, as the Friends lost their innocence and the Indians lost their civilization. The story circles even as it moves forward, and what it circles around is the central portrayal of Penn's spiritual struggle and enlightenment. When dealing with this religious experience Hoffman opts for a plain, almost transparent style, reflecting the austerity of Quaker worship. Set against some of the bravura efforts already described, such writing comes as a notable counterpoint. Plain though it is, it has its own moments of splendor, as when Penn in prison has a vision of the City of Brotherly Love that he will one day found:

He is alight with his knowledge in which all propositions are fused in one arc of brightness

As all colors are fused in one arc of brightness unbroken

Save when a prism of droplets from Heaven spreads it apart

And each of its colors is pure and imperturbable,

The truth of its violet as true as the truth of its faintest blue,

And all in the pulse of pure light alive and shining.[20]

Hoffman's design obliges him to report the disheartening later history in which Penn's noble ideal gave way to the unregenerate impulses that colonialism both nourishes and thrives on. He does this without glossing over the brutal details, as in the French and Indian War government edict that offers "For the scalp of every Male Indian Enemy above the age of Twelve, produced as Evidence of their being killed, the sum of One Hundred and Thirty Pieces of Eight."[21] Nevertheless, in his own balance of the high and low points of his story, he ends with a note of guarded optimism. Returning at the end of the book to the contemplation of Penn's statue atop the Philadelphia City Hall with which he began, he puts the case thus:

We cram the days, put time to use—
no hour but is a rush hour, and where rushing?
Our history grows longer, longer.
It's life that's getting away from us

as the city changes, seethes with being.
Our Founder's feet are stuck
to the cranium of a clock
whose four faces gaze on us unseeing,

yet there's a spirit in this place
that sifts through hands that clasp
what only time can grasp
—Here possibilities of grace

like fragrance from rich compost cling
to leaves where our each deed
and misdeed fall. The Seed
stirs, even now is quickening.[22]

One has to suppose that some readers will find this assertion of "possibilities of grace" a bit of wishful thinking. But perhaps the luster of Penn's example, which continues to serve as a rebuke to those who have not lived up to it, is great enough to suggest a glimmer of redemption.

Such glimmers are harder to find in William Jay Smith's *The Cherokee Lottery* (2000), although in theme and format it offers many parallels with Hoffman's work. Like Hoffman, Smith deals with Native American culture in its losing battles against the white westward expansion. His focus is on the removal of the southern tribes from their ancestral lands to Oklahoma in the late 1830s, a forced migration along a route that became known as the

"Trail of Tears." Also like Hoffman, Smith draws heavily from documentary sources (identified in ample annotation) and accompanies his lines with images (photographs of Indian artwork, paintings and drawings by George Catlin and Charles Banks Wilson). Another similarity is in the handling of verse form, which Smith varies from section to section, availing himself of several kinds of free verse as well as traditional rhyming stanzas. Somewhat shorter than Hoffman's, the work uses the same episodic structure, although there is in it less overall continuity: no doubt conscious of this, Smith sub-titles the volume *A Sequence of Poems*. The greatest contrast is in tone, for this is a darker book than Hoffman's. The evident reason for this is that it has at its center no positive figure or image to correspond to Hoffman's use of William Penn. The unrelenting emphasis is on the chronic bad faith of the United States government toward the Indians and the willingness of white Americans to treat their Indian neighbors as objects for exploitation. The lyric that serves as an invocation, "Journey to the Interior," sounds the dominant note in its image of a wasteland wanderer, whom we may identify with the narrator as much as with any Indian on the Trail of Tears:

> he will pursue each dry creek-bed,
> each hot white gully's rough raw stone
> till heaven opens overhead
> a vast jawbone
>
> and trees around grow toothpick-thin
> and a deepening dustcloud swirls about
> and every road leads on within
> and none leads out.[23]

The vignettes Smith assembles to tell the story are typically harrowing, grotesque, or ironic. Smith succeeds through his thoughtful selection of historical detail and his unobtrusive presentation of it. One does not for-get the eyewitness account of the Cherokees, starving on their journey to Oklahoma, invited by a farmer to scavenge in his pumpkin field:

> Flies swarming to their target,
>   they darted up and down the rows,
> black hair flying,
>   long-nailed tentacles
> protruding, they ripped apart

the pumpkin flesh
until their brown and vacant
    faces merged with jagged pulp,
seeds foaming from
    their hungry mouths, and all I could see,
as on some battlefield, was
    everywhere a wasted mass of orange flesh.[24]

The gruesomeness of Osceola's head, kept as a medical curiosity, is equally memorable, as is the more whimsical episode of the Seminoles on a raid who made off with the baggage of a traveling Shakespearean troupe: "*Hamlet's headgear became the badge of the Seminole medicine man.*"[25]

The sequence loses some of its power toward the end. It overextends itself in passages dealing with material from further west and from a later period (Buffalo Bill, Sitting Bull, Custer all making appearances). The final piece, "Full Circle: The Connecticut Casino," raises some of the same questions that Hoffman's hopeful conclusion does in *Brotherly Love*. In an energetic mix of fantasy and satire, Smith presents the Pequots' casino's huge takings as a long-deferred, fully deserved compensation for all that the whites stole from their ancestors. It is a clever idea, and the writing has verve, but in the end it rings hollow. The Pequots are an entirely different tribe from the Cherokees, and there is something disturbing in treating one tribe's history of deprivation as interchangeable with another's. Then, too, there is a jarring of tone. Smith has been so effective in depicting the sufferings of the Trail that this coda, with all its boisterous comedy, seems forced. It is intriguing to note how frequently endings are a problem in poetic sequences—even highly accomplished ones, as this one is—that are based on history. One explanation that comes to mind is history's stubborn refusal to furnish conclusions of the kind we find in Victorian novels. Loose ends are not tied up neatly; as time goes on, they fray into thinner, even less manageable strands. Unlike history, a book of poetry has to come to an end, and thus it may be that the end is the point at which the poet's presence, will, and artifice are likely to be exposed in a distracting way.

The next example suggests that a more continuous and singly focused narrative line can mitigate this problem. Andrew Hudgins, in *After the Lost War: A Narrative* (1988), takes a more novelistic approach to his material than either Hoffman or Smith. The book has the benefit of a natural coherence and terminus in tracing the life of one historical figure: the poet, professional flautist, and Confederate veteran Sidney Lanier. It is further unified by being cast entirely in Lanier's voice. Perhaps one should place quotation marks around the protagonist's name. As Hudgins candidly states in his preface, "Though the poems are all spoken by a character I call Sidney Lanier, the voice of these poems will be unfamiliar to anyone who knows the writings of this historical figure. Despite his having been dead for over a hundred years now, I'd like to thank Lanier for allowing me to use the facts of his life—more or less—to see how I might have lived it if it had been mine."[26]

Hudgins's decision to fashion a new voice for his character was undoubtedly a correct one, for Lanier's own voice (at least in his writings) is musty with Victorian gentility. Recreating it would have been a stylistic stunt without much to offer to the work's larger aim, which goes well beyond providing a biography-in-verse. The aim, as I see it, is to use the "I" of the poem, a palimpsest, let us say, of Lanier and Hudgins, to evoke the experience of white southerners in the years after the Civil War. One could say the same of numerous novels by Faulkner and others of his generation. Hudgins, coming late in this tradition, shares its sense of the war's savagely enduring impression on the region. As Faulkner said, "The past isn't ended. It isn't even the past." This being the case, Hudgins has opted for a neutral style that, without too much jarring anachronism, seems to suit the dual consciousness of the poem, which views nineteenth-century events through a twentieth-century lens. In this Hudgins differs greatly from Hoffman and Smith, who frequently employ diction that bears the stamp of a particular historical period. The question of appropriateness doesn't arise when a reader is fully absorbed in Hudgins's narrative. If it did, of course, something like Lanier's retrospective disenchantment with his side in the Civil War would be unconvincingly phrased for a speaker in 1881:

> I'm sick of our lost cause—the way
> it's talked about, as if, beneath
> sweet words for suffering, we weren't
> fucked Ivanhoes of wickedness.[27]

Here the attitude and language are obviously tilted toward Hudgins's own era. But such a moment seems accommodated within this particular strategy for reanimating the past. Hudgins's success with this merged persona suggests that, at least in some longer poems, subjectivity is not the trap to be avoided at all costs that one might think it after reading David Mason's account of the New Narrative. In dealing with historical material, an element of subjectivity may be one of a number of ingredients needed to bring the past to life. Of course, the ultimate effect is dependent on the skill of the poet as he not merely recalls but imaginatively inhabits a bygone era.

Besides avoiding a flamboyant ventriloquism in his narrative voice, Hudgins is less flashy as well in his verse forms. Here, too, there is no period allusion evident in the poet's choices. Individual poems in the sequence vary in length of line, some being in free verse, others in a loose blank verse or a shorter, four-beat line. In some pieces the lines are divided in stanzas, but rhyme is not used in any case. The result is that the narrative voice maintains its initial qualities throughout; if there is less surface variety, there is a corresponding gain for unity (and also for momentum). Recurrent motifs and references to previous events as the sequence proceeds also serve to enhance the unity to which all parts contribute. This is a more determined challenge to modernist discontinuity than is mounted by either Hoffman or Smith.

The point of this series of contrasts is not that there is a right way and a wrong way for a poet to write about history but that there are significantly differing, equally viable approaches. Hudgins forgoes some of the flourish and pageantry we find in other works, but his more subdued style and first-person narration prove to be more intimate and psychologically probing instruments. We get more deeply into Sidney Lanier (at least into Hudgins's version of him) than we do in the case of personages in either Hoffman or Smith. Lanier's battlefield experience, his sufferings as a prisoner of war, the lifelong ill health and mental trauma these left him with, his music, poetry, marriage, parenting, metaphysical musings on God, nature, and the human condition—all these have a place in revealing the character to the reader (by virtue of the dramatic monologue form) as the character is revealed to himself by introspection.

One impressive feature of the work is its careful balance of description and rumination. There are Stephen Crane moments, as one would expect, in the war scenes:

> the dull
> inhuman thud of lead on flesh,
> the buckling of a shot man's knees,

the outward fling of arms, and the
short arc a head inscribes before
it hits the ground.[28]

But the same sensory keenness is applied to nature—especially in the several pieces that bring Lanier, at different junctures, to the marsh that is his personal Eden (and the inspiration of his best-known poem, "The Marshes of Glynn"):

>   In winter light,
> the marsh is stark, abstract. Just up
> and down. The hard-edged light is clear,
> incisive as a razor blade.
> In summer, that same light smears everything.
> Trees waver. Bushes merge into
> a haze of gnats, shimmering in air,
> which shimmers too—the whole world dizzy
> and unsure. Meaning falls away.[29]

As one would expect, description merges with moral awareness or meditation in a broader sense when Lanier confronts human mortality, whether in the war or struggling with the tuberculosis, contracted in prison, that eventually killed him. In "Burial Detail" he recalls "the most beautiful thing I've ever seen":

> dawn on the field after the Wilderness.
> The bodies, in dawn light, were simply forms;
> the landscape seemed abstract, unreal.
> It didn't look like corpses, trees, or sky,
> but shapes on shapes against a field of gray.
> In short, it looked like nothing human.
> But the sun broke from the horizon soon enough
> and we could see exactly what we'd done.[30]

And at the end of the book, on his deathbed, he tastes in a last sip of whiskey the power of a nature that has remained incomprehensible, alternately nurturing and imperiling:

> And underneath it all, just barely there,
> I find the scorched-nut hint of corn that grew

in fields I walked, flourished beneath a sun
that warmed my skin, swaying in a changing wind
that tousled, stung, caressed, and toppled me.[31]

Throughout, Hudgins's Lanier serves as representative of his generation of southerners, of the traumatized veteran, of the artist in American society on the verge of modernity, of the lover of a natural world that modernity in ensuing decades would transform. Yet he becomes most vivid as an individual facing death with a sequence of inevitable responses—anger, fear, denial, resignation, final wisdom—expressed in a voice we can accept as believable, even when it fails to indulge in period locutions.

Marilyn Nelson's *Carver: A Life in Poems* (2001) may be usefully placed last in this discussion because it occupies a mediating position between the works of Hoffman and Smith, on the one hand, and that of Hudgins on the other. Like Hudgins, Nelson tells the story of a single life—in this case, the life of George Washington Carver, the renowned African American agricultural scientist. She tells Carver's story for the most part chronologically, through a series of vignettes, just as Hudgins does with Lanier. In other ways, though, her practice is closer to Hoffman's or Smith's. The work is polyphonic, not often cast in Carver's voice. The poet's third-person narration governs most of the individual poems, although some are in the voices of those who knew Carver and a few reproduce his own words. The poems are frequently paired with relevant photographs, both of persons and of objects, and a prose chronology of Carver's life runs through the book at the foot of many of its pages. We are back to documentation, as in Hoffman and Smith, although here the stress is even more on visual exhibits. Finally, it should be mentioned that Nelson's economy as a writer sets her book apart from the works previously discussed. The book as a whole, and its individual segments, are notably compact; certain pieces have almost a snapshot quality which seems harmonious with the photographs that accompany them.

Another contrast is provided by the overall tone of the book, which subordinates occasions of sadness to a resilient optimism. There is no dwelling on lost causes or historical betrayals here. Carver's story, even summarized as a bare set of facts, is one of heroic progress and accomplishment, and Nelson is content to let it be just that. Setting down episodes or sometimes merely glimpses of the man in trim, sturdy, free verse sketches, she follows him with a kind of wonder from his birth as a slave to his height of eminence as a scientist; in this, of course, he is also an emblem for the advancement of the first free generation of African Americans. Photographs of Carver's personal effects (his eyeglasses and their case, his Bible and his pocket watch) make the book something of a reliquary, and it is possible to feel that the text is a hagiography, which may provoke in the reader a skepticism to which the writer was immune. Reactions like this probably say more about us than they do about Carver's actual level of merit. We have grown suspicious of heroes in a period populated by instant celebrities whose slick facades corrode almost in a blink. Marilyn Nelson, at any rate, is fully persuaded of Carver's sanctity (no question, after all, about his genius), and her book clearly invites the reader to share in her veneration.

Nelson does make room for the occasional caveat, and even for the voice of the scoffer. "My People" is spoken by an envious colleague soon after Carver began his illustrious career at Tuskegee:

> So high and mighty,
> he must think he's white.
> Wandering around through the fields
> like a fool, holding classes in the dump.
> Always on his high horse, as if his
> wasn't the blackest face on the faculty,
> as if he wasn't a nigger.[32]

But when Nelson allows such naysaying, she typically goes on to counter it. In "Chemistry 101" we see one of those classes in the dump in progress, and the effect is to dismiss the earlier criticism as sour backbiting (if we hadn't done so already):

> He turns, a six-inch length of copper tubing
> in one hand. "Now, what can we do with this?"
> Two by two, little lights go on.
> One by hesitant one, dark hands are raised.
> The waters of imagining, their element.[33]

Nelson even manages to relate one of Carver's failures—an attempt to treat polio with peanut-oil massage—in a way that redounds to his credit. After describing his devoted, prayerful attention to his patients ("his seventy-year-old back, / complaining to him all the time"), the ending of the poem is deliberately flat and undermined by irony:

The results of Carver's Penol experiments
were unsatisfactory and irreproducible,
the cause of those cures being
unquantifiable
and wholly unscientific.[34]

Heartfelt as it is, Nelson's reverential treatment of Carver imposes a certain imaginative limitation. Her depiction of him is controlled not only by the known facts but by her unwillingness to probe these with anything like a critical spirit. In many ways she seems the mirror opposite of Andrew Hudgins, who was willing to create his version of Sidney Lanier out of whole cloth. Nelson's Carver was received by her as an already model figure, and her work enhances the edifying legend without querying it. She can do this only by remaining somewhat remote from her subject; and as a result the portrait, although consistently appealing, lacks intimacy. One of the book's epigraphs is a statement of Carver's, which reads: "A personal relationship with the Great Creator of all things is the only foundation for the abundant life. The farther we get away from self, the greater life will be."[35] The modern reader, with his psychological interests, is bound to wish to penetrate the self of the person he is reading about. But how much can be discovered, exhibited, and analyzed in the case of one who has pursued selflessness rather than self-assertion as his ideal? Given her topic, Nelson might not have been able to offer a more psychologically probing portrait even if that had been her inclination. Perhaps we are best advised to accept Nelson's work as the rare thing it is: a recent, historically based poetic sequence that is more celebratory than critical. Finally, it should be noted that Nelson's uncritical view does not extend to the historical context of her hero's life and achievements. Slavery and its aftermath of Jim Crow oppression are neither evaded nor prettified in her narrative, although it is fair to say that her emphasis is not on these obstacles in themselves but on Carver's ability to overcome them.

Brisk as it has been, this survey indicates that there are distinctive challenges for poets working in this vein. One has to do with the extent to which the poet may feel free to subject historical fact to fictive manipulation. Not every poet would be comfortable in taking the liberties Hudgins does in his makeover of the actual but unexciting Sidney Lanier. Yet all of them filter their material through fictional devices that add something to, and thus alter, the historical record. A host of decisions that may come to seem ethical as well as aesthetic await the poet who attempts this sort of writing. Another knotty problem is that of documentation. Poets must decide how obviously to exhibit their source material—and as we have seen, some are readier than others to flaunt it. While there may be here also an ethical dimension to such choices, the reader will be chiefly aware of the aesthetic consequences. Even a highly sophisticated orchestration of sources, like that of Hoffman or Smith, runs the risk of compromising a narrative's coherence or impeding its pace. (And both these poets, it must be acknowledged, have at times paid such a price.) Background detail has a tendency to usurp the foreground in historical narrative—and perhaps particularly in poetry, when it offers so many symbolic items of interest that can be used to cast light on the main theme. It would appear, in fact, that many poets are still smitten with Pound's advocacy of the "luminous detail," even though they nowadays surround such trophies with an ongoing story line. In any case, some exacting thought about what belongs in the text and what belongs in its apparatus would seem to be recommended.

These considerations overlap with issues of structure. All of the four examples just discussed would be strictly defined as sequences. Even the most unified, *After the Lost War*, is divided into individually titled portions, several of which appeared as free-standing poems in magazines. The fuzzy and shifting terminology of "long poem" versus "sequence" is another legacy of modernism that poets today are still working their way through. It is interesting to note that two contemporary book-length works that manage to sustain an overall unity, Vikram Seth's *The Golden Gate* (1986) and Brad Leithauser's *Darlington's Fall* (2002), are fictional in both characters and plot. They are novels-in-verse by poets who both happen to be accomplished novelists. It may be that history encourages episodic treatment simply because of the selective nature of what primary sources record. Poets have to decide how much they are willing to make up to frame what they are retelling, and ethical qualms about adding fictional touches at will may produce a segmented narrative. There are also aesthetic concerns that have tended to promote sequential form in book-length verse narratives. Ever since the Romantic period, lyric compression—intensity—has been a primary value in poetry, and this has worked against a stress on continuity in longer works. In modernist long poems, cuts are more likely to be found than elaborate transitions. The works we have been looking at accord with this general pattern. The sometimes flimsy joinery of a conservative work like *John Brown's Body* has not, for the most part, crept back into the practice of these poets, who may be seen as adhering to modernist ideas of poetic form in certain respects, even while modifying them significantly in others.

One wonders about the audience for these works, and about a poet's (and, no doubt, a publisher's) calculations regarding it. Such books have the potential for appealing to an audience that may include readers who do not often (or, in some cases, ever) read contemporary poetry. William Jay Smith's book is required reading in schools in Oklahoma, and Marilyn Nelson's is marketed by its publisher, somewhat oddly, as a juvenile title. Hoffman and Hudgins are easy to imagine on the curriculum of a Department of History or American Studies. For many less literarily inclined readers, content rather than style will dominate attention. For poets who have already made a move away from high modernist approaches, this consideration may be a further impetus toward a more accessible style. This tendency is likely to raise the hackles of some critics, who will view it as a "dumbing down" of poetry, and it may visit inner conflict on poets who have not been trained to view their endeavors as art for the masses. One admires the stamina of poets contending with these and other strategic puzzles, as well as the recalcitrant aspects of their material, in the slowly diminishing wake of modernism. They have to worry not only about history but just as much about literary history. One imagines them in the midst of their struggles being accosted by Auden's lines, jumping the bounds of context, filling their ears with a monitory murmur: "History to the defeated / May say Alas but cannot help or pardon."[36] Successes in this field are demonstrably possible, but they are bound to be hard-won and almost certain to be qualified.

Notes

1. T. S. Eliot, "Gerontion," in *Collected Poems 1909–1963* (New York: Harcourt Brace and World, 1963), 30.

2. Ezra Pound, "I Gather the Limbs of Osiris," in *Selected Prose 1909–1965*, ed. William Cookson (New York: New Directions, 1973), 22–23.

3. Pound, "Canto XXV," in *The Cantos* (New York: New Directions, 1948), 115. Pagination is not consecutive throughout the volume.

4. Pound, "Canto LIV," in *The Cantos*, 32.

5. Hart Crane, *The Bridge,* in *The Complete Poems of Hart Crane,* ed. Waldo Frank

(New York: Doubleday, 1958), 55.

6. Ibid., 56.

7. Ibid., 57.

8. William Carlos Williams, *Paterson* (New York: New Directions, 1958), 36.

9. Ibid., 39.

10. Stephen Vincent Benét, *John Brown's Body* (New York: Holt, Rinehart and Winston, 1928), 105.

11. Allen Tate, "Modern Poetry," in *Essays of Four Decades* (Chicago: Swallow Press, 1968), 217.

12. Robert Penn Warren, *Audubon: A Vision*, in *Selected Poems, 1923–1975* (New York: Random House, 1976), 85–86.

13. John Berryman, *Homage to Mistress Bradstreet* (New York: Farrar, Straus, 1956), n.p., stanza 7.

14. Robert Lowell, *History*, in *Collected Poems* (New York: Farrar, Straus and Giroux, 2003), 485.

15. David Mason, "Other Lives: On Shorter Narrative Poems," in *New Expansive Poetry: Theory, Criticism, History*, ed. R. S. Gwynn (Ashland, OR: Story Line Press, 1999), 215.

16. Ibid., 215.

17. Robert Penn Warren's last extended narrative poem, *Chief Joseph of the Nez Perce* (1983), deserves mention along with the works on this theme discussed here. Hoffman's *Brotherly Love* is dedicated to Warren.

18. Daniel Hoffman, *Brotherly Love* (New York: Random House, 1981), ix.

19. Hoffman, "Treating with Indians," section 14 in *Brotherly Love*, 24.

20. Hoffman, "An Opening of Joy," section 40 in *Brotherly Love*, 91–92.

21. Hoffman, "The Structure of Reality," section 55 in *Brotherly Love*, 154.

22. Ibid., 169–170.

23. William Jay Smith, "Journey to the Interior," in *The Cherokee Lottery: A Sequence of Poems* (Willamantic, CT: Curbstone Press, 2000), 1.

24. Smith, "The Pumpkin Field," in *The Cherokee Lottery*, 23.

25. Smith, "The Players," in *The Cherokee Lottery*, 41.

26. Andrew Hudgins, *After the Lost War: A Narrative* (Boston: Houghton Mifflin, 1988), ix.

27. Hudgins, "The Cult of The Lost Cause," in *After the Lost War*, 107.

28. Hudgins, "Serenades in Virginia," in *After the Lost War*, 12.

29. Hudgins, "A Husband On The Marsh," in *After the Lost War*, 74.

30. Hudgins, "Burial Detail," in *After the Lost War*, 21.

31. Hudgins, "The Hereafter," in *After the Lost War*, 132.

32. Marilyn Nelson, "My People," in *Carver: A Life in Poems* (Asheville, NC: Front

Street, 2001), 34–35.

33. Nelson, "Chemistry 101," in *Carver*, 37.

34. Nelson, "The Penol Cures," in *Carver*, 88–89.

35. Nelson, *Carver*, vi.

36. W. H. Auden, "Spain 1937," in *Collected Poetry* (New York: Random House, 1945), 185.

ELOQUENT SILENCES

Lyric Solutions to the Problem
of the Biographical Narrative

APRIL LINDNER

In his essay "Reader's Life," Stephen Dobyns writes, "In much poetry what is important is the lyric moment, a sort of fervent crescendo when the emotional world of the writer joins with the emotional world of the reader. The primary function of narrative in poetry is to set up these moments. We are more interested in these moments than we are in the story."[1] In this view, the narrative serves the lyric and can be seen as either a vehicle for it or a background against which the lyric moment can shine. Dobyns's statement makes explicit an assumption held by many contemporary poets and embodied in much recent poetry: the narrative serves as mere scaffolding propping up the truly important lyric moment—the poem's reason for being.

From this assertion, it is just a small step to the position that narrative can and should be stripped away wherever possible. In "Disruptions, Hesitation, Silence," Louise Glück theorizes her preference for the lyric over what she sees as a trend toward expansive poems with "long lines, long stanzas, long poems which cover an extended sequence of events." "I do not think that more information always makes a richer poem," she writes. Moreover, she prefers those poems that make do without narrative: "I am attracted to ellipses, to the unsaid, to suggestion, to eloquent, deliberate silence."[2] Glück's partiality to poems that aspire to the purely lyrical is, despite her assertion to the contrary, a commonly held preference of poets of her generation. A cursory survey of literary magazines published since the 1960s would reveal a marked preponderance of brief, neoconfessional lyric poems, often to the exclusion of anything else.

Since the sixties, the lyric has flourished, and the long narrative poem, for a time, all but disappeared. In "The Dilemma of the Long Poem," Dana Gioia illustrates the lack of diversity in contemporary poetry by imagining the reaction of a hypothetical eighteenth-century reader to the late twentieth-century poetry scene: "Where are the narrative poems, he would ask, the verse romances, ballads, hymns, verse dramas, didactic tracts, burlesques, satires, the songs actually meant to be sung, and even the pastoral eclogues? Are stories no longer told in poetry?"[3] In reaction to this lack of diversity, a handful of poets (including Gioia) began in the 1980s to speak up on behalf of neglected modes and techniques. One of these neglected modes was narrative. These New Narrative poets, as they came to be called, argued for the return of storytelling values to poetry and insisted on narrative as aesthetically valuable in and of itself. They maintained that an educated general audience lost to television and the novel might be won back by poems that offered the entertainment values of fiction, including a gripping plot and fully drawn characters, presented in poetic language made memorable by rhyme and regular meter. *The Reaper*, a journal founded by the poets Mark Jarman and Robert McDowell, issued the movement's edicts: "*No emotion without narrative. Emotion is inconsequential unless it is the result of a story. The story is communal; it is for others.*"[4] In this view, narrative has a wider social value, in that it might appeal to those fans of the novel who would ordinarily never consider picking up a book of poetry. Moreover, David Mason, another practitioner of the New Narrative, makes large social claims for the narrative poem:

> There are at least two good reasons why contemporary poets might use verse to create characters and tell stories. One reason is that it can rejuvenate their art by compelling them to reevaluate the subjects they write about, to look more closely at lives usually deemed insufficiently flashy or spectacular. By involving us in the nuances of social and individual problems, narrative poetry can address issues beyond the narrow confines of the poet's life, or it can focus emotions too painfully personal to be revealed

directly in a lyric. It is also possible that the line has advantages lacking in prose, the chief one being that it contributes to memorability, helping to sustain a literary culture most of us would agree is in danger of extinction.[5]

In this view, narrative is presented as healthy for the individual poet, for poetry itself, and even for society. Reaching beyond the self to inhabit a character is for poet and audience an act of empathy, what Mason calls "a civilizing process."[6]

The 1980s and 1990s saw the publication of a small but noteworthy crop of book-length narrative works, including Jarman's *Iris*, McDowell's *The Diviners*, and Andrew Hudgins's *After the Lost War*. Other collections, including Gioia's *The Gods of Winter*, Mary Jo Salter's *Sunday Skaters*, and Mason's *The Country I Remember*, offered long narratives among the lyrics. Clearly emerging from the tradition of Robert Frost and Robert Browning, these poems often are dramatic monologues, and often are in blank verse. Always, these poems employ plot and character development. Most important, these poems aim, as realistic fiction does, to summon the reader into what the novelist John Gardner called "a 'vivid and continuous dream.' "[7] Continuity, in fact, is the quality that sets these narrative poems apart from modernist "narrative" poems, as well as from lyric poems that hint at a narrative underpinning. The way in which story is handled is more a defining attribute of the New Narrative poem than is the presence of story itself.

When Dobyns claims that every lyric poem implies a narrative, he is getting at something important: story is implicit in most lyric poems, if not every one. While certain poems and poets aspire to platonic ideals of either pure lyricism or pure narrative, most poems dwell somewhere along the continuum between the two. Louise Glück points to Rilke's "Archaic Torso of Apollo" as a "magnificent example of lyric poetry" in that it "begins with the unknowable . . . and ends with the unknown."[8] She locates the poem's value in its absence of narrative, in how it creates a "space which is potentially an alternative to information." However, just as the torso in Rilke's poem is lent gravitas by the missing "legendary head / with eyes like ripened fruit,"[9] so this almost purely lyric poem is lent weight by its lacunae, in this case, the statue's history, cast in the missing parts we can never know; the loss of an attending narrative is what makes the statue so poignant. We can make a distinction between poems, like Rilke's, that strive toward the purely lyric and those that expand to include the volume of information one finds in realistic fiction: whereas a narrative poem may achieve its most rewarding moments in resting spots of lyricism, those moments feel earned by plot and character development. One example is Mason's *The Country I Remember*. While the sweep of the long New Narrative poem confounds swift summation, a stanza or two may reveal some of its characteristic elements. The following passage introduces a monologue by Lieutenant Mitchell, a Civil War veteran captured at the Battle of Chickamauga:

> Someone told me that mankind always moves
> from east to west, but in my day I've traveled
> back and forth like a saw blade cutting wood.
> When I was young I worked my father's farm,
> but when at twenty-one I became a man
> I left the farmwork and the biting flies
> to drive an ox team out to Oregon.[10]

That these lines are in iambic pentameter and have the spoken quality of a dramatic monologue are only two of the attributes that mark this poem as an example of New Narrative poetry. Its length—fifty-three pages—is another. The poem covers vast time and space, giving it an epic quality that signals narrative intentions. It is broken into long sections that include exposition to help the reader navigate the poem's vast temporal and geographic terrain. Though not without lyric high points, lacunae, and temporal leaps, this poem falls close to the "pure narrative" end of the spectrum, just as "Archaic Torso of Apollo" falls close to the "pure lyric" end.

For poets at any point on the spectrum, achieving a balance between the two elements presents challenges and opportunities. While moments of clumsily handled exposition have marked many a lyric poem as amateurish, the tension between lyric and narrative within a poem can serve as a source of interest and energy. Successful poems milk that tension. In fact, some of the most interesting long narrative poems of the last two decades have sought new ways of enacting the tension between the lyric and the narrative. Three of these—Marilyn Nelson's *Carver: A Life in Poems*, Stephanie Strickland's *The Red Virgin*, and Rita Dove's *Thomas and Beulah*—deliver complicated narratives via lyric strategies. While any long narrative presents challenges for the poet, I have chosen to address the biographical sequence as the epitome of those problems, since its author must distill something as complex as a life into a poem and in doing so provide moments of lyric payoff as well as plot.

Carver: A Life in Poems

With a Newbery Medal of Honor and a Coretta Scott King Award sticker festooning its cover, *Carver: A Life in Poems* is clearly marketed to the high school classroom. Readily accessible and rich in photographs, the book has potential appeal for a young audience. Like its photographs and Newbery Medal, the book's narrative clarity might put off young adult readers of poetry (admittedly a smaller and less sought-after audience anyway), but, packaging aside, *Carver* has pleasures to offer beyond the merely educative. The book's reader-friendly appearance and its accessibility by both sophisticated and unsophisticated readers of poetry are in keeping with the New Narrative goal of winning a wider audience for poetry, and Nelson has frequently been grouped with the New Narrative and New Formalist poets. In *Carver*, brief lyrics spoken by a polyphony of voices—some in third person, some dramatic monologues, some in the form of letters—are interspersed with photographs to create the illusion of a documentary history. An occasional biographical footnote supplies narrative information not conveyed by the poems or photographs themselves. Essentially a collage of words and images, *Carver* provides one solution to the problem of the long biographical narrative. Nelson hits on the highlights of her subject's life, leaving gaps between these events in place of the connective tissue of narrative exposition.

Like any skillfully told story, *Carver* establishes tension from the start. "Out of 'Slave's Ransom,'" the book's first poem, is narrated by John Bentley, the white man who recovered the infant George Washington Carver after he and his enslaved mother were kidnapped. The baby would be raised by Moses Carver and his wife, and the book's first poem sets up the white man's incomprehension of this arrangement:

> When I handed him to Missus Carver,
> you never seen such carrying-on.
> All that over a puny black baby.
> You'd have thought that Mary
> was her sister or something.[11]

While Bentley is blind to Carver's worth as a human being, other characters, white and black, perceive his genius and struggle to nurture the fragile young man, who remains essentially an oddity to most of the world. Another poem,

"The Prayer of Miss Budd," is narrated by a teacher at Simpson College, where Carver majored in art:

> I'd known he was enrolled, but still
> the sight of a sepia boy
> trembled my foundations,
> I must admit. Thanks
> for your patience.
> They say each teacher
> gets one student. Thanks
> for giving me mine.[12]

Carver would go on to found the Agricultural Department at Tuskegee Institute and to break important ground as a botanist and inventor. *Carver* quickly establishes its hero as sensitive, curious, and marked by greatness, at least to those who have eyes to see. The book's reverence for Carver is conveyed by its lesser, more human characters, who serve as lenses through which we view the greatness of Carver. These varied depictions of Carver have vivid and memorable moments, as in "Watkins Laundry and Apothecary," when a neighbor tells us:

> He was sweet with the neighbor children.
> Taught the girls to crochet.
> Showed the boys
> a seed he said held a worm
> cupped hands warmed so it wriggled and set
> the seed to twitching.[13]

But the respect with which Nelson portrays Carver often keeps the man himself at arm's length. The poem continues:

> Gave them skills and wonders.
> Knelt with me at bedtime.
>
> He was the child the good Lord gave
> and took away before I got more
> than the twinkle of a glimpse
> at the man he was going to be.[14]

George Washington Carver hardly speaks in the book that bears his name. Though Nelson depicts the man primarily through the viewpoint of the host of characters that surrounds him, she does offer a few moments in which we glimpse his subjectivity. "The Perceiving Self" is one of these. In this poem, the fifteen-year-old witnesses a lynching, and for a moment, he is less the future great man and more "the perceiving self," slowly coming to terms with the scene before him. The poem begins by obscuring its true subject with benign natural images:

> The first except birds
> who spoke to us, his voice high
> and lilting as a meadowlark's,
> with an undertone of windsong,
> many-petaled as the meadow,
> the music shaped and colored
> by brown lips, white teeth, pink tongue.[15]

The horrific nature of what is being described dawns slowly on the reader, with the violence of the event clearly established near the poem's end:

> Then he squealed, a field mouse taken
> without wingbeat,
> with no shadow.[16]

Even this violent natural image, though, is benign compared with the reality of what the speaker is witnessing. The poem's conclusion affords a more direct description of a "torched deadman, barking laughter / from the cottonwoods at the creek." This gradual movement from metaphor to direct statement implies denial giving way to horror. The poem in its entirety establishes the general backdrop of racism and deprivation against which Carver's achievements shine even more impressively.

In its narrative arc—from the sickly child of a slave to elder statesman of science—Nelson's book implies that Carver's greatest achievement was symbolic: he showed what was possible, bridging the distance from slavery to a fully realized freedom. A sonnet titled "From an Alabama Farmer" establishes the poverty and near illiteracy from which Carver escaped:

> Dere Dr. Carver, I bin folloring
> the things I herd you say last planting time.
> I give my cow more corn, less cottonseed
> and my creme chirns mo better butter.[17]

More than an expression of gratitude for the practical benefits of Carver's advice, the poem ends by revealing the farmer's hunger for knowledge, a hunger that will go largely unsated:

> It do fele grate
> to see the swet off your brow com to bloom.
> I want to now what maid my miricle.
> Your humbel servint, (*name illegible*)[18]

Circumstance and talent allowed Carver to transcend the racism that held back so many other African Americans, but he himself was often resented by his people and threatened by the Klan, and his life was shaped in a meaningful way by subtler brushes with discrimination. "The Sweet-Hearts," a poem in the form of a suicide note, is spoken by the light-skinned Sarah Hunt, who rebuffed Carver's romantic advance, put off by his rumpled scholar's appearance and his dark complexion. She begs forgiveness from her children and husband because she "can live no longer / this life of a fool."[19] As a young woman, Hunt valued her ability to pass as white more highly than she valued Carver, and later she cannot live with this mistake.

Carver's value—as a historical figure, a scientist, a teacher, an artist, and a man—is, of course, precisely what this book labors to establish. Carver himself rarely speaks in these poems; others speak *of* him, reverently or uncomprehendingly, but always in service of the book's main task: defining the great man's legacy. (The book's last page finds a neat symbol of that legacy in a pair of commemorative postal stamps, issued in 1948 and 1998, respectively.) But these pat official symbols are less persuasive than Nelson's choice to insert herself obliquely into the book by ending with the poem "Moton Field," in which her own father, one of the famous Tuskegee Airmen, makes a cameo appearance. The poem juxtaposes Melvin Moton Nelson performing a victory roll with our final view of Carver, a bedridden old man answering his mail and lamenting the war. In a photograph opposite the poem, Melvin Nelson cuts a dashing figure in uniform, clearly representing the brighter future ushered in by Carver and the students who carried on his legacy. This unusual rhetorical move underscores the book's already emphatic message, but because it surprises and disarms the reader, it is ultimately one of the book's most effective expressions of that message.

Because the book sets out from its start to convince us of Carver's greatness, because we ultimately understand the man more from the outside than from the inside, and because we see only his good qualities, the collection flirts with hagiography. *Carver* means to inspire and enlighten its readers, and that, more than anything, defines it as classroom reading. This intention, of a piece with the book's packaging, distracts from Nelson's spare and understated poetry, from her nuanced portraits of those who are disturbed and edified by Carver's achievements, and from her elegant solution to the formal problems posed by the biographical narrative poem.

The Red Virgin

In its intentions, Stephanie Strickland's *The Red Virgin* bears a superficial resemblance to *Carver*. Like Nelson, Strickland writes of a figure she clearly admires, the philosopher Simone Weil. Like Nelson, she weaves herself into the narrative of Weil's life. Strickland too takes a quasi-documentary approach, juxtaposing poems that pose as letters, partial transcripts of interviews, lists, and the accounts of others to add up to a life story. *The Red Virgin*, however, is an elusive work, yielding up its literal meaning gradually. Weil's short life was full of remarkable undertakings. Born to a wealthy family, she chose to work in a factory and became a trade unionist. As a soldier in the Spanish Civil War, she was injured in an accident, but would later work for the French Resistance during World War II. Weil starved herself to death in an expression of solidarity with the destitute, her body destroyed by her ideas just as her ideas were weighed down by the limitations of her body.

In *The Red Virgin*, Strickland struggles for equipoise among three different modes: the lyric, the meditative, and the narrative. The effort both to interweave the facts of Weil's life with the complexity of her ideas *and* to soar to occasional lyric heights isn't always successful, but it is always interesting. While a chronology at the book's start obviates much exposition, Strickland still packs a fair amount of factual information into the poems themselves, and the book's first half feels clumsy and journalistic as a result. Individual poems often are sunk by the weight of ideas and exposition. While many New Narrative poems use the music of iambic pentameter to smooth the way for facts, in the free verse of *The Red Virgin*, logistical information can fall with a thud: "Crisis in '32 becomes Depression and Simone / has joined rival Unions in order to unite them."[20]

In contrast, poems like "Comic Progression, 1939—," which rely on lyric means—disruption, hesitation, silence, compression—telegraph facts more entertainingly, and more movingly:

1. *Send me. I'll organize a Front Line Corps*
   of Nurses. Men, who would otherwise die from shock
   and loss of blood, will live. Send me.

   Rejected.

2. *Since Nazis are inflamed by prestige, by the mystique*
   of the SS, the persistence of services offered
   at great risk, from great love, in the center
   of our battles, will serve as a symbol, a rallying
   image. I will train the women. Send me.

   Rejected.[21]

Lists, fragmented letters, scraps of essays, and interview transcripts are interspersed with brief lyrics spoken by Weil, those who knew her, and an authorial persona. These shifts in style and perspective lend the narrative interest and variety. As in *Carver*, the insight and misperceptions of those who knew Weil enable us to see her more clearly, and to empathize with her struggles. Her physical presence—the absentminded intellectual as a young woman—is quickly established:

Awkward hips, long

tent skirts. Stuffing an inkpot
down the pocket
of her beige one—the stains,

huge, black suns
spreading on
the skirtfront, Simone![22]

Awkward, convinced of her intellectual inferiority to her older brother, André, the young Simone frequently was thwarted in her longing to serve humanity. Consumed by her longing to be of use, Weil is simultaneously passionate and virginal; hence the book's title, taken from disparaging remarks by the director of young Simone's school. "Names/Ugliness" establishes the disjunct between Weil's soul and her physical self, viewed by Paul West, that same director, as somewhere between a "pensive doll" and "the head-mistress type, owl-eyed through excessive perusal."[23] The authorial persona responds to West's judgment:

They don't know love when they see it.
They think ugliness unfits her for it,
or nicotined fingers, grating voice,
that low monotonous tone, never known
to concede.[24]

The gulf between Weil's soul and her outward appearance is one form
taken by the mind/body split at the book's center. A later poem, "Your Death:
What Is Said," depicts Weil struggling to balance her ideals with a body that
enables her to act on those ideas even as it weighs her down. As someone
passionately involved in many forms of resistance, Weil recognizes that
struggle matters only when there is something to struggle against. The
authorial persona must struggle herself to make sense of Weil's suicide.
She interrogates her protagonist:

Did you judge your death to be a more effective
witness than your life? If so,
you were correct
about us, we leap upon it to hold
against your work. By this
resistance, brought to keep them both

—your thought, your death—

in the mind, polar.[25]

The book's explorations of the limitations the body places on the mind sheds
light on Weil's lifelong preoccupation with hunger, violence, war, rape, and
slavery—all physical conditions that can limit the soul's potential. As the
chronology tells us, Weil demonstrated against police brutality and worked
as a trade unionist, a field hand, and even, for a time, as a soldier in the
Spanish Anarchist Union's militia until she was injured in an accident. In
"Revolution: Simone at 27," Strickland depicts Weil's preoccupation not
with battle itself but with the feelings of the peasants for whom she fights.
Weil's participation in the Spanish Civil War ends abruptly when she trips
into a cooking pit and is scalded by burning oil, her high intentions thwarted
by her clumsiness.

As concerned as the book is with the ways in which the vulnerable body
can compromise the mind, we're made no less aware that the body enables

the mind to be. In "Still Darning a Sock," Weil watches her landlady iron-
ing and realizes how a woman's soul is both weighed down and "washed
through" by domestic work. The title of another poem, "Zealot in a Zoo,"
speaks for itself. At the book's climax, a momentary equilibrium is reached
with the realization that "the body is not the soul's opponent." Instead,

the opponent of the soul

is the soul's own words, made to serve,
made-to-measure, to grasp all things
by its grammar.[26]

Weil's struggle for equilibrium is mirrored throughout the book by that
of the authorial persona, forced to approach Weil's life through the filter of
those who wrote about her but who knew her imperfectly:

Coming to me
soured, brought by the distaste
you cause some man or woman; no one

saw what you are doing, not even
you, although you knew
the price you paid.[27]

The poet reckons, like any biographer, with artifacts and documents. The
opening poem, an invocation of sorts, announces her methods:

I would descend
lower still, bring her near me, gossip
about her, paraphrase. If I distort,
I don't abandon.[28]

Piece by piece, Strickland builds her understanding of Weil's ideas and
character, to convey the complexity of Weil's own ideas. The payoff is a
window into Weil's preoccupations and, especially toward the volume's
end, quite a few soaring lyric moments, as provided by the following brief
poem, "My *Not* Burns":

What burns in hell?
Divines, doctors, say self-will.
But I say *not*.

If I am not
fire, fire consumes me.
My *not* burns me.[29]

Like much of *The Red Virgin*, this poem takes on greater resonance when
read in sequence. Fragment by fragment, Strickland builds her portrait of
a woman haunted by her inability to merge with the world she so loved. In
refusing food, Weil chose to serve the living by refusing life itself, and that
refusal—her *not*—consumed her. Throughout *The Red Virgin*, Strickland
conveys Weil's ideas without simplifying them, and the result is a demanding collection charged with the excitement of the poetic process itself—with
the energy of its own creation.

Thomas and Beulah

A double portrait of Rita Dove's grandparents, the acclaimed *Thomas and
Beulah*, winner of the 1987 Pulitzer Prize for Poetry, provides a chronology
at the book's end, where the reader is least likely to look for it. This choice,
like much else about the book, signals its intention to make the reader an
active participant. The first-time reader is likely to be puzzled by the book's
literal element. Clearly, it's meant to be a narrative; the dedication page
tells us so. But *Thomas and Beulah* relies heavily on lyric means, including
compression, disruption, hesitation, silence, and a large dose of imagery, to
tell its tale. Dove herself has described her intentions as an effort to convey
"the grandness that narrative can give, plus the sweep of time" without letting the book "bog down in the prosier transitional moments."[30] She says,

> I didn't see very many long narrative poems that really weren't smaller poems
> linked together. So one of the things I was trying to do was string moments
> as beads on a necklace. In other words, I have lyric poems which, when
> placed one after the other, reconstruct the sweep of time. I wanted it all. I
> wanted a narrative and I wanted lyric poems, so I tried to do them both.[31]

What differentiates *Thomas and Beulah* from narrative sequences made
up of "smaller poems linked together" (like *Carver* or *The Red Virgin*) is its
resistance to a simple one-time, start-to-finish reading. While the poems
in most narrative sequences are connected primarily in linear fashion and
can be rewardingly read from start to finish, those in *Thomas and Beulah*

demand a recursive reading. A first-time reader is likely to go through the book with some frustration, then stumble across the chronology and go back and reread the work to make better sense of the story. For a narrative, *Thomas and Beulah* makes few concessions to exposition. Some of its brief lyric poems provide enough information to situate the reader, but many aspire to the purely lyric, presenting isolated moments that make narrative sense only in relationship to other isolated moments.

The format of the book—like so much else about it—makes multiple rereadings necessary. Though its primary subject is a marriage, *Thomas and Beulah* delivers all its poems about life as perceived by Thomas before doubling back chronologically to give us Beulah's take on events. This arrangement emphasizes the separateness of experience; despite their shared lives, Thomas and Beulah in many ways don't know each other. This format also adds to the narrative's central tension: even a long, successful marriage has its dissatisfactions, misunderstandings, unbridgeable gulfs. One of the book's many pleasures is reading Beulah's version of an event and doubling back to reread Thomas's version, and noting how the two versions fit together—or fail to. The gaps between Thomas's story and Beulah's call into question the reliability of any narrative.

In other ways, too, *Thomas and Beulah* uses unconventional means to convey, in Dove's words, "the essence of my grandparents' existence and their survival, not necessarily the facts of their survival."[32] The book begins reassuringly, with a lyric that makes concessions to exposition. In "The Event," we meet the young Thomas headed north on a riverboat with his friend, Lem. Though the two have "nothing to boast of / but good looks and a mandolin," the mood mingles festivity with a hint of danger:

> They spat where the wheel
>
> churned mud and moonlight,
> they called to the tarantulas
> down among the bananas
>
> to come out and dance.[33]

What happens next is startling: on a drunken dare, Lem swims out to what appears to be an island. As Thomas watches, Lem and the island disappear under water. A moment later, Lem is gone forever, with nobody but Thomas to notice:

At his feet

a stinking circle of rags,
the half-shell mandolin.
Where the wheel turned the water

gently shirred.[34]

This fleeting but decisive moment sets the tone for the rest of Thomas's life. The mandolin the two men shared pops up throughout the book as an emblem of Thomas's survivor guilt and of the soured promise of youth. Thomas pierces his ear to remind himself of his lost friend, and travels on solo to Akron, Ohio, a nattily dressed ladies' man with a gift for music. It's telling that Thomas's half of the book bears the subtitle "Mandolin"; music throughout the book has potent associations. In "Straw Hat," we see Thomas in Akron, where he sleeps in a work barracks. We learn that

To him, work is a narrow grief
and the music afterwards
is like a woman
reaching into his chest
to spread it around.[35]

Music and romance are associated for Thomas, and both are bittersweet.

In "Courtship," we encounter other emblems that recur throughout the book. Out with Beulah, Thomas "wraps the yellow silk / still warm from his throat / around her shoulders."[36] The expensive scarf Thomas gives away with pride and reluctance will make an appearance in Beulah's section. In the companion poem, "Courtship, Diligence," in Beulah's section, we get her less than ecstatic take on Thomas's gift: "A yellow scarf runs through his fingers / as if it were melting." We glimpse her opinion of his beloved mandolin: "*Hush*, the strings tinkle. *Pretty gal.* // Cigar-box music!"[37] We learn that she would "much prefer a pianola / and scent in a sky-colored flask // Not that scarf, bright as butter. / Not his hands, cool as dimes."[38] We also learn why Beulah ultimately accepts his proposal anyway: "She is getting on" and can't be too fussy. The emblem of Beulah, the daughter of prosperous parents whose life together has its own tensions, is a canary, and the subtitle of her section is "Canary in Bloom." The caged bird is a familiar symbol of the oppressed housewife, but the way in which Dove pits

Thomas's emblem against Beulah's to imply the tensions of their household is far less usual. "Compendium" offers a terse summary of the marriage and its compromises and disappointments. This poem, more than any in the book, illustrates Dove's use of lyric strategies to advance her narrative. The poem in its entirety reads:

> He gave up fine cordials and
> his hounds-tooth vest.
>
> He became a sweet tenor
> in the gospel choir.
>
> Canary, usurper
> of his wife's affections.
>
> Girl girl
> girl girl.
>
> In the parlor, with streamers,
> a bug on a nail.
>
> The canary courting its effigy.
> The girls fragrant in their beds.[39]

Hung on the wall, his mandolin—reduced to "a bug on a nail"—stands off against his wife's canary. The bird is caged, the musical instrument is silent and reduced to mere ornament. Both emblems are diminished. The fourth stanza tells with magnificent compression of Thomas's primary disappointment: instead of the son he hoped for, he fathered four daughters. The poem's last line, however, offers a hint of consolation as the father thinks fondly of his sleeping daughters, the fruit of this less than idyllic marriage.

To make sense of poems like this one, and of *Thomas and Beulah* as a whole, the reader must stay alert to recurring images. The standoff between Beulah's emblem, the canary, and Thomas's, the mandolin, stands in for tension between the story's two protagonists, and other poems expand on this tension, as when Thomas takes the mandolin down from the wall and finds himself unable to play:

> Each note slips
> into querulous rebuke, fingerpads
> scored with pain, shallow ditches

to rut in like a runaway slave
with a barking heart.[40]

This passage helps make sense of the earlier one in which "the canary courts its effigy." Thomas's resentment is revealed in his perception of his wife's singing pet as the real thing while his own emblem, the mandolin he can no longer play, has been reduced to an "effigy." Recurring images like these advance the story and let Dove sidestep the need for ponderous exposition. Another such emblem is the couple's sky-blue Chandler, a token of prosperity that brings them humiliation and the threat of violence when, broken down by the side of the road, their car catches the attention of "a carload of white men."[41] Similarly, the river, glimpsed at the book's start, returns at the end of Thomas's life, when, dying of a heart attack in the drugstore parking lot, he remembers Lem and "laughed as he thought *Oh / the writing on the water.*"[42]

In Beulah's section, we see that she too is haunted by her missteps. While dusting, she remembers a boy from her past:

> What
> was his name, that
> silly boy at the fair with
> the rifle booth?[43]

Here as elsewhere, Dove's free verse lines are spare and musical. The images speak for themselves. Even so, a complex, multilayered story emerges. The limitations of Beulah's life come across powerfully in "Daystar," in which we see the beleaguered young mother's hunger for a

> place that was hers
> for an hour—where
> she was nothing,
> pure nothing, in the middle of the day.[44]

In painting a finely detailed portrait of a marriage, the book manages to do something more surprising: it gives us a glimpse of the historical forces that contribute to shape the lives of Thomas and Beulah. Just as Dove establishes the class difference between Thomas and Beulah with a few carefully chosen images, she deftly suggests the backdrop of racism behind her story's main action. In "The Great Palaces of Versailles," Beulah alters the clothes of white women with breeding less fine than her own, while remembering a book she has read about Versailles:

> French ladies at court would tuck
> their fans in a sleeve
> and walk in the gardens for air. Swaying
> among lilies, lifting shy layers of silk,
> they dropped excrement as daintily
> as handkerchiefs.[45]

Beulah's married life, a diminishment of her dreams, meshes seamlessly with the bitter knowledge that wealth and privilege don't necessarily coincide with merit.

Though large historical events are not its primary subject, *Thomas and Beulah* illustrates how events like the Great Depression, the Great Migration, and the civil rights movement can shade an individual life. Unlike Thomas, Beulah lives to witness the civil rights movement. In "Wingfoot Lake," her daughters bring her to a Goodyear company picnic. It's 1964, and the party is segregated. Beulah muses bitterly over recent history:

> Last August she stood alone for hours
> in front of the T.V. set
> as a crow's wing moved slowly through
> the white streets of government.
> That brave swimming
>
> scared her, like Joanna saying
> *Mother, we're Afro-Americans now!*
> What did she know about Africa?[46]

Changes wrought by the civil rights movement come too late in Beulah's life to seem anything but vaguely threatening to her. This larger communal turning point is mirrored by a smaller, personal one: Beulah comes to appreciate her marriage too late for it to make much difference. The book's narrative arc finds completion when Beulah tells the dying Thomas, *"listen: we were good / though we never believed it."*[47] Though Beulah has long felt alienated from, even superior to, her situation in life, she finally comes to appreciate her marriage in all its imperfection.

With the fullness of a novel and the grace of a lyric poem, *Thomas and Beulah* is a unique achievement, every bit as ambitious in its own way as the more tradition-bound epics of the New Narrative. In its eloquent silences, its disjunction, its often extreme compression, its luminous images and musical free verse, *Thomas and Beulah* provides a powerful example of how a long poem can strive for the swift immediacy of the lyric without sacrificing the breadth of the narrative.

Having It Both Ways

In response to Steven Dobyns's assertion that every lyric implies a narrative, Ellen Bryant Voigt (the author of *Kyrie*, a book-length narrative lyric sequence) counters that, similarly, "every narrative poem obscures a lyric."[48] She goes on to explain:

> The man in a restaurant crushing a wineglass in his hand acts out an emotional complex not wholly explained by a hard day at the office, or being cheated in the taxi, or what his companion just said. If the narrative writer is instinctively curious about the individuating "story," is hard-wired for the distinct sequence of events preceding that table and that wineglass, the lyric poet may be as naturally drawn to the isolated human moment of frustration, distilled, indelible, the peak in the emotional chart.[49]

The lyric moment is more than the result of those events that caused it, Voigt argues, implying that the image often can best speak for itself, unmodified by exposition. Narrative—the journalistic where, when, what, and who—is no substitute for the transcendent lyric moment conveyed by a striking image or an emotional outcry. And yet, as a punch line is all the better for a skillful setup, the lyric moment isn't necessarily obscured by the narrative that surrounds it. It can both transcend context and benefit from it. In trying to have it both ways, to obscure neither the lyric nor the narrative, Dove, Strickland, and Nelson encompass both the "individuating story" that provides historical and biographical context and the "isolated moment" of high drama that can be clarified but not wholly explained by context. In playing all the stops along the continuum from pure lyric to pure narrative, the narrative sequence can encompass the fullness of human experience—the deeply personal, ineffable self as well as the wider world that surrounds that self.

Notes

1. Stephen Dobyns, "Reader's Life," in *Best Words, Best Order: Essays on Poetry* (New York: St. Martin's Griffin, 1997), 45.

2. Louise Glück, "Disruptions, Hesitation, Silence," in *Twentieth Century American Poetics: Poets on the Art of Poetry*, ed. Dana Gioia, Meg Schoerke, and David Mason (New York: McGraw-Hill, 2003), 378.

3. Dana Gioia, "The Dilemma of the Long Poem," in *Can Poetry Matter?* (St. Paul, MN: Graywolf Press, 1992), 23.

4. Mark Jarman and Robert McDowell, "The Reaper's Non-Negotiable Demands," in *The Reaper Essays* (Ashland, OR: Story Line Press, 1996), 40.

5. David Mason, "Other Lives: On Shorter Narrative Poems," in *New Expansive Poetry: Theory, Criticism, History*, ed. R. S. Gwynn (Ashland, OR: Story Line Press, 1999), 216.

6. Ibid., 215.

7. John Gardner, *The Art of Fiction* (New York: Vintage Books, 1991), 87.

8. Glück, "Disruptions, Hesitation, Silence," 379.

9. Rainer Maria Rilke, "Archaic Torso of Apollo," in *Selected Poetry of Rainer Maria Rilke*, trans. Stephen Mitchell (New York: Knopf, 1982), 61. In German, "sein unerhörtes Haupt, / darin die Augenäpfel reiften," 60.

10. David Mason, *The Country I Remember* (Ashland, OR: Story Line Press, 1996), 32.

11. Marilyn Nelson, "Out of 'Slave's Ransom,'" in *Carver: A Life in Poems* (Asheville, NC: Front Street Press, 2001), 9.

12. Nelson, "The Prayer of Miss Budd," in *Carver*, 22.

13. Nelson, "Watkins Laundry and Apothecary," in *Carver*, 14.

14. Ibid.

15. Nelson, "The Perceiving Self," in *Carver*, 17.

16. Ibid.

17. Nelson, "From an Alabama Farmer," in *Carver*, 39.

18. Ibid.

19. Nelson, "The Sweet-Hearts," in *Carver*, 53.

20. Stephanie Stickland, "Airdrill," in *The Red Virgin: A Poem of Simone Weil* (Madison: University of Wisconsin Press, 1994), 14.

21. Strickland, "Comic Progression, 1939–," in *The Red Virgin*, 17.

22. Strickland, "Absent from Dances, 1925," in *The Red Virgin*, 5.

23. Strickland, "Names/Ugliness," in *The Red Virgin*, 47.

24. Ibid.

25. Strickland, "Your Death: What Is Said," in *The Red Virgin*, 69.

26. Strickland, "Soul Learns Everything from Body," in *The Red Virgin*, 70.

27. Strickland, "How You Are Withheld From Me," in *The Red Virgin*, 35.

28. Strickland, in *The Red Virgin*, 3.

29. Strickland, "My *Not* Burns," in *The Red Virgin*, 46.

30. Quoted in Steven Schneider, "Coming Home: An Interview with Rita Dove," *Iowa Review* 119.3 (1989): 117.

31. Ibid., 117.

32. Ibid., 116.

33. Rita Dove, "The Event," in *Thomas and Beulah* (Pittsburgh, PA: Carnegie Mellon University Press, 1986), 11.

34. Ibid., 12.

35. Dove, "Straw Hat," in *Thomas and Beulah*, 15.

36. Dove, "Courtship," in *Thomas and Beulah*, 17.

37. Dove, "Courtship, Diligence," in *Thomas and Beulah*, 50.

38. Ibid.

39. Dove, "Compendium," in *Thomas and Beulah*, 28.

40. Dove, "Definition in the Face of Unnamed Fury," in *Thomas and Beulah*, 29.

41. Dove, "Nothing Down," in *Thomas and Beulah*, 23.

42. Dove, "Thomas at the Wheel," in *Thomas and Beulah*, 43.

43. Dove, "Dusting," in *Thomas and Beulah*, 52.

44. Dove, "Daystar," in *Thomas and Beulah*, 61.

45. Dove, "The Great Palaces of Versailles," in *Thomas and Beulah*, 63.

46. Dove, "Wingfoot Lake," in *Thomas and Beulah*, 72.

47. Dove, "Company," in *Thomas and Beulah*, 74.

48. Ellen Bryant Voight, "The Flexible Lyric," in *The Flexible Lyric* (Athens, GA: University of Georgia Press, 1999), 94.

49. Ibid., 94–95.

HISTORICAL NARRATIVE IN THE LYRIC SEQUENCE

The Challenge of Robert Penn
Warren's *Audubon: A Vision*

CHRISTINE CASSON

The poetic sequence is a relatively new genre that has evolved over the past century and a half and is, according to M. L. Rosenthal and Sally M. Gall, who have written extensively on the subject, "the outgrowth of poets' recognition and pursuit" of what Hart Crane called, as they indicate in a different context, "new thresholds; new anatomies."[1] Likened to a modern version of the epic poem,[2] the poetic sequence emerged in the mid-nineteenth century "to accommodate the complexities and passions of contemporary experience," and encompasses "a shift in sensibility" that "goes many-sidedly into who and where we are *subjectively*."[3] According to Rosenthal and Gall, the sequence, emerging in response to the pressures and circumstances of a changed world, fulfills the need for "encompassment of disparate and often powerfully opposed tonalities and energies" and is structured "neither to resolve a problem nor to conclude an action but to evoke the keenest, most open realization possible." "Like a piece of music," it "establishes an initial poetic pitch more than a theme or character," an emotional center that moves toward a state of equilibrium that balances its otherwise "conflicting and logically irreconcilable energies." Primarily lyric in structure, the sequence "concentrates on something other than logical . . . narrative, [or] thematic links" and places increased emphasis on "a complex music of feeling" achieved through "the succession and interaction of units of affect" that reveal "intensities" of "emotionally and sensually charged awareness."[4] Liberated from a narrative or thematic framework, the sequence, then, like a musical composition, must have its shape, something that allows the reader, as Aaron Copland says when speaking of a musical score, "to find his way around."[5] The poet's task is to provide this shape, to determine the length, character, and arrangement of its parts, to organize what Rosenthal and Gall call its "progression of affects"[6]—its moments of emotional and sensual awareness—so that, as in music, "ever new relations and ever new shapes are created,"[7] shapes that build one upon another to form, finally—Copland, again—a "coherent whole where "everything [is] in its place."[8]

In light of the traditionally lyric nature of the sequence, the integration of historical or biographical information pertinent to the portrayal of a historical subject—be it an event or an individual—that incorporates into its structure the chronology of a distinct time and place or the life and sensibility of a particular individual promises to be difficult. How does a writer include the narrative—the necessary information of a subject's life or of events—and still sustain what Rosenthal and Gall call the sequence's "radiant tonal centers" of intensity that "accommodate the complexities and passions of contemporary experience?"[9] How does one sustain a "complex music of feeling"[10] when confronted with the chronology of the subject's life or a historical event that claims a progression of its own and that must also have its part in the organization of the whole? After all, it is from the unfolding of time underlying all human experience that moments of emotional and psychological intensity arise and meaning accrues. The chronology of those moments, then, is significant and compels us to confront the temporal world, which is, as Paul Ricoeur says, the hallmark of narrative. As he posits in *Time and Narrative*, "time becomes human time to the extent that it is organized after the manner of a narrative; narrative, in turn, is meaningful to the extent that it portrays the features of temporal experience."[11] If human experience occurs in and over time and takes on resonance through narrative constructions, the poet must, in composing a historical sequence, take chronology—and narrative—into account, two elements that Rosenthal and Gall claim have little place in the sequence. Is the genre changing and becoming less lyric than it was at its inception? Perhaps, but that is the basis for a much longer

discussion of the poetic sequence than there is room for here. More important, the facts and chronology of an event or a life can easily strangle *any*
poem's potential that in its most effective incarnation utilizes language to
push through and beyond mere description of the referent toward utterance
that more fully reveals human experience. The poem's discourse, Ricoeur
writes, "brings to language aspects, qualities, and values of reality that lack
access to language that is directly descriptive and that can be spoken only by
means of the complex interplay between the metaphorical utterance and the
rule-governed transgression of the usual meanings of our words."[12] How,
then, can the poet successfully transform the enumeration and succession
of events into something meaningful and, in the case of the sequence, into
an orchestration that will sustain the music of the whole?

To explore these questions, I have selected Robert Penn Warren's *Audubon:
A Vision*, which takes a historical life as its subject. The poem provides a rich
example of a sequence that reveals the dance—and at times the struggle—of
narrative necessity and lyric impulse in the act of guiding the poem's "progression of affects."[13] The interplay is a curious one. The narrative information
underlying the poem is, of course, Audubon's life, a non-negotiable fact
that Warren as poet had to address in writing this work. Warren was first
introduced to Audubon after reading histories of Kentucky and Tennessee in
preparation for writing *World Enough and Time*. Later, when he was working
with Cleanth Brooks and R. W. B. Lewis on *Understanding American Literature,*
he wrote the section on Audubon. Yet, although he read Audubon's journals,
in an interview with the *New England Review* he recounts that when he finally
decided how the poem should progress, he envisioned that "each element in
the poem would be a 'shot' on Audubon rather than a narrative."[14] His intent,
then, was to write a lyric sequence, a succession of poems that would focus on
significant moments of intellectual and emotional intensity in his subject's
life or, as Dave Smith describes it in his essay, "Warren's Ventriloquists," "a
poem of lyric voice performing narrative tasks."[15]

That a good deal of this poem is lyric is, perhaps, testament to his success. Yet the poem is challenging in its structure. The work is divided into
seven movements, each individually titled. It is the second movement that
is most narrative.[16] In fact, it is almost pure narrative, though Warren uses
line breaks, stanza breaks, and sentence fragments to disrupt its otherwise
linear direction. The second movement accounts for 200 lines of a 399-line
poem, or half the entire sequence. In light of its length, one question that

immediately arises is what event should receive such prominent treatment. In this section the speaker of the poem relates in the third person an incident involving the poem's "he," or Audubon, in which Audubon witnesses the hanging of a woman and her sons. We are never clear why he is at their home and why he witnesses their capture and death; the poem's explanatory epigraph casts doubt on whether this incident ever occurred or whether it might be one of Audubon's fantastic "embellishments" of his life.[17] So this narrative is, on the one hand, extremely suspect. On the other hand, its placement and length suggest that the encounter affected Audubon deeply and was instrumental in the development of his passion for wildlife, a passion that led to his slaying of that wildlife so that it might be reproduced in art, embodied in such a way that we might see what Audubon saw, who, according to this poem, "knew the lust of the eye" (V.[A].1).[18]

Therefore, we should consider what in this poem is—or at least announces itself to be—biographical information, and how that information is presented and utilized in pursuit of more lyric concerns—specifically, the intellectual and emotional life of the poem's subject. To those ends it seems useful to turn to movement I, "Was Not the Lost Dauphin," where Warren works to integrate lyric and narrative moments as he introduces his poem's subject. Warren gains the reader's trust in the authenticity of what is revealed here by immediately referring back to that part of the biographical note he provides as epigraph to the poem. The epigraph discusses the most famous legend about Audubon that arose after his death, that he was the lost dauphin of France, son of Louis XVI and Marie Antoinette. The first lines of the poem emerge directly out of this assertion and, as we would expect of our trustworthy speaker, deny its validity. This first attempt to define Audubon arises out of what he is not, a move particularly interesting in light of the sequence's epigraph, from Carlos Drummond de Andrade, that speaks of his subject's "strict shadow" that "remain[s] silent," and suggests the difficulty of determining who another really is.[19]

In the first three lines of the poem, then, we are provided with a good deal of historical information that agrees with what we've already learned in the biographical note and suggests that the speaker is attempting to circumvent the legends, to reveal the real Audubon. Yet in the next two lines the poem asserts that a man is other than the biographical information of his life, that somehow such details are secondary to who we really are, and an individual's true self is revealed through his emotional and intellectual life: "What / Is man but his passion?" Interestingly, these lines suggest that the lyric poem's modus operandi is more conducive to approaching such a truth than the historical record can ever be. Still, the poem insists in its first lines that it is only through those initial narrative steps, the ones that define Audubon's social status and struggle to survive, that the leap toward some embodiment of his intellectual life can be made. Yet in this first stanza we are only told of the leap, of its importance. It is not until the next stanza that the poem itself—its language—moves into lyric and begins to embody a moment of intellectual and emotional awareness.

That awareness is achieved through vision—through our experience, as readers, of Audubon's own vision that appears, in these lines, like writing in the sky. The white space between stanzas is the physical terrain of that movement toward seeing; the fragmented sentence that begins with "Saw" provides a linguistic disjunction through which the reader can break with purely narrative information and enter a space in which what happens—what is seen—has metaphorical significance and achieves that timeless quality that defines the lyric. What is seen is mysterious, as though the bird were a puppet not moving of its own volition, an encounter that resonates with meaning. The otherworldliness of Audubon's vision is conveyed through Warren's use of color—the dawn that is "redder than meat," the color of "God's blood spilt," which so profoundly suggests sacrifice. A price is attached to Audubon's vision, its beauty intimately and inextricably bound up with violence and death. The rhythm of the lines also works to pace the vision: the "dawn" of line 6 doesn't "break" until the end of the following line; the "large bird" appears, then in line 8 moves, traces the "slow calligraphy" written on the horizon in a writing "crank, flat, and black," the insistent stress of these one-syllable adjectives regulating how this event, "pulled by a string," unfolds slowly across our field of vision. It is an occurrence that takes place in time but, in the context of the poem, never concludes. This, in combination with its visionary quality and Warren's careful working of description and language, pushes it into timelessness, into a moment that gains great significance in our emotional understanding of Audubon's "passion" for birds. Even though in line 13 we see the great heron "proceed across the inflamed distance," lines that suggest the linear notions of distance and time, we are never released from the vision but are thrust into Audubon's thoughts, in which the bird, "*Ardea occidentalis,* heron, the great one," takes on mythical significance. By the end of this section we are still caught at the moment of dawn, a moment one might think impossible to hold because it is so transitory, our experience of it always so instantaneous and brief. Perhaps most significant, the other, more obvious use of the dawn as a trope to suggest beginnings, the onset of awareness, is so well embedded in the poem's mystical vision as to become almost imperceptible to that part of our mind that parses meaning.

It is significant, then, that Warren ends section I.[A] with the question, "and what is your passion?," turning abruptly from third-person narration to direct address. The section folds, like an envelope, back on itself, echoing the rhetorical question of lines 4–5, "what / Is man but his passion?," but stepping well beyond the rhetoric of the first stanza to address a "you" that remains undefined, a "you" that might be Audubon, the reader, or the speaker questioning himself. It is the first sign that this poem may well concern itself with more than historical subject, that its reach extends into the present and, perhaps, the personal.

Yet moving into the next section, I.[B], we return immediately to the third-person narration, to a recounting once again of story, as the narrative eye observes the motions of a bear as it settles down to hibernate. This poem, written in two-line stanzas, does not suffer the syntactic disjunctions of the previous section. Instead, we follow a linear narrative line: the bear "yawns"; we see its tongue and teeth; we see its drowsiness, revealed here as a gentle intoxication; and we assume that, like the "last bee," it will soon enter a long sleep. We witness the bear at its most vulnerable moment, when it is "daft in the honey-light" and "yawns," its "tongue, pink as a baby's." Clearly, this bear is unaware of the speaker's observing eye; its guard is down as it prepares for its winter sleep, and in that unguarded moment it is as innocent and as unsuspecting as an infant. Yet this imagery is complicated by the following lines, which further describe its tongue, and then its teeth. Like the blood-colored dawn of the previous section, the "black blood" stain of the blueberry that so effectively conveys how the berries are crushed as they are consumed reveals the ruthlessness of the feeding bear. The blueberry juice that flows like blood further suggests the bear's potential to harm if disturbed or angered, an event that could lead to blood being spilled. This, juxtaposed with the bear's "importantly white" teeth, pulls us away from the tranquilizing imagery of the first three lines and toward a recognition of the violence this animal is capable of. Our response to the narrative is more unsettled, perhaps; the unusual gentleness of the bear brought on by the season is, we are reminded, only temporary, a lull in the course of natural events, the preying of one animal on another. Indeed, as the following lines show, death itself is the intoxicant in this poem: the bee is equally "bemused" by the actions of the bear and the blueberries' pungent scent.

The significance of this imagery seems related to the season, to the natural progression from fullness or ripeness to hibernation or death. It isn't until the final stanza that we understand its full importance, and its relationship to Audubon and his life. It is in this final stanza that the disjunction of the poem occurs, and it is not a syntactical disjunction but one in point of view. The observing eye, the camera's lens, if you will, shifts dramatically. The alteration in point of view, so subtle between stanzas four and five as to pass almost unnoticed, where the bemusement of the bee could as easily be the bemusement of the bear, is wrenched dramatically as we enter this last stanza:

He leans on his gun. Thinks
How thin is the membrane between himself and the world. (I.[B].3–14)

Suddenly, the ursine hunter has become the hunted; "he," now a man, "leans on his gun" and observes the bear. We are in the presence of Audubon; we experience the inner workings of his consciousness as he witnesses the bear's preparations for sleep. As readers, we are struck by the potential cruelty of this moment when Audubon could, if he wished, easily shoot the bear, having come upon it, as he has, when it is unaware. More significant, Warren observes Audubon engaged in this very thought; when he "Thinks / How thin is the membrane between himself and the world," we witness the cool, scrutinizing eye of the observer who understands how fine the line is between life and death, and who is as fascinated by one as by the other. Death is as intoxicating for Audubon as it is for the bee in stanza five. Just as the "black blood" of the blueberry is revealed and comprehended only after it is crushed, so the observing eye does its best work in close proximity to its subject, knowing that the intimacies of any creature are manifest as much in death as in life. Yet the "membrane" the poem refers to in its last line is a timeless one, and fragile, a moment of thought that falls between the one who would act violently and the one who stands to be acted upon.

Repeatedly, then, in sections [A] and [B] of the poem's first movement we are jettisoned out of time into timelessness or stasis, and into spaces where all is stilled for a moment, long enough to reveal Audubon's emotional and psychological state. Yet the narrative information and its relation to the passage of time—how one thing follows on another—are critical to these revelations. We gain insight into when and in what circumstances his obsession with wildlife began, and witness how experiences that followed Audubon's initial insight reinforced and intensified those obsessions. That narrative relies on time is a given, yet the complexity of the relationship that unites the two, particularly when utilized in a historical sequence where, one might argue, the task is to convey the "story" of the subject's life, needs to be explored. Furthermore, the poem makes numerous references to time in its following movements.

Interestingly, Warren conveyed very specific ideas about time in an interview with Ralph Ellison and Eugene Walter, first published in the *Paris Review* in 1957. Ellison, referring to an essay by Warren in the *New Republic*, queries Warren about his notion of the "still moment" in William Faulkner's art, what Ellison then observes as "a suspension, in which time seems to hang." In his response, Warren refers to "the frozen moment" and "freeze time" that can "harden up an event, give it its meaning by holding it fixed." Clearly, Warren is deeply aware of time and how its progression and suspension inform a work of art. "Time spreads and is the important thing, the terrible thing," he adds, continuing to speak of Faulkner's novels. "A tremendous flux is there, things flowing away in all directions. Moments not quite ready to be shaped are already there, waiting, and we feel their presence." He refers then to the "sweep of time over things" and "the balance of the frozen, abstracted moment" in Faulkner's novels.[20] How this delicate interplay informs the shape of Warren's sequence is particularly important here, and his notion of time—its immanence, its passing, and its potential fixedness—is expanded in interesting ways if one takes into account, as Paul Ricoeur does in *Time and Narrative*, Augustine's inquiry into time in his *Confessions*. In book 11 Augustine asks, "Who can lay hold on the heart and give it fixity, so that for some little moment it may be stable, and for a fraction of time may grasp the splendour of a constant eternity?" (xi, 13).[21] Though he asks this question in order to illustrate to his reader that there is no way God's eternity and the human experience of "temporal successiveness which never has any constancy" can be compared, his impulse to "lay hold on the human heart and make it still" so that it might comprehend this difference reverberates with Warren's language describing the "still" or "frozen" moment that would bestow "meaning."

Augustine's aporia, as Ricoeur calls it,[22] and Warren's discomfiture arise from a similar question, namely, whether one can say that time exists. As Augustine notes, how can the past and future " 'be' when the past is not now present and the future is not yet present," and the present, which is not an eternal present, "is so made that it passes into the past" (xiv, 17)?[23] Similar to Warren's notion of time "flow[ing] away in all directions,"[24] Augustine posits early in his discussion that time seems only to exist "in the sense that it tends towards nonexistence."[25] Yet, as Ricoeur observes, "we say that things to come *will be,* that things past *were,* and that things present are *passing away*,"[26] noting that it is language usage that provisionally provides the resistance to the thesis of nonbeing. To escape this thesis is critical for Warren as it flies in the face of the meaning he seeks to reveal. Interestingly, Ricoeur's conclusion that the "speculation on time is an inconclusive rumination to which narrative activity alone can respond"[27] is one that Warren in his novels and, I would argue, in this sequence has already assimilated. Ricoeur's attention to Augustine's argument becomes the means by which he can reveal more fully the function of narrative in history and in art. In both instances, it is important that time be revealed as something that exists and can be measured as "long" or "short" and can be distinguished from eternity. Yet this is difficult: if the past no longer exists and the future does not yet exist, it is only the present that can be measured, but Augustine observes that "if we can think of some bit of time which cannot be divided into even the smallest instantaneous moments, that alone is what we can call 'present' "(xv, 20).[28] As such, he continues, it has "no duration" and "occupies no space," and therefore cannot be measured.[29] The intention here is not to follow in detail the progression of Augustine's argument but to consider how he solves the conundrum, and why for Ricoeur the theologian's meditation is critical to an understanding of narrative.

Augustine insists, then, that the past and the future exist in the images we have of them in the present—in memory and in premeditation—or, as he suggests, "a present of things past, a present of things present, and a present of things to come" (xx, 26).[30] But if the present passes away as soon as it comes into existence, and if time has no space (*spatium*), there still is no "extension" of time that can be measured. Nevertheless, he knows "no body can be moved except in time" (xxiv, 31),[31] be it human or animal, natural or celestial, though moving objects don't comprise time. After a continued meditation, during which once again he considers our experience of the passing of time, where it comes from and where it goes, reiterating again that it can't be measured, he finally turns to sound—to the human voice, and then to language; to the recitation of words comprised of syllables of varying length; and finally to the arts, specifically to a poem that is longer or is shorter than another, and to the recitation of that poem (in his case, one of the psalms)[32]—to reveal at last how time can be measured. Augustine locates our experience of time in the mind that is the "active agent" of "three processes":

> For the mind expects and attends and remembers, so that what it ex-pects passes through what has its attention to what it remembers. Who therefore can deny that the future does not yet exist? Yet already in the mind there is an expectation of the future. Who can deny that the past does not now exist? Yet there is still in the mind a memory of the past. None can deny that present time lacks any extension because it passes in a flash. Yet *attention* is continuous, and it is through this that what will be present progresses towards being absent. (xxviii, 37; italics mine)[33]

The "attention" that Augustine speaks of actively confronts the "multiplicity of the present."[34] As Ricoeur notes, it "stretches" this "threefold present" in "opposite directions, between expectation, memory and attention." He continues, "*Only a mind stretched in such different directions can be distended.*"[35] That mind also has *intention* (italics mine) when it recites a poem, and it is that "present intention (*praesens intentio*)"[36] that actively "transfers the future into the past"[37] and transforms experience. The resulting distention or *distencio amini* (in Augustine, of the soul) reveals the mind's active en-compassment of time's threefold present and might also be called *duration*, a word that could quell any misgivings Warren might have about time's "tremendous flux" that confounds meaning. Time is transformed from a moment into something constant and prolonged enough to recite a psalm, as Augustine does, and to experience through anticipation and memory the full import of the song.

Of course, the theologian's intent is to understand God's creation, so "it is *in* the soul . . . as an impression," Ricoeur notes, "that expectation and memory possess extension." More important, "the impression is in the soul only inasmuch as the mind *acts*, that is, expects, attends, and remembers."[38] This observation is critical as it opens the door to a consideration of how the mind that acts on impressions can be likened to one that acts narratively. The work of narrative is just the same: to anticipate, to experience, and to remember, and the work of the storyteller is to orchestrate events in such a way that will reveal not necessarily all that happens but the *impression* of what happens. Another convergence comes into play here as well, for, as Ricoeur notes, the pursuit of time Augustine engages in leads him to lament how the *distencio* of human experience pales in light of God's eternity, how it is "a lack that is felt at the heart of temporal experience."[39] As such, Augustine's intention moves beyond recitation of a psalm to a hope of "leaving behind the old days" so he "might be gathered to follow the One, 'forgetting the past' (Phil. 3:12) and moving not towards those future things which are transitory but to 'the things which are before' [him]" (xxix, 39).[40] This pursuit of the eternal revealed in his desire to " 'contemplate [God's] delight' (Ps. 26:4) which neither comes nor goes"[41] reveals the active intention of the soul as it works to hold that which is distended more firmly. It returns us to his initial entreaty for the heart held still that might "for some little moment . . . be stable, and for a fraction of time . . . grasp the splendour of a constant eternity." Likewise, when Warren speaks of his own work, he would infuse events with meaning and "harden them up," thereby creating for them a temporal space that would approach what Ricoeur calls "the pole of eternity."[42] It is the creation of that space that concerns us here, and how, in the orchestration of the sequence, the poet creates "a hierarchy of levels of temporalization,"[43] each one determined by the significance of events and, in the case of the historical sequence, the effects of those events on the subject's life. We are thrust once again into time, and thereby into narrative, and how that narrative is enacted in a lyric genre. Of note, Ricoeur insists that "speculation on time is an inconclusive rumination to which narrative activity alone can respond."[44] I would argue that this is true for Warren's sequence and that, as Ricoeur observes, "it is to this enigma of the speculation on time that the poetic act of *emplotment* [italics mine] replies."[45] In other words, if one would like to imagine another's life in art, one needs to engage in *distentio*, the meaningful drawing out of significant *moments* in human experience, through narrative device. Again, Ricoeur turns to Augustine, who posits that the attention of reading the psalm, in which the speaker engages memory and expectation within the attention and recognition of the present, "is also valid of the entire life of an individual person, where all actions are parts of a whole (xxviii, 38)."[46]

At this juncture, Ricoeur turns to Aristotle, and to *mimesis* (Ricoeur's term is "mimetic activity") and *muthos* ("emplotment")[47] as defined in Aristotle's *Poetics*: the former "the active process of imitation or representing something" and the latter the "art of composing plots."[48] Based on the discussion above, both are integral to the composition of the historical sequence. *Mimesis* as the "imitation or representation of action" inclines to the life of the sequence's subject—what he or she did, thought, experienced. *Muthos* is the organization of the events of that life or, as Ricoeur says in his discussion of Aristotle, "the 'what' of the mimesis."[49] Pertinent to this discussion is Ricoeur's reiteration of Aristotle's idea that both these terms are related to *poiesis*, to the *act* of creating, and as such, both imply "production, construction, [and] dynamism . . . which have to be taken as *operations* [italics mine], not as structures."[50] In other words, mimesis and muthos are artistic activities that serve "narrative," or the "organization of events,"[51] and require the active engagement of the artist, reminiscent of Augustine's "present intention," which measures and configures time. It is the *act* that is significant and the attention it requires that lends significance to the events that occur.

This is complicated by the nature of narrative, which, as Ricoeur elegantly reminds us, is "a model of concordance" and an "exigence for order,"[52] with a beginning, middle, and end. Nevertheless, like Aristotle's "tragic model that has its own logic,"[53] any narrative or plot is enacted in "virtue of poetic composition"; the "succession [of events] . . . can be subordinated . . . to some logical connection . . . because the ideas of beginning, middle, and end are not taken from experience. They are not features of some real action but the effects of ordering the poem."[54] It is obvious how accurately this prescription applies to the construction of the historical sequence. In my consideration of Warren's first section, which imagines the onset of Audubon's obsession with birds, Ricoeur's observation that "what defines the beginning is not the absence of some antecedent but the absence of necessity in the succession"[55] exactly describes the process Warren engages in to reveal his subject, a process of selection and discrimination. He manipulates time so that it becomes "the work's time, not the time of events in the world,"[56] in order to best reveal the psychological and emotional state of his subject that accrues in light of what he imagines *his subject experiences,* a gesture that is, as Ricoeur notes, "directed more at the coherence of *muthos* than at its particular story."[57] We might still argue that it is through the adept handling of muthos, of narrative, that what is meaningful can be realized. Ricoeur continues, "To make up a plot is already to make the intelligible spring from the accidental, the universal from the singular, the necessary or the probable from the episodic."[58] This is what we all attempt to do with our own lives, and it is what Augustine would wrestle from his meditation on time, a human experience in his case that would—and could—accrue to the intelligible, the universal, the probable, in light of God's existence. In other words, Augustine, in Ricoeur's view, works to redeem human experience from the "discordance"—the "slippage"—of time.[59] For Warren, the accrual is his intention to make sense of the life of Audubon by utilizing a "plot" that suggests one thing is related to or leads to another and affects Audubon's experience as a human being and a naturalist. What this does, then, is create a timeline (not necessarily revealed chronologically), a sequence of events (implicit or explicit) that constructs meaning. Warren's representation is at once separate from and connected to historical events as it seeks to enact in a comprehensible, affecting, and universal way the import of those events for his subject. This ordering of events, or emplotment, is not only about making meaning but is as much about "making" time "*that becomes human to the extent that it is articulated through a narrative mode,* [just as] *narrative attains its full meaning when it becomes a condition of temporal existence.*[60] Story, then, "must be more than just an enumeration of events in serial order; it must organize them into an intelligible whole, of a sort that we can always ask what is the 'thought' of this story."[61] Emplotment is the "operation" that "brings together" and configures "factors as heterogeneous as agents, goals, means, interactions, circumstances, [and] unexpected results."[62] Clearly, Warren structures his sequence to include all these elements—everything from his subject's formative experiences in nature to his dandling babies in section [C] of movement IV, "The Sign Whereby He Knew."[63]

The question remains, how does one structure the lyric sequence to effect "narrative tasks"? Ricoeur's discussion is useful here as well, when he turns his attention to Heidegger's definition of temporality (*Zeitlichkeit*) as the "most authentic experience of time, that is, the dialectic of coming to be, having been, and making present [where] the words 'future,' 'past,' and 'present' disappear and time itself figures as the exploded unity of the three temporal extases."[64] He includes in his discussion Heidegger's "being-towards-death," an idea that emphasizes "the primacy of the future over the present and the closure of this future by a limit internal to all anticipation and every project."[65] This heightens the compass of Heidegger's within-time-ness (*Innerzeitigkeit*)[66] and is also the foundation for Ricoeur's idea of emplotment, which

> combines in variable proportions two temporal dimensions, one chronological and one not. The former constitutes the episodic dimension of narrative. It characterizes the story insofar as it is made up of events. The second is the configural dimensions properly speaking, thanks to which the plot transforms the events into a story,[67]

an emplotment that must include in its configurations the acknowledgment of an "end point."[68] This end point becomes essential in the determination of how the "manifold of events" will be unified into a coherent whole.[69] This is critical to the poetic sequence and very much in line with Rosenthal and Gall's likening it to a symphony in which each movement is orchestrated into a whole that will reveal nodules of emotional and psychological intensities. As Ricoeur notes, it is from the end point that the "story can be seen as a whole,"[70] just as the whole of a symphony, its ebbs and flows, its rhythms and intensities, can only be fully comprehended once the symphony has concluded. Of course, Ricoeur's observation places story even more squarely in the arena of time, and its consequence for human experience is equally as profound. This is complicated by the lyric, and the lyric sequence that would eschew storytelling or any other sense of chronological or configured order yet engages the life of a human subject.

We witness Warren's negotiation of this difficulty throughout *Audubon*. The first movement as discussed above engages in the timely extension of significant moments. In other words, those moments take on resonance—Augustine's duration—that gestures toward the eternal or timeless, yet they also mark time. They are thus significant moments that could have been otherwise, that negotiate and, as each additional moment affects those that have come before, that renegotiate a life, Audubon's life, so that in the end it seems "Simple, at least, in that it had to be" (IV.[A]).[71] What follows this first movement also needs to be discussed, of course, because what one looks for in the sequence is its progression, how the poem is orchestrated to achieve the fullest realization of its subject. How does Warren sustain his subject's life in time? How does he negotiate the implicit narrative of all human experience?

In pursuit of an answer, I note that Warren's second movement is particularly curious and may raise more questions than it puts to rest. After the lyricism of the first movement, the second movement, "The Dream He Never Knew the End Of," is significantly longer and very much a narrative. Divided into thirteen sections, this "dream" or story has a plot, a cast of characters (of which Audubon is one), and a clear sequence of events, arranged chronologically. At times the "narrative" unfolds smoothly in long graceful sentences; at other times it jerks along, splintered through Warren's use of short or fractured sentences and hard enjambments. The grammatical disjunctions that allow Warren to break from narrative into lyric in his first movement in his second primarily work to break up his extended narrative. Furthermore, unlike the other sections of this poem, in which Warren works to evoke Audubon's life through heightened moments of intense awareness, in the second movement the poem revisits at length an encounter Audubon recorded in his journals.[72]

The first section of movement II begins much like section I.[B]. We are placed in time—the "shank-end of day"—and hear the crow's call, "sweet in the distance." In the next line, however, the unconventional use of "sudden" instead of the adverb "suddenly" creates a disjunction that, rather than break up narrative as it does in movement I, seems to inhibit it, to turn these lines, however briefly, away from their forward motion toward event, or what happens. Warren's use of "sudden" also enacts—and embodies—surprise, a twist of attention away from the "day," the "snow," and the "crow" toward the "clearing" that comes up so unexpectedly, a "wound rubbed raw in the vast pelt of the forest," his metaphor echoing the violence of nature revealed in movement I—in the blood of dawn, and the bear feeding on its prey. Yet the narrative ensues—"there / Is the cabin"—and along with it the narrator's own observation of "The human filth, the human hope" it reveals.

From here the narrative steadily moves forward, although Warren manipulates sentences and line breaks as if to make the story less real, to push it toward that dream that the title implies. Warren's stanzas work cinematically: first we see the clearing, then the cabin with smoke coming from its chimney, then Audubon as he "leans on his gun," and finally Audubon's approach to the front door of the cabin. Yet in the third stanza, Warren turns to disjunction to disrupt his narrative. Audubon "thinks," then "thinks" again. Warren's use of a colon emphasizes the presence of a third-person narrator, which is not necessarily a departure from story but as enacted here augments the awkwardness of the storytelling. In this section Warren also inverts syntax, uses hard enjambment, and employs sentence fragments.

The sharp line break that describes how Audubon's "hand / Lifts, hangs" before knocking on the door lends a strangeness to what would otherwise be a very natural and expected action. The question that needs to be answered, then, is what is the effect of this broken narrative? If the poem isn't reaching toward lyric, what purpose do the disjunctive moments serve? Are they to suggest the dreamlike nature of Audubon's experience and the strangeness of the woman he encounters on his journey across America? Or are they to suggest dream itself? Though the section title suggests the latter is the case, one can't help but be reminded that dreams, when experienced, seem to be real; the events that take place unfold like a narrative that cannot be stopped unless the dreamer awakens. In the next section, Warren continues to break up his narrative. Here the interlude allows the narrator once again to interject, to question and judge his protagonist. The tone of these lines is one of utmost seriousness. Certainly, they strongly suggest that we are to interpret this story as event rather than dream, that the "sloven" human condition revealed in the first section reflects the nightmarish "dregs of all life." Still early in the narrative, Warren backs away from such a conclusion. His "Unless. // Unless what?" that closes this section suggests that perhaps these "dregs" can become something else.

To find out, we are returned to the narrative in the ensuing section, though once again, the story seems surreal:

> The face, in the air, hangs. Large,
> Raw-hewn, strong-beaked, the haired mole
> Near the nose, to the left, and the left side by the firelight
> Glazed red, the right in shadow, and under the tumble and tangle
> Of dark hair on that head, and under the coarse eyebrows,
> The eyes, dark, glint as from the unspecifiable
> Darkness of a cave. It is a woman. (II. 1–7)

Warren inverts the syntax in the opening sentence, disrupting the story's forward movement before launching into a syntactically complicated description of the individual who opens the door, a description that leans clumsily on the main clause that describes "the eyes, dark" that "glint" as from a cave. Not until line 7 is this individual acknowledged as a woman. Warren's repeated attention to "hands," this time hers, that "hang," just as her face "hangs" a few lines above, augments the strangeness of the encounter and places us at a distance from the narrative. Yet in the following lines, which conclude this section, Warren launches into dialogue; this woman speaks, and we reenter the narrative more fully once again.

In "The Dream He Never Knew the End Of," Warren engages in an introduction and reintroduction of narrative that is consistently disrupted. The problem that lingers as we continue through this section, then, is to understand what is achieved by its length and Warren's narrative interruptions. How does it speak to Audubon's life as a whole, or to the "vision" Warren seeks to convey of a man who finally learns to accept his fate?[73] If one reads Audubon's journal, one is immediately aware of how greatly Warren transforms and heightens Audubon's account of his experience. Still, it is not Warren's embellishment of the facts that is problematic; in fact, this manipulation of the original "story" suggests that Warren would like this experience to represent something more than it did, to give it greater emotional resonance. Instead, it is his insertion of this extended, chronological narrative section that in its length dominates the entire poem that raises questions. Why recount this particular event? Audubon notes in his journal that it "was the only time at which my life was in danger from my fellow creatures"[74] during twenty-five years of traveling all over America, and observes one paragraph later how this particular locale, virtually uninhabited when the incident occurred, is, at the time of his entry, populated and settled. How, then, does this encounter and Warren's imaginative adaptation of events transform the poet's subject? If Warren's intention is to suggest Audubon's cool, scrutinizing eye that can as easily look at a dead human as at a dead bird and see the beauty and knowledge that arise from both, why not encompass this response to the woman in a shorter lyric section, as he does with birds in movement VI? And why engage in a narrative that is constantly arrested and reintroduced? Though Warren's stanzas progress cinematically, the grammatical and syntactical disjunctions primarily work to interrupt what John Gardner in The Art of Fiction calls the "profluence"[75] of the story, its "vivid and continuous"[76] forward motion, like a dream in the reader's mind. If this is the "vision" of the poem's title, one would expect it to be intense and continuous; instead, its disruptions emphasize the presence of a third-person narrator, and as a result, the "story" becomes more self-conscious. Further, in light of the entire sequence, this narrative section seems disproportionate, almost burdensome, taking on perhaps more significance than it should through its extended length and dramatic content. Certainly, it invests this particular moment in Audubon's life with hypertropic significance, but is this significance enough to resist the section's narrative pull? Furthermore, how does the imbalance achieved by focusing at such length on this specific encounter affect the entire poem and work to reveal the emotional complexity of Audubon? And what does it reveal of Warren's relation to his material, particularly in light of those sections I've already discussed in which his orchestration of historical fact is so deft that we don't so much feel informed as located in the life of his subject?

It's productive to consider once again Warren's own attitude toward time. Robert Jackson in an essay on time in Warren's poetry turns to Heidegger's *Being and Time* and the philosopher's notion of "presencing"[77] that "uncovers lost possibilities, a going back to go forward."[78] According to Jackson, Heidegger's "moment of vision," a phrase that suggests deep connection to the title of Warren's sequence, "cannot be clarified in terms of the simple 'now,' as a simple 'making present,' but rather temporalizes itself in terms of a future, the emerging structure of the moment that cannot be summed up in a single instant." Jackson continues, "the focus, for both Heidegger and Warren, is always upon potential, possibility; the moment is always futural, always a function of will and conscience."[79] We see this is the case throughout Warren's sequence: in movement I when he leans on his gun but doesn't act; in movement II, when the "face, in the air, hangs," and the recognition that it is a woman's is suspended for six lines; in movement III's revelation, "We never know what we have lost, or what we have found, / We are only ourselves, and that promise," and in movement IV, when "The world declares itself" and "its end / Is its beginning." It is most obvious, of course, in the body and the title of the narrative second movement, "The Dream He Never Knew the End Of," where we are repeatedly reminded of a potential ending (Audubon's death by the woman's knife) that never occurs, at the same time that a very certain and non-negotiable conclusion transpires: the hanging of the woman and her sons. The dream of death, to be at the receiving end of a kill, would certainly have relevance in light of Audubon's vocation, yet the means Warren engages in to reveal this revelation still seem overly protracted. It suggests that time is as much the subject of this sequence as Audubon, but time that is so divergent as to be characterized as "nothingness" in section [J] of movement II, "for / There is no Time," as a condition presented as *other* than the protracted moment of recognition Audubon has in movement IV, section [A], when he sees his life—past, present, and future—"as though down a rifle barrel, lined up," and as "story" in the final section of the sequence. This may well be Jackson's "deferral of ends," where the narrative "emerges as the duration"[80] so that what we perceive of as driven by time—story—is made to evoke Jackson's "temporal expansiveness." In light of the sequence, this lends new possibilities to what can be accomplished through a historical subject and raises some profound questions about how much the genre needs to remain or has remained a primarily lyric one.

Undoubtedly, there is an impulse in Warren to resist time at the same moment he would embrace it through history and story. His long narrative second movement is reconfigured as dream, and dreams have their own inner workings of time, very much as Augustine's soul or mind configures time in a way that is particular to itself. In an effort to confound time further, the remaining poems of Warren's sequence are primarily lyric. Only section [A] of "The Sound of That Wind" delves more fully into narrative detail through Warren's use of seven fragments from Audubon's journals, and even in this instance, whatever chronology exists is bound to the here and now, as these accounts of Audubon's life are funneled into and compressed in the event of his death. In fact, Warren manipulates time so thoroughly in this movement that in section [B] he jettisons us into the speaker's experience of his present, when night "now leans off the Atlantic . . . on schedule," and the "Northwest Orient plane . . . has passed, / winking westward." Yet it may be mistaken to label this as primarily lyric. Instead, as Jackson says in his essay, paraphrasing Heidegger, "the *moment of vision* manifests itself as a 'span,' a 'stretching along' of 'historical temporality'" that is, as Heidegger posits, "fatefully whole in the sense of the authentic historical *constancy* of the self."[81] The self revealed here is twofold—it is Audubon's and Warren's. Not surprisingly the final two poems in the sequence move far from the chronology of Audubon's life, so far, in fact, that in "Love and Knowledge" (IV) we are in the presence of the "footless dance" of the birds themselves, which "cry / In a tongue multitudinous," the sound becoming part of a continuous present that is both historical and imagined. In the final movement, "Tell Me a Story," we leave the world of Audubon entirely and enter instead the consciousness of the poem's speaker, the "I" that would remember his own youthful experience of the "great geese hoot[ing] northward" and that would demand, in the sequence's final section, to be told a story.

It is this turn toward story—toward story as narrative structure, as revealing of time and history, and story as timeless, as existing in an eternal present—that Warren seeks to evoke and explore, and what better way to reveal this aporia, this enigmatic intersection of time and timelessness, but through an insistent conflation of the two. "Vision" is to see in the present, but it also is to see into the past and into the future, to see "the self that was, the self that is, and there, / Far off but in range, completing that alignment, your fate."[82] It is also imagination, to be able to "dream / Of a season past all seasons," as Warren writes in "The Sound of That Wind," to reveal time and the timeless, each through the other. "In this century, and moment, of mania / Tell me a story,"[83] the speaker demands at the conclusion of this sequence in response to a configuration of cultural and psychological pressures different from those of a century before but still very much a part of what Rosenthal and Gall envision as central to the genre's development. "The name of the story will be Time, / But you must not pronounce its name." In a reversal of expectations, it is narrative and time the speaker seeks, not timelessness. It is in time that the imagination configures meaning. It is in narrative that its essence is revealed. "Tell me a story," the speaker insists, "of deep delight."

Notes

1. M. L. Rosenthal and Sally M. Gall, *The Modern Poetic Sequence: The Genius of Modern Poetry* (New York: Oxford University Press, 1983), 3.

2. Ibid., 10.

3. Ibid., 3.

4. Ibid., 3–15 passim.

5. Aaron Copland, *What to Listen For in Music* (New York: Signet, 2002), 24.

6. Rosenthal and Gall, *The Modern Poetic Sequence*, 15.

7. Erwin Stein, *Form and Performance* (New York: Limelight Editions, 1989), 83.

8. Copland, *What to Listen For in Music*, 24.

9. Rosenthal and Gall, *The Modern Poetic Sequence*, 15, 8.

10. Ibid., 7.

11. Paul Ricoeur, *Time and Narrative*, vol. 1, trans. Kathleen McLaughlin and David Pellauer (Chicago: University of Chicago Press, 1984), 3.

12. Ibid., xi.

13. Rosenthal and Gall, *The Modern Poetic Sequence*, 15.

14. Interview with Eleanor Clark and Robert Penn Warren," *New England Review* 1.1 (Autumn 1978), reprinted in *Robert Penn Warren Talking: Interviews, 1950–1978*, ed. Floyd C. Watkins and John T. Hiers (New York: Random House, 1980), 276.

15. Dave Smith, "Warren's Ventriloquists," in *Hunting Men: Reflections on a Life*

in *American Poetry* (Baton Rouge: Louisiana State University Press, 2006), 61.

16. In light of this poem's configural complexities, I've found it useful to refer to the larger sections as movements and the subsections as sections. The designation of movements to these larger sections is appropriate in light of my own interest in sequential orchestration and resonates with Rosenthal's and Gall's likening of the lyric sequence to a "piece of music."

17. Robert Penn Warren, *Audubon: A Vision* (New York: Random House, 1969), 2.

18. Warren, *Audubon*. All references to the poem are indicated by movement, section, and line number.

19. Carlos Drummond de Andrade, "Travelling in the Family," trans. Elizabeth Bishop, in Warren, *Audubon*: "I caught at his strict shadow and the shadow released itself with neither haste nor anger. But he remained silent."

20. Ralph Ellison and Eugene Walter, "Warren on the Art of Fiction," in Watkins and Hiers, *Robert Penn Warren Talking*, 41.

21. Saint Augustine, *Confessions*, trans. Henry Chadwick (Oxford: Oxford University Press, 1991), 228–229. All references to Augustine's text include Chadwick's chapter and paragraph divisions.

22. Ricoeur, *Time and Narrative*, 5.

23. Augustine, *Confessions*, 231.

24. Ellison and Walter, "Warren on the Art of Fiction," 41.

25. Augustine, *Confessions*, 231.

26. Ricoeur, *Time and Narrative*, 7.

27. Ibid., 6.

28. Augustine, *Confessions*, 232.

29. Ibid.

30. Ibid., 235.

31. Ibid., 238.

32. In an interesting coincidence, the second epigraph to Warren's sequence is taken from Psalm 56, verse 8: "Thou tellest my wanderings: put thou my tears into thy bottle: are they not in thy book?"

33. Augustine, *Confessions*, 243.

34. Ricoeur, *Time and Narrative*, 16.

35. Ibid., 18.

36. Augustine, 243 (also quoted in Ricoeur, *Time and Narrative*, 19).

37. Ibid.

38. Ricoeur, *Time and Narrative*, 19.

39. Ibid., 26.

40. Augustine, *Confessions*, 244.

41. Ibid.

42. Ricoeur, *Time and Narrative*, 28.

43. Ibid.

44. Ibid., 6.

45. Ibid., 21–22.

46. Augustine, *Confessions*, 243.

47. Ricoeur, *Time and Narrative*, 31–32.

48. Ibid., 33.

49. Ibid., 35.

50. Ibid., 33.

51. Ibid., 36. Important here is Ricoeur's explanation that what he calls narrative is the same as what Aristotle calls *muthos;* both can be defined as the organization of events.

52. Ibid., 38.

53. Ibid., 39.

54. Ibid.

55. Ibid., 38.

56. Ibid., 39.

57. Ibid., 41.

58. Ibid.

59. Ibid., 21.

60. Ibid., 52.

61. Ibid., 65.

62. Ibid.

63. Warren, *Audubon*, 22.

64. Ricoeur, *Time and Narrative*, 61.

65. Ibid.

66. Ibid., 62.

67. Ibid., 66.

68. Ibid., 66, 67.

69. Ibid., 66.

70. Ibid., 67.

71. Warren, *Audubon*, 20.

72. Audubon, *Audubon and His Journals,* ed. Marie R. Audubon and Elliott Coues, 2 vols. (New York: Dover, 1960), 2:225–230.

73. Peter Stitt, "An Interview with Robert Penn Warren," in Watkins and Hiers, *Robert Penn Warren Talking*, 235.

74. Audubon, *Journals*, 2:230.

75. John Gardner, *The Art of Fiction* (New York: Vintage, 1991), 55.

76. Ibid., 33.

77. Richard Jackson, "The Generous Time: Robert Penn Warren and the Phenom-enology of the Moment," *boundary 2* 9.2, "Supplement on Contemporary Poetry" (Winter 1981): 2.

78. Ibid., 3.

79. Ibid.

80. Ibid., 7.

81. Jackson, "The Generous Time," 8.

82. Warren, *Audubon*, 20.

83. Ibid., 32.

PART III

The Experimental Contemporary

Narrative Poem

ONE ARC SYNOPTIC
Plot, Poetry, and the Span of Consciousness

DANIEL TOBIN

O Choir, translating time
Into what multitudinous Verb the suns
And synergy of waters ever fuse . . .
—HART CRANE, *The Bridge*

Dancing on the Bridge

There is a scene near the beginning of *Saturday Night Fever* in which Tony Maniero, after another late-night sojourn with his friends in the discos of 1970s Brooklyn, parks his blue-collar, hand-me-down sedan in the middle of the Verrazano Bridge. What follows is a ritual of testosterone-fueled whooping and strutting as Tony, hardware store clerk by day and aspiring dance sensation by night, climbs over the guardrail onto the span of girders, where he begins a sequence of pirouettes that requires him to balance precariously several hundred feet above the churning Narrows where the Hudson River opens into Gravesend Bay and the Atlantic beyond. This macho flirtation with death is a rite of passage, and Tony is the hero who must survive the film's "epic" trials, not least of which is overcoming his blue-collar upbringing to become an artist, battling a gang of Puerto Ricans from Sunset Park with his own tribe of Italian Americans from Bay Ridge, and, finally, winning the woman he loves—his ideal dance partner—by entering the big contest of 2001. The movie is a late twentieth-century American male bildungsroman (counterpointed by the high falsetto voices of the Bee Gees), and its plot, true to the roots of Western narrative, follows a dramatic arc replete with temptations, reversals of fortune, and the birth of a new identity in the form of a more mature consciousness for the hero. Before he can leave the world of his youth he must, at the crucial turning point, or peripeteia, refuse the dance prize he so desired and award it himself to the Puerto Rican couple whose dancing he judges to be better than his own and his partner's. He must also return to the girders of the bridge high above the flowing water of the Narrows between the human city and the vast inhuman ocean to witness the death of his sidekick, the pathetically sycophantic Ralph, who plummets into the swell below while drunkenly trying to perform the same leaps his idol had mastered at the beginning of the film. It's as though Tony's transformation has to be sealed by the loss of his alter ego, his antiself—the part of him that was mindlessly subservient to his origins. In the end, he must even forgo an erotic relationship for a purely platonic one with his beloved. In short, it's not until the "Ralph" in him is dead that he can cross the other bridge—Hart Crane's bridge, it so happens—into the promised land of Manhattan.

However we interpret *Saturday Night Fever*, the figure of the bridge presides over its plot from beginning to end and may be taken as an analogue of plot itself—in Greek, *muthos*, the dynamic span of a story's essential action as it is structured through the succession of details and events. Plot is, in Robert Scholes and Robert Kellogg's succinct definition, "the dynamic sequential element in narrative literature."[1] Working directly from Aristotle, Thomas Leitch defines plot as "a sequence of events or actions (*praxis*) which display a particular end (*telos*)."[2] Given that Aristotle defines a poet as a maker of plots rather than of verses, it seems plausible that this definition of plot should hold for narrative poetry as well as for fiction and film. Surely the narrative poems of Robert Frost and Robinson Jeffers have plots. Yet, when I think of the situation of narrative poetry at the beginning of the twenty-first century, the first name that comes to mind is neither E. A. Robinson, nor Frost, nor Jeffers, nor any of the significant contemporary poets working with narrative in our own time, nor even a poet in the strict sense at all, but Virginia Woolf. "Examine for a moment an ordinary mind on an ordinary day," Woolf enjoins us in her essay "The Novel of Consciousness":

The mind receives a myriad impressions—trivial, fantastic, evanescent, or engraved with the sharpness of steel. From all sides they come, an incessant shower of innumerable atoms; and as they fall, as they shape themselves into the life of Monday or Tuesday, the accent falls differently from of old; the moment of importance came not here but there; so that, if a writer were a free man and not a slave, if he could write what he chose, not what he must, there would be no plot, no comedy, no tragedy, no love interest or catastrophe in the accepted style. . . . Life is not a series of gig lamps symmetrically arranged; life is a luminous halo, a semi-transparent envelope surrounding us from the beginning of consciousness to the end.[3]

Woolf's observations, revolutionary in their time, construe plot as anything but sequential. As a translation of time's endless flow into a narrative's beginning, middle, and end, plot becomes profoundly diminished, if not entirely marginal, in Woolf's formulation. Indeed, her remarks are observed here for the purpose of undermining what she called "the tyranny of plot," and while the genre she had in mind clearly was fiction, her implication that there is something contrived, artistically stultifying, and epistemologically deluded about plot begs the question of how poets both in her time and ours might effectively construct a narrative poem.

The legacy of modernism in both fiction and poetry asks writers and readers to rethink if not eschew traditional machinations of plot, or at least to make them secondary to character or other kinds of temporal organization. Through the experiments of Joyce, Faulkner, Lawrence, Woolf, and many others, the "realistic" novel of the nineteenth century becomes atomized and recast in the flow of modernist stream of consciousness. Often contemporary realistic novels minimize plot designs for character development, and the postmodern metanarrative tradition often manipulates plot in outrageous ways for the purposes of parody. In Woolf's case the realistic novel is anything but "real"; it is a warping of reality into false constructs, a lie of order that transgresses against time's inherent flow. What was for the mythic storyteller truth—the shaping muthos of some sacred or near sacred idea of order—becomes an impediment to representing the world as it is in all its radiant complexity. What was for Aristotle the hallmark of art as well as life, plot, for Woolf seems almost an intrusion upon life and an impediment to art.

Aristotle's notion of plot as the mimesis or representation of an action and not of character emerges from that first world of ritualized narrative, of storytellers re-creating strictly defined plots within the confines of oral tradition. Again according to Robert Scholes and Robert Kellogg, traditional plot evolves from this mythic world on its way to what they call "the secular narrative."[4] Moreover, for Scholes and Kellogg, though plot is dynamic in its construction of sequence, "the whole movement of the mind in Western culture . . . has been a movement away from dogma, certainty, fixity, and all absolutes in metaphysics, in ethics, and epistemology," and so by extension the very idea of plot as a plausible ordering of reality becomes ever more undermined even as it reaches its dominance in the "traditional story."[5] If Scholes and Kellogg are right—and it is hard to argue against this prevailing sense of things regardless of one's philosophical, religious, ethical, or aesthetic persuasions—then the idea of plot is linked to fundamental issues of human self-understanding and desire for a world at once conceivable and representable in the truth of time's fugitive nature. In short, modern and contemporary questions of plot find their roots in primordial questions of time, consciousness, and the sacred. As always, one's idea of poetry, narrative or otherwise, emerges implicitly if not explicitly from one's idea of the order of things, even if one believes there is nothing but chaos at the ontological heart of experience.

Surely Woolf's misgivings about plot were expressed in support of her own narrative art, which is, paradoxically, intensely inward, character-driven, and lyrical. The lyric movements of her novels are, in a profound sense, a scandal to temporal structure. Her novels portray consciousness immersed in the fluid medium of time. How would Woolf represent the action of Tony Maniero's passage from dancing thug to the sadder and wiser aspirant we see at the movie's end? Perhaps the question isn't fair, since Woolf may well be the least cinematic of twentieth-century novelists, and the thought of any adaptation of plot in the traditional sense would be anathema to her. If one could imagine Virginia Woolf in 1970s Brooklyn, I doubt the bridge would loom so boldly in her exploration of Tony's consciousness. Still, plot as an orchestration and sequencing of events does not disappear entirely from Woolf's actual work, though it is minimized in favor of the envelope of accrued luminous details. Plot closure in Woolf is Lily Briscoe's final brushstroke through the center of her painting at the end of *To the Lighthouse*, almost an afterthought even as it satisfies the reader's sense of closure: "It was done . . . I have had my vision."

In addition to her disaffection with plot, Woolf's view of consciousness also reflects the diminishment of individual identity before the powers and dominions of modern life, and is not this reflection the inevitable consequence of Romantic claims to self-empowerment? At the same time, the rejection of the Romantic ethos by the modernist poets who were Woolf's contemporaries—most notably Pound and Eliot—ironically reveals a longing for the security of plot in the face of what appears to be a thoroughly atomized world, and this longing persists perhaps most visibly where plot seems most absent. Though as an epic it achieves far less closure than Woolf's *To the Lighthouse*, the structure of Pound's *The Cantos* is predicated on the submerged plot of Odysseus's journey home. Despite its seeming cacophony of allusions and voices, Eliot's *The Waste Land* achieves a kind of discordant symphonic coherence through its "subsumptive" myth. The action it represents is that of the dying and reviving god, assumed like an archetypal code beneath its fragments, juxtapositions, and associations. To some it might seem ridiculous to mention *The Waste Land* in the same breath as narrative, but in addition to what one might call the poem's intertextual plot, *The Waste Land* has distinct narrative as well as dramatic elements. It is above all an orchestration of intertextual stories or fragments of stories that would fit together into one ur-narrative. In a profound sense, Eliot's assumption of his intertextual, archetypal plot brings him nearer to the muthos found in ritual, where the action is sacred action, worthy of ritual repetition, to be later embellished by "the singer of tales," but not to be essentially departed from. Remarkably, in *The Waste Land*, potentially the most secular of all plots—the fracture of civilization into incoherence and disorder, into the profane—is also the most sacred: a repetition of the eternal struggle between order and chaos, leading, hopefully, to spiritual regeneration. Though one would be hard-pressed to defend *The Waste Land* as a narrative poem in the strictest sense, plot understood as the essential action of muthos orchestrated through events and details is necessary for the poem's artistic success and integrity.

When Aristotle spoke of plot as a representation of action, or more specifically a sequence of actions leading to a justifiable end, he was speaking of Sophoclean drama as the highest form of poiesis. What, however, is the nature of a poem's action, its muthos? For the lyric, that action might ideally be described as an action of voice. Unbounded by story, the pure lyric gathers forward motion through an intensity of voice that gestures ultimately toward a suspension of time. Beginning, middle, and end exist as staging for the voice's aspiration to sing out of a state of pure being, or perhaps into that state through language, as in Rilke's *Sonnets to Orpheus*—"Gesang ist Dasein." Song is existence. In contrast, the essential action of narrative poetry, like that of any narrative, must be accomplished with reference to time's forward motion, that is, in reference to becoming. Of course, it's debatable whether there is a pure lyric as described above, though if there were, Rilke's poetry would come near to achieving that standard. Still, plot, as Thomas Leitch observes, is an essential part of the rhetorical structure of the English sonnet,[6] and Edward Arlington Robinson's Tilbury sonnets show him to be an essentially narrative poet within this lyric form. More broadly, in his essay "In Praise of the Impure: Narrative Consciousness in Poetry," Alan Shapiro demonstrates how narrative informs such lyric poems as William Carlos Williams's "The Road to the Contagious Hospital" and Robert Hayden's "Those Winter Sundays."[7] Conversely, to be successful the narrative poem must have a strong lyric dimension; it must combine story with song in the sonic and rhythmic textures of its lines, or otherwise it might as well be written in prose. To complicate matters further, Paul Ricoeur in his magisterial work, *Time and Narrative*, reminds us that even in Aristotle's *Poetics*, the representation (*mimesis*) of an action (*muthos*) manifests itself through "the medium of metrical language."[8] From this standpoint, the adaptation of muthos into the belated world of prose is secondary to its fundamental presence in poetry. At the very least, it suggests that the terms lyric and narrative are not strict generic markers but point toward something more fluid. At the root of the matter, song and story are not mutually exclusive but rather are mutually implicated in the reordering of time through which stories are told and meaning gets made in poems.

Questions over the nature of narrative's reordering of reality certainly fuel the discussions of narratologists, and ought to be entertained by poets in their more extended musings about their art. "Plot alters . . . the world even as it provides an interpretation of it": so Thomas Leitch describes what he sees as the fundamental paradox of narrative, its ability to at once comment on the world from a stance that transcends the world, a vantage point of wisdom "outside the particular represented situation," and operate through the narrative's sequence of events, its "process of development" or essential action.[9] This is exactly what Woolf finds so transgressive about plot—its presumption of having staked out the truth about life when it is merely a warping of life away from the truth of its elusive nature. There is no outside for Woolf, no vantage point except within the luminous envelope—hers is a narratology approaching pure immanence. Hers is a mimesis of consciousness rather than a mimesis of action or even character.[10] At the same time, without some dimension of plot, neither a story nor a poem could achieve closure. Plot, therefore, may be understood as a fundamental trope of the poet's imagination, a shaping action or "organizing mimesis," to use Paul Ricoeur's phrase, that transforms a fluid temporal experience into self-conscious unity.[11] Plot for Ricoeur is "a synthesis of the heterogenous"[12] by which the fluid multiplicity of life achieves livable order on the human scale. To use Woolf's *To the Lighthouse* again as an example, it is in the middle section, after Mrs. Ramsey dies and the nonhuman life of the house rises to narrative focus, that life outside the human experience of time comes into focus as the wider truth of existence. The whirling line of light from the lighthouse, like plot, can reach only so far across the flow surrounding it. It inevitably disappears. The human world is an island world, and its plot concerns, even world wars, pale before the nonhuman flux that composes the greater elusive sum of reality. At its core, plot constitutes an ontological countermovement against the flow even as it intends to articulate that flow. That is the core of its paradox. Plot therefore lives a double life, and finds in Frost's "West-Running Brook" an apt figure for its contrary nature:

> Speaking of contraries, see how the brook
> In that white wave runs counter to itself.
> It is from that in water we were from
> Long, long before we were from any creature.
> Here we, in our impatience of the steps,
> Get back to the beginning of beginnings,
> The stream of everything that runs away.
> Some say existence like a Pirouot
> And Pirouette, forever in one place,
> Stands still and dances, but it runs away,
> It seriously, sadly, runs away
> To fill the abyss' void with emptiness.[13]

How tempting it would be to compare Frost's Pirouot and Pirouette with Tony Maniero's dance on the bridge above the Narrows, but such mindfulness about the ontological and epistemological roots of things really never enters the human neighborhood of *Saturday Night Fever.* In any case, plot as an arc of action assumes a vantage point outside the flow of time, a contrary movement like Frost's white wave, since without that outside vantage point time itself would not exist as a succession of comparable moments: without plot, time would not be time but "undifferentiated flow."[14] The paradox cuts in both directions at once, not unlike Frost's brook. Plot not only exists as a presumption that would impose order as if from outside time, it is an invention of time without which time would not exist. As the poet Eleanor Wilner remarked once at a poetry reading, "We are hot-wired for narrative." We are, it seems, hot-wired more specifically for muthos, at least in some measure, and the managing of plot in poems as well as stories is a dance of degrees that at once marks the human span, clarifies its longing, and admits its own countervalence in a flow that otherwise cannot be known.

It is interesting that poetic intelligences as unlike each other as Woolf's and Frost's would be drawn in their contrary ways to the same experience of time's flow and ultimately to the question of how human experience seeks to determine meaning through the reordering of time. Both writers are ultimately concerned with consciousness, and in the human sphere that also means inherently living a double life, being at once a part of the flow of life, as Frost sees things—"It flows between us, over us, and *with* us," Fred reflects in "West-Running Brook"—and existing counter to the flow by our mind's awareness of its seeming separateness from nature. I think, therefore I am: the Cartesian formula with its primacy of thinking over being speaks to the phenomenological truth of our inherent contrariness. Similarly, according to Colin McGinn in *The Mysterious Flame,* consciousness is a phenomenon that by its essential properties eludes our ability to describe it since, by his estimation, we cannot determine its true nature simply because we exist *as* humanly conscious beings. For humans to see consciousness for what it truly is would be for an eye to be able to see itself without the aid of a mirror. "Our ignorance here," he observes, "is an ignorance of a hidden architecture of the self. Something about the hidden structure of the self determines its unity and identity, but we do not grasp this hidden structure, which is why we cannot answer questions about unity and identity with any reliability. It is not that we know the essential nature of the self but fail to understand under what physical conditions it exists; rather, we are ignorant of what the self intrinsically is."[15]

Speaking as a philosopher, McGinn writes persuasively and compellingly about the failure of both science and religion to answer this most fundamental question, but both Woolf and Frost in their own idioms brilliantly portray the essential action of consciousness reflecting on itself and, perhaps, reveal art's most basic mimetic aim—to represent the "hidden architecture" of our humanity. Though Woolf's art, in Ricoeur's estimation, is "a masterpiece from the point of view of the perception of time" precisely through her ability to make "the incompleteness of personality, the diversity of levels of consciousness . . . and the evanescent character of feelings" the center of her portrayal of human beings,[16] her minimizing of plot in story does not eradicate what he calls "emplotment" as an indelible feature of narrative and, I would claim, a necessary feature of human self-reflection. From the first cave painting, art has sought to represent the essential action of the human consciousness seeking to see itself for what it is intrinsically and in relation to the world. If McGinn is right, that is an impossible task, though what may be a failure for philosophy could well be a boon to art, and to poetry specifically, for with each failure the spur to represent, to create in an image the true nature of ourselves that forever eludes us, is renewed.

Does this scenario lock us into a postmodern hall of mirrors, the product of a tragic tautology or a fruitfully recursive journey inside the most formative of hermeneutical circles? The fundamental aporia, the seemingly "unbridgeable gap," as Ricoeur calls it,[17] falls between the representation of time in a reality independent of us and the representation of time as the condition for our experience in the world. Ricoeur's answer is to claim that "emplotment"—muthos as a creation of the structure of human consciousness—clarifies the gap but does not offer a solution to the problem. The bridge itself is a dance above that serious, sad running away of everything from everything else and from itself that is, finally, the emptiness that fills Frost's couple in "West-Running Brook" with "a panic fear." At the same time, the multifarious presence of plot in ways not normally construed in poetry permits us to extend our understanding of how poetry might be orchestrated outside the traditional "gig lamp" design and still maintain a dimension of narrative as well as coherence and viable closure. This is what Ricoeur means by "emplotment" as opposed to plot: it is the deep structure of the work that brings the intention of single action to the succession of events linked together by causality, and it is the product of that "rage for order" Stevens found a concomitant of the poetic impulse. In my view, such causality in poetry need not be apparent in the traditional sense but may exist through narrative elements and non-narrative elements in a poem's orchestration; hence my example above of *The Waste Land*. Ricoeur's understanding of emplotment might also allow us to see more traditional narrative designs in the manner of Robert Frost's dramatic narratives as being far less the series of gig lamps they may at first appear to be, particularly when the poet effectively confronts themes that resist the human order of things, which is something Frost does all the time in his best work. Finally, it may help us begin to rethink some of the assumptions that have led to a Balkanization of American poetry into mutually exclusive camps whose artistic assumptions are underwritten by profoundly antipathetic views of reality and of how reality, self, and time ought to be represented.

Macrocosm: Polyphony and Configuration

Beginning. Middle. End. I am riding in the back seat of my family's new Rambler station wagon on a Friday afternoon in Brooklyn, my father having left work early to beat the traffic. We have driven the ten blocks to 95th Street along Fourth Avenue, made the left turn just before the Harbor Theater, resumed the trip after the red light on the corner of Fifth by the White Castle—a light we always seem to catch whatever time of day—and now with the next right after Vesuvio Italian Restaurant and Joe's Garden World we're merging along the on-ramp of the Verrazano. It's 1968, and the Vietnam War is still raging just before the catastrophic events—King's assassination, Kennedy's assassination—that would transform history occur. We glide along the rise over the Narrows between the two towers I watched ascending through some of my earliest memories and down the gradual arc to the toll plaza cut into rock beside Fort Wadsworth and above the emptying Hudson, one brief leg of the trip west finished, an ending to be followed by other markers—the Outerbridge, Perth Amboy Refineries, the Wishing Well Tavern on Route 206, signs for Lake Hopatcong, Andover, Newton, Don Bosco College—that had become my way of pacing the journey that ended, at least until Sunday night, when we started back, at Cherry Wood Trail in Crandon Lakes, New Jersey. This paced organization, the way of finding significant milestones as a means to mark time, is, I think, a way of not only enduring *chronos*—what Frank Kermode in *The Sense of an Ending* calls "waiting time" or "passing time"—but of shaping it into "significant time," what he in contrast identifies as *kairos*.[18] Though Joe's Garden World and the Wishing Well Tavern hardly stand as significant markers outside my own memory, and only then in retrospect, it is this reconfiguring of time from mere chronology to meaningful order that most distinguishes the Western conception of history, particularly in the Judeo-Christian tradition. We find the significance of our place in time by seeing our lives somehow in concert with the *kairoi*, those events that stand out as emblematic of an encompassing story that lifts us above the passing flow, that configure the plots of our lives within the purview of some larger and deeper emplotment.

Assurance of the validity of such an overarching conception of temporal order has, of course, been greatly undermined, as much for most poets as for theologians and philosophers. If the grand arc of a world-defining story could be believed any longer, it would have to be believed with the provision that its truth claims provide only a glimpse at best of the reality to which the grand scheme points, itself having become one story in a potentially infinite number of stories all pointing in their limited ways to some still grander and ever-elusive universal emplotment. At the same time, the urgency of so eminent a design exists like a ghost in the machine of poetry. Stephen Dobyns, a poet notable both for his narrative gifts and for his skepticism in matters of ontology and epistemology, endorses as much when he reflects, "the way a poem is created is a metaphor for the ordering of chaos, not only through the use of pattern, but also through structure, which is the presence of a beginning, middle, and an end."[19] Dobyns's insight is profound, for it makes the poet's task akin to the mythmaker's. The poet's ultimate success is an image of order wrested from a disordered world—the representation of a single essential action that is the poem, realized through the formal patterns established by the poet's various choices. Beginning, middle, and end—their deep structural integrity—achieve meaningful unity of time in a victory of concordance over discordance.[20] This is, as Dobyns observes, a structural victory, but one that is achieved through the poet's ability to bring all the patterns and textures of the poem into concert with each other—Frost's momentary stay against confusion.

The most astounding example of a poem that organizes itself at every level according to the scheme of some grand emplotment is Dante's *Divine Comedy*. The beginning of the poem is the middle of the poet's journey— "Nel mezzo del camin di nostra vita"—though his life is also "our" life, the one life, the one archetypal plotline. The poem's terza rima, its thirty-three cantos in each book but for the *Paradiso*, which has thirty-four and brings the poem's number to a perfect hundred, the tripartite structure of the whole—all reveal an orchestration of scale reflective of the Trinitarian unity of Dante's spiritual and physical universe. The fiction of Dante's journey of descent and ascent—the epic romance of the soul—is a passage through scales of one divinely ordered muthos for human being, history, and the entire universe. Dante's encounters along the way, with both the damned and the saved, are personal *kairoi* that further and deepen his spiritual knowledge and, finally, enable him to represent that which paradoxically cannot be represented: the Divine Life itself, which is ultimately the beginning, middle, and end of human life. Whether one still believes in Dante's universe is beside the point. In *The Divine Comedy*, time has become fully humanized. What the narratologist would call the prevailing "discursivity" of life, its absence of plot, has been reconfigured to achieve teleology, a configuring end, one that is conducive to meaning and therefore human habitation in time. Narrative becoming has arrived at the lyric apotheosis of being only to find that it has been being all along!

Like Stephen Dobyns, Alan Shapiro envisions poetry, and in particular narrative poetry, as intimately bound to human self-definition and reflective of human consciousness as well as of our innate desire to create order in a world that sorely resists our efforts in these matters. Shapiro's sense of narrative, though far removed from Dante's cosmic unity of scale, nonetheless retains the idea of unity of action, emplotment, as a dynamic structural organization that necessarily involves all aspects of the poem. "I regard narrative," Shapiro declares, "as having more to do with a particular activity of consciousness than with technical matters, or with anecdote, or with the mere sequential nature of external happenings." He continues,

> Narrative involves what W. S. DiPiero calls "states of becoming," the enactment as well as imitation of action (mental, physical, emotional, or intellectual) in the unfolding of the verse. The complete rendering of an action implies an arc connecting origins and ends—how have I come to this (past) is implicit in what I am doing (present), and what I am doing is unintelligible from what I am doing it for (future). Anything in the poem which clarifies or contributes to the rendering of this action has narrative meaning. Thus it is possible to talk about meter and syntax as narrative elements, and about how the evolving shape of the sentence,

for instance, or the developing contour of a particular rhythm, forms a segment of the arc which the poem as a whole describes.[21]

Shapiro's observation here is important because it shifts our attention from the contrivances of plot that so troubled Woolf to the very matter of consciousness that Woolf sought to better represent by removing plot in any conventional sense from her fiction. In turn, it adapts DiPiero's concept of "states of becoming" in a manner that amends the Aristotelian notion of muthos as an imitation of action. For Shapiro, plot is an "enactment," an idea that in one sleight of word restores the fundamentally dramatic emphasis of Aristotle's *Poetics* and makes it central to narrative poetry. Finally, it reiterates the likewise fundamental connection between narrative and lyric poetry, seeing correctly the difference between the two as a difference of inclination and degree, and reaffirming implicitly if not explicitly that a successful narrative poem must have something lyric about it in its employment of rhythm, sonic texture, syntax, and form.

The linking of narrative to states of becoming in Shapiro's thought underscores what Scholes and Kellogg affirm is the now long-standing shift in narrative literature "from myth seen in the context of a cyclical concept of time, to myth seen against a linear concept."[22] For these two critics, moreover, "this change in the human conception of time is an aspect of that universal movement toward a rational understanding of the cosmos which tends to make itself felt in most cultures but is virtually the identifying characteristic of our Western culture."[23] The birth of narrative literature in the West, which by and large coincides with the epic vision we identify with Homer, may itself be understood as a secularization of myth into progressive narrative. Dante's sacred journey combines his soul's linear state of becoming with an encompassing cyclical revelation at the visionary summit of the *Paradiso*—the whirling, kaleidoscopic Rose that is the poet's admittedly feeble figure for the communion of divinity and humanity, transcendence and immanence, that is being in its essence. Dante's poem unites being with becoming, linear time with cyclical time, by joining microcosm with macrocosm in a final commanding figure that seeks to represent that which cannot be represented. In contrast, Odysseus's journey home after Troy, fraught as it is with delay, binds action to character. He is *polytropos*, the multifaceted man, and by inscribing the arc of his journey the plot of *The Odyssey* manifests the same polytropic character. What Thomas Leitch calls "the polytropic principle"[24] is essentially a conception of plot that would reconcile its discursive dimension—the potentially endless narration of events in the manner of Scheherazade—with its equally necessary teleological impulse, the requirement for closure.

In modern poetry, the mythic impulse at the root of narrative finds its expression in the modernist "epic" sequence. Of course, there is no modernist (or postmodernist) epic in the pure sense of the word since we no longer have the luxury of a shared, all-encompassing paradigmatic story. Homer, Virgil, Dante, Milton—all assumed a unifying muthos for their cultures. Blake invented his own mythology. In Wordsworth's *The Prelude* we see the displacement of the epic impulse into the poet's own "becoming"—a psychological epic, the inward journey. In the twentieth century, Pound's *Cantos* reflect the epic impulse, but the sequence's failure rests in its unbridled discursiveness. Despite their roots in Homer (and their multifaceted cultural allusions, ranging from Confucian China to troubadour France), the *Cantos* finally have no telos. The modernist and postmodernist epic plot from Williams to Olson displays itself as a quest for the very organizing principle that would provide it with closure, a discursive search for the end that never comes. Dana Gioia's remark in "The Dilemma of the Long Poem" that the modern long poem is "doomed to failure" reflects his stance, and the New Formalist stance in general, that only the narrative structures of epic can satisfy narrative teleology. The narrative poet should adopt traditional narrative structures to avoid the pitfalls of endless discursivity, according to this analysis, since by Gioia's estimation the need to create "the form" of one's own poetic discourse assumes an outright rejection of received methodologies.[25] However, Gioia's assumption that the modern long poem refuses to adopt traditional narrative structures simply does not hold, unless one is limiting the phrase "traditional narrative structure" largely to blank verse. Though Pound does not write in blank verse, the *Cantos* do attempt to incorporate the essential narrative structure of the journey as a way of organizing the poem's discursivity. Pound fails mightily to infuse his poem with a formal telos, but his failure is not born of rejecting all traditional narrative structure. Rather, he fails to adapt the Homeric motif sufficiently to the poem, becoming ever more distracted by his own centripetal wanderings in the vast storehouse of human cultures. Both *Paterson* and *The Maximus Poems*, as brilliant as individual parts might be, likewise lack teleological focus, though in both cases it is due not to the utter rejection of traditional narrative structures but, I would argue, to the failure of the poets to adapt tradition in a way conducive to reconciling the long poem's need for discursiveness with a reliance on teleology to achieve satisfactory closure. They fail, in short, at being polytropic, at reconciling these two fundamental elements of plot.

One modernist long poem that does not fail to achieve adequate closure despite its incorporation of multivalent perspectives that amplify the discursive aspect of its structure is Hart Crane's *The Bridge*. Most believe Crane's poem to be, in Dick Allen's words, "a noble failure,"[26] and there are indeed individual parts of the sequence that do not contribute much to the overall design, or that excel merely as individual moments within the whole. These are "Indiana," the last poem in section 2, titled "Powhatan's Daughter," and section 5, the loosely juxtaposed "Three Songs." There are also moments of vatic bombast, excesses of Crane's ambition and operatic conception of the poem. Nevertheless, the governing action of *The Bridge,* its plot, is the eternal metamorphosis of divinity into time through history and the human effort of creation in material form by which new incarnations are made. Every section of the book intends to be revelatory of that end. The Brooklyn Bridge is the representative figure or trope for this action, and it is anything but static. One could also identify lines and parts of individual poems, but these sections do not achieve sufficient import within the pattern of the whole. Dick Allen's observation, then, that the noble failure of the modern long poem results from attempts by poets to extend the "imagistic lyric" into epic form without regard for "narrative and dramatic elements"[27] does not quite hold for Crane's ambitious work. Indeed, the opposite is true: the sections identified above fail because they are imagistic relative to the scope of the whole, and the sections that do further the poet's vision are at once more lyrically vital and more vitally formed within the structure of the narrative. Through its multiple perspectives and its multiple voices, *The Bridge* is Hart Crane's attempt to realize a modern myth. It is an affirming myth, shaped by our shared belief in progress, perhaps the one popular overarching, largely untested value of our culture despite the high modernists' demurrals to the contrary. In *The Bridge*, by virtue of the poet's orchestration of this muthos through a variety of voices and temporal vantages, satisfactory reconciliation between discursivity and teleology is achieved in the poem as polyphony, the many songs of its various embodiments resounding in the "One Song" of the poem.

Many voices are heard in *The Bridge*. There is the poet's voice, sometimes animated by Orphic rapture, as in the opening "Proem: To Brooklyn Bridge" and particularly in the sequence's final section, "Atlantis," sometimes more quietly meditative, as in "Cutty Sark" and "The Tunnel," and sometimes punctuated by slang. The variety of tones is so great, and the shifts sometimes so sudden, that this "authorial" voice actually becomes multivalent in the poem. The poet's voice shifts abruptly from slang to biblical rapture, at times within the span of a line, as though the poet had suddenly become an oracle. It is, in fact, the integrity of the plot that gives the presiding voice a core intention that runs through its variety of tones. In addition to this dominant voice, there is the voice of Columbus in "Ave Maria" and the voices of women throughout the individual poems of "Powhatan's Daughter," each of whom is a historical permutation of the female archetype or anima that is also the continent itself. There is the sailor in "Cutty Sark," whom the poet meets on one of his night wanderings. Then there is the voice-over prose narrative running alongside the verse that provides yet another, more omniscient perspective on events. The polyphonic orchestration of voices in Hart Crane's poem achieves its unity of action primarily through the poet's recursive figuralism. The looming figure of the poem is, of course, the Brooklyn Bridge itself, which is as much the embodiment of the poem's nameless deity as it is the material structure:

And Thee, across the harbor, silver-paced
As though the sun took step of thee, yet left
Some motion ever unspent in thy stride,—
Implicitly thy freedom staying thee![28]

One of the bridge's prevailing attributes is its status as a figure that unites opposites, a *coincidentia oppositorum*, a figure whose ambition Dante certainly would have admired. From the start, Crane depicts the bridge as theophany, a revelation of the divine that combines both motion and stillness, at once spiritual manifestation and product of the creative libido of the world: "O harp and altar, of the fury fused, (How could mere toil align their choiring strings!)," the poet exults. Yet the bridge is matter shaped by human design to manifest its destiny as spirit incarnated. Thus it can "condense eternity."[29]

The figure of the bridge recurs throughout the poem in literal form when, for example, the poet encounters the sailor on South Street in "Cutty Sark," whom he eventually leaves to walk home back across the bridge. In "Cape

Hatteras," Crane's great evocation of Walt Whitman—the true presiding spirit of the poem—the bridge is identified not merely as a physical entity but as the fulfillment of Whitman's imaginative vista:

> Our Meistersinger, thou set breath in steel;
> And it was thou who on the boldest heel
> Stood up and flung the span on even wing
> Of that great Bridge, our Myth, whereof I sing![30]

This is Crane at his bardic and operatic best. The figure of the bridge permits him to mythologize his imagination's hero and thereby channel his vision into his own. The bridge is the myth of America, carried forward from Columbus's "spanning" the ocean—*Te Deum laudamus*, for thy teeming span!" Columbus exclaims in "Ave Maria." Or is it the poet, or a fusion of the poet and the historical figure? The metaphorical span of the bridge, its ability to incorporate and designate the "amplitude of time," is made manifest through the plot of the poem, and it is precisely this figural trope that allows Crane's voices to metamorphose in their archetypal fusions across the span of the poem. Though the poem constitutes a myth of America, its true subject and aim, its action, as confessed to Walt Whitman, is "To course that span of consciousness thou'st named / The Open Road. [. . .]."[31] Like Columbus and Whitman, the other principal human figures in the poem manifest the bridge's attribute of "spanning" space and time by configuring it anew through the power of their imaginations. Edgar Allan Poe is yet another figure who appears in "The Tunnel" as the shadow side of the poet's imagination, the destructive antiself who must be expiated, something, tragically, the suicidal Crane was unable to do in his life. The feminine principle of "Powhatan's Daughter" in turn seeks to infuse Native America into the poem, though the contemporary reader might well cringe at her appearance as at an earnest but insensitive and overly lavish stage production. Nevertheless, she and her manifestations introduce a conception of cyclical time, which moves counter to the apparent linear organization of the sequence from Columbus in "Ave Maria" to the utopian future of "Atlantis." The reconciliation of these two conceptions of time, cyclical and linear, is another fusion of opposites the poem seeks to accomplish through its plot.

Motion is a central theme in *The Bridge*. "Proem: To Brooklyn Bridge" begins cinematically with the pivot of a seagull's wings above New York

Harbor, and the poem places the reader inside that motion, as if there were a camera fastened to the seagull's breast. Then, in a series of movements, "elevators drop us from our day," and we are with the "multitudes" in the "panoramic sleights" of cinemas to which they hasten. A "bedlamite speeds" to the parapets of the bridge to jump into the East River, noon accelerates down Wall Street, derricks turn, traffic lights "skim" along the bridge's own "unfractioned idiom." In the midst of all this movement the bridge stands, an embodiment of both movement and stillness. The bridge "vaults" both the sea and "the prairies' dreaming sod" as the poet prays for it to descend to us, the lowliest. All of this motion at the outset of the poem puts me in mind of Philip Glass's film *Koyaanisqatsi*, whose rapidly modulating score accentuates the scenes of urban energy. Glass's film is meant to portray life out of balance, but Crane's poem intends the opposite. All the movements in the poem coordinate and ultimately dovetail with its singular action, its muthos: the ever more encompassing revelation of the bridge as a figure of divine energy incarnating itself in matter.

This short exegesis of *The Bridge* from the standpoint of plot does scant justice to the brilliance of Hart Crane's orchestration, of every aspect of narrative and lyric texture in the poem, despite its rhetorical excesses and the insufficiencies of some individual poems in the sequence. Though not a narrative poem in a strict sense, Crane's long poem demonstrates that a strictly held conception of narrative poetry perhaps hides more than it discloses, and in so doing limits the possibilities of narrative structure in contemporary poetry, as well as how we understand narrative's role for poets like Crane, who play off tradition without abandoning its teleological imperative. Some contemporary narrative poets see narrative as antithetical to modernist and certainly to postmodernist experimentation. Crane is from the second generation of modernists, and his eclectic use of various poetic methods places him outside the tradition of Frost and even Jeffers, both of whom loom large as models for New Narrative poets. However, if we look even briefly at a major long narrative poem such as Andrew Hudgins's *After the Lost War*, it becomes clear that Crane's modernist methods and Hudgins's stricter adherence to traditional narrative structure have common ground.

The major difference in plot structure between *The Bridge* and *After the Lost War* is that while Crane's poem develops recursively to achieve closure, Hudgins's poem adopts a linear chronology. Discursiveness in Crane's poem is given teleological form through a muthos that incorporates an earlier cyclical conception of time. To use Paul Ricoeur's term again, in *The Bridge*, plot operates through a highly ritualized brand of configuration, something close to myth. Plot as configuration in Hudgins's poem operates according to a principle of linear selectivity rather than ritual circularity. In *After the Lost War*, Hudgins renders the life of Sidney Lanier univocally rather than polyphonically, and most often in blank verse. He also places us in Lanier's life in medias res, after the war, and allows Lanier's speech to render the character's consciousness as overheard by the reader, and as reimagined by Hudgins himself. By Hudgins's own estimate, Lanier as portrayed is a hybrid character, part nineteenth-century American poet and part Hudgins. As Hudgins remarks in the preface, "I'd like to thank Lanier for allowing me to use the facts of his life—more or less—to see how I might have lived it had it been mine." As such, the univocal nature of the poem is perhaps not as stable as it first may appear. More significant to the notion of plot, however, is that Hudgins's long poem, like Crane's, is a sequence of poems and that, like Crane, Hudgins uses recurrent figures to create continuity. The figures of the child, Lanier's flute, bees, and insects continually resurface in Lanier's meditations, which turn as often to metaphysics as to history. As such, the two poems share thematic concerns as well. Most important, while the tone of Hudgins's poem shows he aims to demythologize a life more than mythologize a paradigm, as in Dante or Crane, the principle of selection the poet uses to choose what facts and experiences of Lanier's life on which to focus is essentially a principle of gleaning *kairoi*—representative "spots of time"—from the available chronological record of Lanier's life, and often inventing them. These *kairoi*, as in the stories told by Dante's shades, reveal the life, and, as in Wordsworth's "spots of time," they offer perspectives on the hope of transcendence, or at least moments of clarity within the life that constellate into a pattern of coherence. The plot structure of *After the Lost War* is the sequence of these *kairoi* that, while arranged in chronological order, nonetheless configure into an order of time that is not merely discursive but teleological:

> For so long I have thought of us as nails
> God drives into the oak floor of this world,
> it's hard to comprehend the hammer turned
> to claw me out.[32]

Chronologically, death is the end of life, where the beginning and the middle find their completion and, hopefully, fulfillment. "Only through time, time is conquered," Eliot wrote in *Four Quartets* with somewhat greater faith. The passage just quoted, from the last poem of Hudgins's long sequence, reveals, however, that Lanier's life has been shaped all along by the plot or muthos of the Christ story. Though Lanier expects death to be death, unlike Crane, who expects transfigurations on the operatic scale, that does not prevent his fictive life here or Hudgins's poem as a whole from being organized by a more subtle orchestration of the paradigm in the very process of demythologizing Lanier's life. Indeed, because it requires attributing equal value to time as well as eternity since the figure of Christ is both human and divine, the Christ story as a shaping paradigm allows ample room for discursiveness, digression into time and along the flow of time, for time is the medium through which the eternal is made known. Regardless of Hudgins's assent to belief, this paradigm provides the narrative of the poem with its figural organization. Though *After the Lost War* does not seek to "condense eternity" in the manner of *The Bridge*, both poems in their different idioms use plot as a principle of configuration to shape narratives that ultimately engage supreme questions of human destiny.

Microcosm: Plot as Sentence Sound

Both Crane's *The Bridge* and Hudgins's *After the Lost War* are book-length works that depend on large-scale figural strategies of emplotment to orchestrate their parts into a whole greater than the sum of those parts. Such orchestration necessarily depends on what chaos theorists call recursive symmetries between scales. Such symmetries become operative through each poet's use of figures, despite the obvious differences in the kinds of figures each poet employs. In both cases, successful closure is achieved, paradoxically, through the extravagance of the individual poems and sections, their individual narrative and lyric satisfactions. Still, in the current postmodern milieu, the idea of closure accruing out of individual parts has become seriously undermined. More than a century ago, Edgar Allan Poe proclaimed the long poem impossible. In a paradigmatic conceptual problem the Greek philosopher Zeno proposed that in reality, an arrow fired toward a target never reaches its mark since the space traveled can always be divided by half and half again, into a minimalist infinity. A like problem is encountered today when we consider a fractal shoreline whose size reaches infinity as one conceives of its surfaces measured in ever-finer dimensions of space. Measurement depends on scale. To build a bridge across that fictional shoreline to the other side would be to span infinity, according to this paradox of scale. That is what plot does in narrative, the nominalist's refusal of universal claims surmounted by the realist's impossible dream. In his essay "Nature," Ralph Waldo Emerson makes this paradox constitutive of human life and consciousness when he affirms, "We live in a system of approximations. Every end is prospective of some other end, which is also temporary; a round and final success nowhere."[33] Such a vision of reality is near to Virginia Woolf's idea of life as a transparent envelope and implicitly foreshadows both what Alan Shapiro calls "the subjectivist esthetic"[34] of modernism and the acceptance of some postmodern writers of a world devoid not only of approximations but of linguistic reference. It also presages our own historical and cultural moment, characterized by Tony Hoagland in his essay "Fear of Narrative and the Skittery Poem of Our Moment" as evincing "a widespread mistrust of narrative forms, and, in fact, a pervasive sense of the inadequacy or exhaustion of all modes other than the associative."[35] Behind this current fashion, among undoubtedly other converging influences—historical, cultural, and academic—is a pervasive skepticism about language itself.

Based on Ferdinand de Saussure's notion that linguistic signs comprise the foundation of discourse and that such signs become knowable through difference among each other rather than through any intrinsic quality of self-identity, one of the core ideas of postmodernism as it is usually advanced is that language constitutes a field of play in which meaning endlessly slips and defers so that neither the world nor the play-space of language itself is anything more than a shifting approximation of a reality that, to echo Fred in "West-Running Brook," "seriously, sadly, runs away." Where Fred articulates the fact of reality's "slippage" from our powers of identification, many contemporary poems intend to perform that slippage. By contrast, Paul Ricoeur in discussing this fundamental problem of language refers to Émile Benveniste's alternative conception that holds the sentence and not the sign to be the basic unit of discourse.[36] "If," Ricoeur proposes, "we take the sentence as the unit of discourse, then the intended of discourse ceases to be confused with the signified correlative to each signifier in the immanence of a system of signs."[37] The difference between these two conceptions is a difference in the perception of scale within the space of language proper. Like those who might see a shoreline as infinitely divisible by virtue of a fractal reality and make that prospect the ground of their understanding of the world, those who hold with Saussure that signification is founded on difference see the world of language as a world of difference in the most profound sense. There is no bridge outward from language to the world, or even across signs within the field of language itself. The idea founds the most extreme nominalism. In such a world, narrative as anything more than a parody of its endlessly faltering intentions cannot exist. Ricoeur, after Benveniste, essentially affirms that the sign as a vehicle of discourse is the wrong order of scale to describe how language operates in the reality we inhabit. A bridge can be built from language to reality, for "with the sentence reality is oriented beyond itself."[38] Likewise, Alan Shapiro sees narrative as a "going toward" the other.[39] Paul Ricoeur again summarizes the issue neatly when he states that "narrative time is like a bridge set over the breach speculation constantly opens between phenomenological time and cosmological time," that is, between time as it is humanly experienced and time as it exists physically on the still larger scale of universal motion. The breach must be bridged. To deny this is to deny that reality has a ground in objectivity, though objectivity may be only a series of approximations that, as Emerson would have it, we must plumb again and again with no final success. To refuse the validity of this higher order of scale in language is self-defeating, for to do so is to subvert one's own claims to meaning (the meaning in this case that there is no meaning, only difference) as a categorical a priori—the figure of a snake eating its own tail and wholly swallowing itself.

Between Schema and Scheherazade

Nevertheless, as soon as one mentions plot, one conjures its shadow side: the scheme and not the design, the contrivance and not the storyline—in short, Woolf's gig lamps. This is particularly problematic in our postmodern milieu, in which Woolf's universe of impressions resists the ordering vehicle of a shared frame of reference. Without this shared cultural context it becomes exceedingly difficult if not impossible, and more often than not debilitating, for poets to aspire to the epic ambition if not its satisfaction. "Overall is beyond me," the late A. R. Ammons wrote in "Corsons Inlet." Ammons sought to create a shared culture in the context of a science with cosmic significance. Though he eschewed traditional narrative, the plot for Ammons was motion in his long poems, a transfiguring in the poem of nature's endlessly creative action. In other hands, plot as such becomes transposed into an errancy endlessly rehearsed, like one of John Ashbery's dazzling ruminations or Woolf's transparent envelope devoid of its letter. In a situation lacking anything resembling common poetic consensus, the reliance on traditional narrative strategies can gain appeal, at least for those poets for whom an ethos of radical skepticism proves unsatisfactory and ultimately a brand of decadence. Still, the question remains: How can individual contexts resonate beyond the confines of their own self-referentiality, if not in epic terms then in terms that appeal to a deep human circumstance, not simply for popular or political or personal appeal?

In contrast to some postmodern views on the subject of narrative, John Barth in his "4 1/2 Lectures" affirms the traditional Aristotelian conception of plot as a representative action in light of contemporary physics. For Barth, plot is "the incremental perturbation of a homeostatic system and its catastrophic restoration to a complexified equilibrium."[40] Barth's definition is only superficially tongue-in-cheek since he goes on to translate his admittedly amateurish adaptation of science to narrative into explicit Aristotelian terms. The point he intends to make is that chaos theory does indeed constitute a shared cultural context in the way that Thomism infuses Dante's *Divine Comedy* through what Barth calls "the principle of metaphoric means," that is, "the writer's investiture in as many aspects of the text as possible with emblematic significance."[41] Barth's principle clearly resonates with Leitch's polytropic principle. In both, muthos is an essential aspect, even to Barth as an avowedly postmodern writer. Moreover, as he elaborates his discussion of chaos theory in the essay, and in a manner that recalls the figuralism of Crane and Hudgins, Barth likens the kind of nonlinear models of narrative production to "recursive symmetries between scales—swirls within swirls within swirls, replicated over numerous scale levels."[42] Though as we've seen, Crane's myth organizes itself recursively to orchestrate closure, for Barth the narrative exemplar for such organization is Scheherazade, whose stories within stories within stories are told to fend off death by her captor, King Shahryar. Such storytelling is the model for the teleological narrative, the narrative that potentially digresses endlessly without closure. Reified in this manner, Scheherazade's narrative is all flow, but if Barth is right, that doesn't mean it is without muthos, without order, without plot. At the same time, Barth's claim that stories formally deploying the principle of metaphorical means "will be stronger and richer than those that do not"[43] suggests that works exhibiting contrary structural principles to those seemingly untested by contemporary ontological claims (the "linear" novel uninformed by experimental design, the "straight" narrative or lyric poem, as I heard one avant-garde poet quip derisively) are at best lower-order achievements, at worst nostalgic holdovers from an outmoded aesthetic.

Of course, exponents of the New Narrative and the New Formalism contest such claims vigorously. In appealing to Yvor Winters's "the fallacy of imitative form," Christian Wiman urges us to be skeptical of the simplistic notion that because the world is disordered, chaotic, and resistant to meaningful representation, poetry likewise should reflect formally that distressing condition. The critic Marjorie Perloff is guilty of this fallacy when she claims that only poets who write in "indeterminate forms" avoid the nostalgia for some determined order.[44] Against this fallacy Wiman opposes the proper claim that good poems, narrative or otherwise, allow their ideas of order to be "contested" by the disorder of the world.[45] Such poems effectively assume disorder like an antibody into the poem. The assumption need not be a formal one, or at least not in the most obvious sense. Frost's work is highly formal, but few have assumed disorder so effectively into the work by means of such formal control. His "momentary stay against confusion" is achieved not by denying the disorder of the world but by plotting it, in every sense, into the poem. Certainly the sheer disruptiveness of sense at times in Crane's operatic myth of modernity assumes the very disorder out of which he would construct his paradigm. Like Frost, Wiman also maintains "it's sometimes precisely in those works which exhibit the greatest degree of formal coherence . . . that a reader may experience, and thereby more likely endure, the most intense anxiety and uncertainty."[46] To claim otherwise, it seems to me, is to delude oneself into believing that one's particular sensibility is somehow reflective of some ultimate reality and therefore no less an uncontested idea of order as any religiously held belief. The like is true for those who hold that only a return to traditional forms can save contemporary poetry from its own cultural and artistic irrelevance. Between plot manifested as schema, an abstract structural organization used to shape a poem's action as it assembles toward completion, and plot as Scheherazade, discursivity for discursivity's sake, for which closure is an afterthought or mere cessation of speech, narrative poems find a range of efficacious, compelling, and even emblematic formal investitures of intense human significance.

If there is any poet who inhabits the dynamic space between plot as an abstract structural organization and the kind of discursivity that eschews closure as an afterthought, it is Elizabeth Bishop. She is equally adept at writing highly formal verse as she is at writing free verse, and in particular a free verse that plots the poet's perceptions in a resolutely discursive way. There is a seemingly random recounting of the speaker's travels in "Over 2,000 Illustrations and a Complete Concordance," though her strategy of letting her precise and brilliant eye linger on each detail of the unfolding scenes makes for the poem's gradual but no less powerful revelation of the "missed" nativity that would have permitted us to "look and look our infant sight away." Bishop's poem is about the fall away from a guiding revelation, the divinely inspired muthos of Christ's birth as the central moment of God's plan for the world's salvation, into travels that indeed appear plotless:

> Entering the Narrows at St. John's
> The touching bleat of goats reached the ship.
> We glimpsed them, reddish, leaping up the cliffs
> Among the fog-soaked weeds and butter and eggs.
> And then at St. Peter's the wind blew and the sun shown madly.[47]

Between the speaker's recollection of the Narrows and her recollection of being at St. Peter's, time is telescoped by a simple "And then." What follows is a catalogue of places—Mexico, Dingle Harbor, Marrakesh. Her travels in the poem, vivid as they are, trace the errancy of life lived without muthos, of life in which everything is "only connected by 'and' and 'and.'" From its opening lines, "Thus should have been our travels: / serious, engravable," the poem announces that it will lead us through a discursive world, a world without any true telos, however vivid its digressions may be. At the same time, Bishop's arrangement of these brilliantly observed details reveals a plotted shapeliness resolving into closure. The poem's first stanza leads the reader through a series of illustrations that depict time and space from the vantage point of sacred history: Christ's tomb, the pit, the sepulcher, the decorative arrangement of emblematic signs seemingly infused by Barth's "principle of metaphoric means." All proceed to the image of "God's spreading finger-print" in the storm images made by the burin that, in turn, ignite "in watery prismatic white and blue." In short, the stanza moves the reader from the emblems of truth to the nearest truth of God's identity—his fingerprint. The stanza also progresses in a manner that reflects the poet's method in that the arrangement of illustrations mirrors Bishop's own strategy of focused detail accruing larger and larger significance as the reader lingers over the poem. The "page alone" and the "page made up / of several scenes," "when dwelt upon, all resolve themselves." That is, the seemingly chaotic scales of association begin to reveal order, emplotment, reconfiguration at higher levels.

If the first stanza of Bishop's poem constitutes the speaker's record of a bygone sacred muthos puzzled together through crosscuts of emblematic scenes, then the second stanza represents its antithesis: the travels that are mere digressions in a world devoid of sacred history. Cunningly, Bishop segues from the first stanza to the second by carrying over the water imagery associated with God's signature into the water journey into the Narrows. The arrangement of travels in the second stanza in turn brings us to paynims, that is, back to the beginning of the poem with its ironic Arabs "plotting against our Christian empire." As a plot, then, the poem begins with a thesis that is elaborated in the first stanza. The second stanza constitutes the antithesis. The poem's final stanza, not unexpectedly now, constitutes Bishop's synthesis of the contraries in an optative revelation that never actually occurs—the fulfillment of the "should have" at the poem's outset in the implied "would have" of the Nativity. The poem likewise therefore organizes itself from sepulcher to manger, from death to birth, or from end to beginning. That beginning, the Nativity scene, is also a most vivid and satisfactory end, the perfect closure to a poem that shrewdly contests both the idea of muthos as teleological ground and the reliance on discursivity or digression as an associative method of organization and resolves them in a way that includes both brilliant divergences—Barth's "incremental perturbations"—and strong closure that, as in all great poems, resonates beyond "the system" of the poem itself and into our being in the world.

Elizabeth Bishop's "Over 2,000 Illustrations and a Complete Concordance" is exemplary for its achievement in dynamically joining contrary organizational imperatives, though Bishop's greatness as a poet stems from her larger achievement of succeeding over and over again in this regard. In poems like "At the Fishhouses," "In the Waiting Room," and "The Moose," to name only a few, her strategy of employing digression as a way of realizing closure makes for astonishing resolutions and at times revelations in a world that is supposed to be devoid of such measures. Her poems typically move by peripheral vision to an unforeseen center, as in "The Filling Station," where filth and grease, an arrangement of oil cans ("Esso-so-so"), and a briefly but crucially sustained anaphora on the word "somebody" lead to the explosive and completely convincing insight in the context of the poem that "somebody loves us all." At the end of "At the Fishhouses," Bishop declares that "our knowledge is historical, flowing, and flown," though that revelation is likewise prepared through the painstaking arrangement of details, a configuration through peripheries of an essential action revelatory of our fragile place in the universe. Bishop's genius is her ability to shape that flow to include closure without transgressing against the world's luminous details or our consciousness of its fleeting nature. As such, she manages by a sleight of perception worthy of Escher to include Scheherazade in the defined schema of beginning, middle, and end.

Entering the Narrows at St. John's with the poet in "Over 2,000 Illustrations and a Complete Concordance" is to place oneself *in the middest*, apart from the sure path, with no hope of recovering the security of a Dante ascending, however uncertainly, toward paradise. Tony Maniero's cinematic dance above another Narrows likewise placed him and the viewer in medias res on his path to maturity, though like my own journey with my family over the same bridge above the same Narrows in real life and now only in memory, such travels inevitably point to possibilities outside the frame of immediate reference. At the same time, it is the poet's job not merely to mimic the ongoing in a dispersal of recursive associations but to shape the time of the poem to human ends. Even a poet like Robinson Jeffers, wary on an ontological if not metaphysical scale of human ends, places the human story in the context of ends that transcend human time as its stands in relief of a natural sublime. After Frost, Jeffers's work constitutes the purest narrative impulse in modern poetry—perhaps more so than Frost, since Jeffers's narratives are less dramatic and more plot-driven. Not surprisingly, along with Frost he constitutes an important model for New Narrative poets such as Mark Jarman, who would, as in the book-length poem *Iris*, use Jeffers's model to tell a story in verse. By contrast, Robert Hayden's "Middle Passage," for example, uses pastiche and association, shards of narrative lyrically arranged, to tell the story of the slave trade and in particular of the *Amistad*—"passage through death to life upon these shores." Though less ambitious in scope than *The Bridge*, it is nonetheless a poem of epic travel that demythologizes Crane's sublime vision of the modern world—his skewed vision of history untainted by brutality. Given the span of possibilities for narrative in our time, is one mode really more vital or viable than the other? Imaginative vitality as always rests in the poet's employment of poetic craft in a manner that surpasses the mere execution of craft in poems, regardless of one's aesthetic temperament.

Emerging from the crowd of poets born during the time modernism was at its height and coming to prominence after modernism had "morphed" into that various cultural and creative state of affairs known as postmodernism, John Ashbery has written a lifetime of poems that from the first seem to have breathed the same air as Scheherazade. This is certainly true of Ashbery's longer productions—"Flow Chart," for example, or "Litany," or "A Wave"—that unreel in an associative flow that would forestall closure indefinitely. Ashbery's productions, however, both large and small, whether strictly formal in the traditional sense or more open and experimental in their formal appropriations, resist plot and closure first and foremost on the scale of sentence organization. One could say, strangely enough, that, like Frost, Ashbery is primarily concerned with "sentence sounds," though unlike in Frost, living speech in an Ashbery poem becomes "warped" through an intellectual prism that has dislodged itself from the requirements of objective representation. There is not much world in an Ashbery poem, except as an occasion for manifesting a linguistic sublime. Though one moves through an Ashbery poem when reading it, the poem has no movement in the traditional sense. Instead, as in "Self-Portrait in a Convex Mirror," what one typically encounters is a sequence of beginnings without end. Time itself in such an art, and hence plot, never advances:

> The time of day or the density of light
> Adhering to the face keeps it
> Lively and intact in a recurring wave
> Of arrival. The soul establishes itself.
> But how far can it swim out through the eyes
> And still return safely to its nest?[48]

The answer to Ashbery's question is that the soul cannot travel past each new beginning, and so "Self-Portrait in a Convex Mirror" articulates an aesthetic of continual emergence, poems that are journeys composed of departures alone, no middle or end, for there is only the moment-by-moment: "The soul has to stay where it is, / Even though restless, [. . .] /

Longing to be free, outside, but it must stay / Posing in this place." There is no "going towards" in such a poem, only gestures that finally round to self-enclosure—consciousness enwound in its own subjectivity.

Ashbery's poetry puts into ideal practice the prevailing ethos that muthos is impossible. For Ashbery, this is a matter beyond contention, beyond testing in any dramatic way, as even in Frost's more ambiguously constructed forays. It simply is the world his poems inhabit or, more rightly, construct. Since plot requires movement, the poems may be read as brilliantly textured rehearsals for journeys that never take place beyond the moment, or perhaps only just beyond. The moments are vivid and lush, but they must be savored for themselves, like the swirls of recurrence in Barth's "homeostatic system," though without resolution, catastrophic or otherwise:

Other dreams came and left while the bank
Of colored verbs and adjectives was shrinking from the light
To nurse in shade their want of method
But most of all she loved the particles
That transform objects of the same category
Into particular ones, each distinct
Within and apart from its own class.
In all this springing up was no hint
Of a tide, only a pleasant wavering of the air
In which all things seemed present, whether
Just past or soon to come.[49]

These lines from "Scheherazade" are indubitably gorgeous, an ontological meditation that envision, among other possible readings, the making of poetry as Scheherazade's potentially endless process of generation, though there is no tide, no passage, and hence no time. The lines also unmistakably echo Wallace Stevens's "The Idea of Order at Key West"—"She sang beyond the genius of the sea"—though in Ashbery's poem the "blessed rage for order," "the maker's rage to order words of the sea," has become a pleasant receptivity to the patterns or order momentarily revealed by the chaotic system of the sea itself. The stories that the poem rehearses as it shifts tones slightly and continues on give evidence of an obstinacy that borders on delusion, the notion that "none knew the warp / Which presented this major movement as a firm / Digression." That major movement, ironically, is merely "the new fact of the day," which is no different from the old fact of the day before, composed as it is merely of moments juxtaposed. It is as if the poem's stream of sentences unfolds from discrete present to discrete present, luminous as photons beamed from Woolf's proverbial lighthouse, and blotting out any afterglow of gig lamps. As the poem later states, the echo of stories become merely "Anticipation that was only memory after all, / For the possibilities are limited." Where Bishop admits a world in which "everything is connected by 'and' and 'and,'" her poems are organized in such a way as to position a counterforce against mere discursivity unshaped by human ends. In contrast, Ashbery in a superficially dazzlingly way divests teleology of any force whatsoever except as it is realized in the luscious surfaces of language encountered in the moment.

The argument to be made against such a poetry has nothing to do with its lush articulateness, its dazzling spikes of grandeur and tonal amplitude, its surface elegance and flow, but with an aesthetic that refuses, like Blake's Thel, to enter the fraught world of experience, and so to make the journey beyond its own protected self-defined and self-enclosed boundaries—its own self-enwound luminous envelope of what Sven Birkerts calls his "semantic slippages" and non sequiturs.[50] It is this refusal that distinguishes Ashbery's poetry from Frank O'Hara's work and the work of A. R. Ammons, two poets of his generation with whom he is often compared. Where O'Hara captures the moment in the context of ordinary human time, Ammons shapes his poems in such a way as to inhabit in language the larger motions of order discovered in nature. There is much of Scheherazade in both these poets, though there is also some engagement with the world that makes the idea of endless digression something to be contested, though not an endorsement of strict closure. In contrast, those poets of the same generation, such as Anthony Hecht and Richard Wilbur, who have become models for formalist and narrative poets of recent years, clearly embraced a contrary aesthetic in which the scheme of form and plot shapes the utterance of the poem. These two broad orientations in the art define a gap that needs to be bridged for American poetry to advance beyond the mere reiteration of disputing traditions.

Given the legitimate doubts in our time about language, culture, knowledge, and consciousness itself, what, we might ask again, could be more intransigently rooted in the nostalgia for plot, and so the determination of identity, than narrative? In "Fear of Narrative," Tony Hoagland likens the present shift to "crop-rotation,"[51] though the shift itself suggests that the more serious impact on the culture portends a loss of confidence in the authenticity of meaning-making in our poems as well as our institutions.[52] The characteristic mistrusts of such poetries—"a fear of submersion or enclosure by narrative,"[53] the limitations and presumptions of the confessional poem including serious epistemological and metaphysical doubts about the veracity of something we might call the self—have generated "elliptical" work attractive in Tony Hoagland's view for its "speed, wit, and absurdity."[54] At the same time, he likewise identifies the potentially trivial nature of such poetry when it becomes a mere homage to dissociation. Indeed, if the danger of narrative is that it might enable us to relax into "the pretense of order,"[55] then the danger of dissociative modes is that they may perform and perpetuate the vacuity of sense that so pervades the culture at large. Such untested "disorderliness" is potentially as culpably self-indulgent as narrative's rage for order. This is not to confuse poetry with propaganda or to prize the message over the medium of the art but merely to affirm with Hoagland that "one of poetry's most fundamental reasons for existing" is "the individual power to locate and assert value"[56] and that to abscond from that purpose may be in the long run to render one's work irrelevant.

Nostalgia for permanently stable orders has its own culpabilities, of course, that surely breed irrelevance at best and, at worst, far graver legacies. If, however, the guiding muthos of our time is that there is no muthos, and that any shaping plot for our identities as well as our art must be held provisionally (if at all) to have any hope of authenticity, then perhaps as a matter of course poetry need not be as atomized and ephemeral as the world it inhabits. "There is something in disorder that calls to me," Louis Simpson writes in "Searching for the Ox." Rather than passively and performatively reiterating the scattered atoms of his world through an artifice utterly mimetic of that world, Louis Simpson's speaker dramatizes the crisis of consciousness. At the same time, Paul Ricoeur's claim that "we tell stories because in the last analysis human lives need and merit being narrated"[57] stands as a cautionary observation for any poet who would turn away wholly from the world. For, as he continues, "this remark takes on its full force when we refer to the necessity to save the history of the defeated and the lost. The whole history of suffering cries out for vengeance and calls for narrative."[58] American poets employing narrative in various ways are mindful, in practice at least, of Ricoeur's affirmation. For example, Eleanor Wilner's re/visions of myths and biblical narratives use narrative itself as mode of inquiry into the sources of culture with an aim toward reenvisioning those sources and redressing cultural injustice at the level. She aims, among other things, to awaken us to a counter feminine tradition—her version of the Shekkinah—hidden inside the prevailing Western religious and mythic narratives. In contrast, Rita Dove's *Thomas and Beulah*, though it claims to tell a personal story, convinces primarily as a lyric sequence, though it is a sequence shadowed by the history of civil rights. The plot of the two sides of her grandparents' lives together provides chronological and circumstantial scaffolding for the lyric epiphanies. Though book length, *Thomas and Beulah* finally affirms an aesthetic of compression rather than expansion, and that is its particular success. Like Wilner's work, it is also a testimony to the underrepresented who have been largely absent from the historical narrative. In their own spheres, both Eleanor Wilner and Rita Dove seek to give amplitude to their poetry by engaging cultural and historical contexts, the story lines that shape our lives as a matter of course and not merely as a matter of personal circumstance.

This, it seems to me, is a condition for truly expansive poetry—not length alone but breadth and depth of vision, the desire to portray as fully as possible the complexity of the human journey. The admirable desire to link the individual consciousness to the collective life may likewise be found in Ellen Bryant Voigt's *Kyrie*, her justly praised sonnet sequence that takes as its subject the flu pandemic of 1918. Here, in a manner that takes inspiration from Frost, though with a strong infusion of montage, Voigt blurs dramatic, lyric, and narrative genres. Her shorter narrative work, particularly in *The Lotus Flowers*, as well as powerful lyric narratives written by a diverse retinue of other poets, shows that a strong narrative cast still is present in American poetry regardless of any affiliation with the New Expansive poetry or claims of nostalgia from the imaginative heirs of Scheherazade. Among the expansive poets linked to the New Formalism by association and temperament, Mark Jarman and B. H. Fairchild stand out, with Andrew Hudgins, as among the most significant practitioners of narrative in contemporary American poetry. Poems like Fairchild's "Beauty," "Body and Soul," and "The Blue Buick" and Jarman's book-length *Iris*, as well as an array of shorter narratives, have achieved critical recognition beyond the confines of the New Formalist canon. Regardless of affiliation, it should go without saying that in the case of every successful poem, especially narrative poems, the line and the story line are intimately related. It should go without saying that, like memory itself, narrative works by selection, though like life it must leave ample room for the intractable, the unexpected, the disorderly, which is to say that the linear impetus of plot of course requires digression and diversion into the textures. This is so much more the case in the narrative poem, which by necessity must embody plot, the arc of the whole, in image and metaphor, line, syntax, and poetic structure. Perhaps, then, it also goes without saying that any poem, large or small, lyric, narrative, or dramatic, is nothing without intensity. That being said, poetry is consciousness released from its dream of accident into a new dream of achieved form that, like any good plot, surprises and satisfies, and in the end may illuminate us with a clarity and recognition never entirely foreseen.

Notes

1. Robert Scholes and Robert Kellogg, *The Nature of Narrative* (New York: Oxford University Press, 1966), 207.

2. Thomas Leitch, *What Stories Are: Narrative Theory and Interpretation* (University Park: Pennsylvania State University Press, 1986), 130.

3. Virginia Woolf, "The Novel of Consciousness," in *The Modern Tradition*, ed. Richard Ellmann and Charles Feidelson, Jr. (New York: Oxford University Press, 1965), 123.

4. Scholes and Kellogg, *The Nature of Narrative*, 13–14.

5. Ibid., 276.

6. Leitch, *What Stories Are*, 139–143.

7. Alan Shapiro, "In Praise of the Impure: Narrative Consciousness in Poetry," *Triquarterly* 81 (Spring–Summer 1991): 5–30.

8. Paul Ricoeur, *Time and Narrative*, trans. Katherine Blamey and David Pellauer, 3 vols. (Chicago: University of Chicago Press, 1984), 1:33.

9. Leitch, *What Stories Are*, 131.

10. Ricoeur, *Time and Narrative*, 2:156.

11. Ibid., 1:33.

12. Ibid., 1:ix.

13. Robert Frost, "West-Running Brook," in *Collected Poems, Prose, and Plays* (New York: Library Classics of the United States, 1995), 237.

14. Wallace Martin, *Recent Theories of Narrative* (Ithaca, NY: Cornell University Press, 1986), 86.

15. Colin McGinn, *The Mysterious Flame* (New York: Basic Books, 2000), 163.

16. Ricoeur, *Time and Narrative*, 2:9–10.

17. Ibid., 3:19.

18. Frank Kermode, *The Sense of an Ending* (London: Oxford University Press, 1966), 47.

19. Stephen Dobyns, *Best Words, Best Order* (New York: St. Martin's Press, 1996), 140.

20. Ricoeur, *Time and Narrative*, 1:20.

21. Shapiro, "In Praise of the Impure," 13.

22. Scholes and Kellogg, *The Nature of Narrative*, 223.

23. Ibid.

24. Leitch, *What Stories Are*, 84ff.

25. Dana Gioia, "The Dilemma of the Long Poem," in *New Expansive Poetry*, ed. R. S. Gwynn (Ashland, OR: Story Line Press, 1999), 206.

26. Dick Allen, "The Forest for the Trees: Preliminary Thoughts on Evaluating the Long Poem" in *New Expansive Poetry*, ed. R. S. Gwynn (Ashland, OR: Story Line Press, 1999), 200.

27. Ibid.

28. Hart Crane, "Proem: To Brooklyn Bridge," in *The Bridge* (New York: Liveright, 1970), 1.

29. Ibid., 2.

30. Crane, "Cape Hatteras," in *The Bridge*, 46.

31. Ibid.

32. Andrew Hudgins, "The Hereafter," in *After the Lost War* (Boston: Houghton Mifflin, 1988), 132.

33. Quoted in Richard Poirier, *Robert Frost: The Work of Knowing* (Stanford, CA: Stanford University Press, 1977), 279.

34. Shapiro, "In Praise of the Impure," 14ff.

35. Tony Hoagland, "Fear of Narrative and the Skittery Poem of Our Moment," in *Real Sofistikashun* (St. Paul, MN: Graywolf Press, 2006), 174.

36. Ricoeur, *Time and Narrative*, 1:77–78.

37. Ibid., 1:78.

38. Ibid.

39. Shapiro, "In Praise of the Impure," 14.

40. John Barth, "4 1/2 Lectures: The Stuttgart Seminars on Postmodernism, Chaos Theory, and the Romantic Arabesque," in *Further Fridays* (New York: Little, Brown, 1995), 340–341.

41. Ibid., 341.

42. Ibid., 332.

43. Ibid., 341.

44. Marjorie Perloff, *Poetics of Indeterminacy* (Princeton, NJ: Princeton University

Press, 1981), 3ff.

45. Christian Wiman, "An Idea of Order," in *After New Formalism*, ed. Annie Finch (Ashland, OR: Story Line Press, 1999), 205.

46. Ibid.

47. Elizabeth Bishop, "Over 2,000 Illustrations and a Complete Concordance," in *The Complete Poems* (New York: Farrar, Straus and Giroux, 1979), 58.

48. John Ashbery, "Self-Portrait in a Convex Mirror," in *Selected Poems* (New York: Farrar, Straus and Giroux, 1985), 188.

49. Ashbery, "Scheherazade," in *Selected Poems*, 169.

50. Sven Birkerts, *The Electric Life: Essays on Modern Poetry* (New York: William Morrow, 1989), 235ff.

51. Hoagland, "Fear of Narrative," in *Real Sofistikashun*, 173.

52. Ibid., 186.

53. Ibid., 177.

54. Ibid., 179.

55. Ibid., 187.

56. Ibid., 186.

57. Ricoeur, *Time and Narrative*, 1:75.

58. Ibid.

GREAT STORIES, LITTLE STORIES
A. R. Ammons and Narrative

ROGER GILBERT

A. R. Ammons's name is probably not the first one that comes to mind when we think of narrative poetry. Ammons is best known for incantatory lyrics such as "The City Limits," discursive ruminations such as "Essay on Poetics," and locodescriptive rambles such as "Corsons Inlet." Yet in a 1980 interview Ammons told Philip Fried that "my greatest interest is narrative."[1] Just what Ammons means by narrative turns out to be rather different from conventional understandings of the term; he explicitly distinguishes it from the mode of the realist novel, for example. Nevertheless the *idea* of narrative seems to have been crucial to the way Ammons thought about his work. In this essay I want to address both the very broad conception of narrative that Ammons invokes in several interviews and prose pieces and the more particular, even idiosyncratic narrative forms that he employs in his poetry. My discussion focuses on three primary narrative strains, which I'll call the mythic, the procedural, and the anecdotal. A fourth, less localizable kind of narrative makes a brief appearance at the end of the essay.

Myths

Despite his avowed interest in narrative, Ammons was among the few poets of his generation who published no prose fiction during his career. In his early thirties he did make a few half-hearted attempts, producing several short stories and an unfinished novel, but the responses he received to these efforts were less than encouraging, and he eventually came to realize that his real talents lay elsewhere.[2] In the same 1980 interview in which he declares his deepest interest to be narrative, Ammons offers some remarkably candid reflections on why he feels unable to write fiction:

> I know that if I tried to write a novel, I would be utterly hopeless and it would be a complete shambles, that I have no fictional ability in the regular way. . . . I can't write fiction because I have a lot of problems with interpersonal situations, and I'm very lonely in life, in myself, and deeply afraid that what I feel about things is a minority view and that it would not stand for what other people—so I don't trust my ability to create a figure and then give him true motivation. Because I never believe when I know another person, such as you or anyone else, that I understand where he is coming from, or that I know what's motivating him. You know what I mean? That makes me feel pretty lonely, but it makes me totally certain that I would not be a fiction writer.[3]

Ammons's profound sense of isolation, palpable throughout his poetry, renders conventional narrative forms that emphasize character and relationship highly problematic for him. Yet from the beginning of his career a strong narrative impulse can be felt in his work. Ammons's first, self-published book, *Ommateum*, consists of a series of stark parables featuring a solitary protagonist named Ezra wandering through desolate landscapes, repeatedly dying and being reborn, and encountering various inhuman entities: the wind, death, the sun and moon, morning, a lioness, an angel. These stories can be characterized as mythic in their archetypal scope and their lack of social context. Even the poems that invoke particular historical settings—Strasbourg in 1349, Antioch in 1098—do so from a distance, calling them up as mere backdrops for Ezra's visionary adventures.

Perhaps the most striking characteristic of the *Ommateum* poems is their deft blending of lyric and narrative conventions. The book's famous first line, "So I said I am Ezra," enfolds an essentially lyric utterance, the speech act of self-naming, within a past tense indicative frame. The word "so" constitutes a minimal narrative gesture, implying causality and continuity, a sequence of events extending before and after the lyric present. At the same time, "so" rhymes with the quintessentially lyric cry "oh," a ubiquitous word in the book that Ammons carefully differentiates into the "O" of apostrophe and the "oh" of exclamation. Both these speech acts figure prominently in *Ommateum*, but Ammons consistently embeds them in the syntax of narrative, as though to mark the limits of the lyric voice, its ineluctable subjection to time, space, and circumstance. (Ammons's blending of narrative and lyric syntax is facilitated by his eschewal of periods in favor of colons, which permit more fluid movements between the two modes.) One might say that the primal words "so" and "oh" encapsulate the tension between lyric and narrative energies that governs much of Ammons's early poetry. The following passages illustrate this dialectical interplay:

> Bathing in the morning river
> I said Oh
> to the reapers
> and stepping out gave
> my white form to morning
> She blushed openly
> so twisting I danced
> along the banks of the river
> and morning rushed up over the hills
> to see my wild form
> whirling on the banks of the river
> Saying O morning
> I went away to the hills[4]
> [. . .]
> The whaleboat struck
> and we came ashore
> to the painted faces
>   O primitives I said
> and the arrow sang to my throat
> Leaving myself on the shore
> I went away
> and when a heavy wind caught me I said
>   My body lies south
>   given over to vultures and flies
> and wrung my hands
> so the wind went on[5]

Jonathan Culler has identified apostrophe as the constitutive trope of lyric poetry, a trope fundamentally at odds with narrative: "Apostrophe resists narrative because its *now* is not a moment in a temporal sequence but a *now* of discourse, of writing."[6] In these passages we see Ammons grounding the intense rhetorical self-consciousness of apostrophe ("O") within a temporal sequence governed by the logic of cause and effect ("so"). The fabulistic character of these narratives does not prevent them from lending a kind of referential solidity to the lyric gestures they circumscribe.

In an interview published in *Diacritics* in 1973, Ammons offers some revealing comments on this early, mythopoeic style. The interviewer, noting that his early work seems "more dependent on specific myths or stories," asks Ammons if he would "not agree that a myth is already . . . the encapsulation of an idea?" Ammons replies,

> No, I don't think so. I think that a narrative provides the configuration from which many ideas may derive. In some short poems, I tell a little story. The story is quite plain; it's the first level of apprehension of the poem, but it becomes mythic in what it might suggest. It can suggest any number of facets. Consequently, it is not formulable into a concept. In other words, I think the narrative is a body in motion and the concept is of a different order.[7]

For Ammons, narrative is valuable precisely for its resistance to conceptual understanding. The phrase "a body in motion" suggests the kind of concrete immanence Ammons often ascribes to poetry; he especially likes analogies that compare poems to such physical activities as walking, surfing, and ice-skating (see his essay collection *Set in Motion*). As an example of his way with narrative, he cites a short poem called "Mountain Talk," written after *Ommateum* but continuing its mythic style:

I was going along a dusty highroad
when the mountain
across the way
turned me to its silence:
oh I said how come
I don't know your
massive symmetry and rest:
nevertheless, said the mountain,

would you want
to be
lodged here with
a changeless prospect, risen
to an unalterable view:
so I went on
counting my numberless fingers.[8]

And here are Ammons's comments:

> It tells a very simple story. Actually the poem investigates the feelings
> that might be said to surround certain objects. A person is walking along
> a dusty highroad. What does a dusty highroad mean? It's almost in a
> religious realm—you know, *dust, height, abstraction, separation* from the
> landscape, in a sense of perhaps being lost in it. And then, the moment
> of recognition when the person who is walking along becomes aware of a
> presence near him and he turns and it is not something that is wandering
> at all. It's a mountain that is always there. It occupies a single position
> and, as the poem says, it retains a single prospect. So the narrative then
> becomes the play of these two possibilities, of being stable and of occupy-
> ing a massive view about things that is unalterable; or being tiny enough
> to go up and down pathways, to become lost. And the speaker finally
> prefers that mobility, that changeability, to occupying a single space.[9]

Despite his earlier protests against conceptual formulation, Ammons could
be accused of committing the heresy of paraphrase in these comments,
yet the poem itself seems to invite such schematic reading. The dialectical
tensions between greatness and smallness, stasis and mobility, singularity
and multiplicity, permanence and change, are all clearly inscribed in the
encounter between the speaker and the mountain; the poem is an almost
perfectly transparent allegory. Yet as the interview continues, Ammons
again emphasizes its narrative aspect:

> it's as if you were reading a newspaper—"I was walking along a dusty
> highroad. . . ." You get to that ordinary level of things and, in a normal,
> almost journalistic way, you go into action, things happen, and then
> they end. Meanwhile they describe a curvature of some sort that's either
> narrative, or myth or structure or whatever, but it is, it exists and is no
> longer susceptible to analysis, to destruction by analysis or to further

creation by analysis. It's there. It was just something that happened and it was a series of actions and somehow those actions were so interrelated that they described a synthesis, a curvature of sentences; and that is the myth, or whatever, lying at the center of the imagination. It's just there; it doesn't do anything.[10]

Given its visionary substance—a man addresses a mountain, and the mountain replies—Ammons's insistence on the brute facticity of this story may seem disingenuous, but for him the poem's narrative frame plays a vital role, acting as a kind of insulation that protects it from reductive analysis. One might easily imagine a more traditional lyric poem in which a speaker first expresses envy of a mountain's "massive symmetry and rest," then reminds himself of his own capacity for change and movement. Ammons instead lets the mountain itself give the counterargument, then ends the poem by rendering the speaker's renewed consciousness in purely narrative terms: "so I went on / counting my numberless fingers." The last two lines might be thought to replace a more abstract, epiphanic summation—something like "suddenly I realized that the world was infinitely rich in particulars." Instead, we get "counting my numberless fingers," a startling trope that implicitly merges body and world as equally inexhaustible resources. But it's the casual phrase that precedes it, "so I went on," with its echo of the similarly offhanded opening, "I was going along," that definitively pushes the poem into another register, muting its didacticism and transforming it from statement to event, "just something that happened." As in the *Ommateum* poems, the word "so" implicitly situates the apostrophic "oh" that precedes it ("oh I said how come / I don't know your / massive symmetry and rest") within a narrative discourse in which events and actions unfold as objective facts.

The Ballyric

The ideas about narrative that Ammons expounds in the 1973 *Diacritics* interview had been gestating in his mind for many years. In part they grew from his instinctive preference for a poetic vocabulary of action over the modernist dogma of the image. As early as 1958, Ammons wrote in a letter to John Logan,

> I am an actamist. That is, an imagist of acts, not images. I build the behavior true, Oh Lord, and let the reader transform the actions into his

own ideas. I can't stand the naked statement of an unclothed, unbodied idea. It hasn't reached the level where the poet works: transformingly transforming.[11]

Lashing out simultaneously against a poetics of static images and one of didactic statements, Ammons proposes action or behavior as an intermediate element that can allow for both concrete and abstract understandings. The rather clumsy term "actamist" suggests a half-hearted attempt to formulate a poetic school along the lines of Pound's imagism, Zukofsky's objectivism, and Olson's projectivism. Four years later Ammons replaced the term with "actionism" in a series of unpublished prose notes. There he defines his new mode as "the marriage of ballad and lyric," which gives rise to another neologism, "ballyric." His essential aim in these notes continues to be the development of a poetics that can mediate between concrete and abstract levels of meaning, now metaphorically evoked by the terms "anchor" and "wing":

> I think I'm going to wind up by talking about the achievement of the concrete in poems by reported acts. I also want to say something about the imaginative range that can be gained by symbolic acts. That is, just as in the lyric objects can convey both a concrete and a general level, acts can in the ballad (and elsewhere, I hope to show) provide both specific anchor and, by the arrangement of the acts, general "wing." I mean by anchor and wing, earth and air, concrete and imagined, specific and general. The better poem is both anchor and wing.[12]

Ammons is juggling many terms and categories here, but his main interest is in the kind of unvarnished narrative he associates with ballads:

> The place to look for acts, events, meaningful sequences of events, is the ballad. There the acts are stated, reported as flatly as possible, as colorlessly, as impersonally. I'm certain this is not a fine accidence but a willed effect, the result of knowledgeable artfulness, even though the ballad originated among the common people, supposedly artless.[13]

Though he initially claims that both ballads and lyrics balance concreteness and generality, or anchor and wing, in a later draft Ammons posits a one-to-one alignment, then elaborates on how ballads anchor themselves in the realm of fact:

The ballad, I think tends to be an anchor: the lyric, a wing. Tends to be. I'm not trying to suggest pure distinctions here. I just want to isolate (and hence to that extent, falsify) certain salient features of ballads and lyrics.

The ballad creates a climate in which the events reported can be accepted as actual: the events are facts, they are as real, specific, concrete, as objects.

"Up and spak an eldern knicht,
Sat at the kings richt kne:"

We are not moved to doubt the actuality of this event. It's too specific. The knight was old, not young, or middle-aged. He sat at the king's right, not left, knee. It is the narrative, then, the series of reported events, that provides earth and anchor. The sky, the wing, are created in the reader somewhat in proportion to the degree of his belief in the actuality, reality, of the events. Since the narrator of the events acts merely as a recording machine, the "truth" content of the events seems even more heightened. People are predisposed to believe that every man tells a story his own way: in telling the story, the man betrays some emotion, indicating that he was more than an impartial observer.[14]

The kind of matter-of-fact reportage that Ammons ascribes to ballads seems to preclude both lyricism and the "wing" of abstract meaning; hence the need for a hybrid genre, the ballyric. Two years later Ammons gave these thoughts further articulation in a short piece called "Actionism":

Many of my early poems were dramatic lyrics. The action was often symbolic, the events rather improbable. Such as

So I left and walked up into the air
and sat down in a cool draft
my face hot from watching the fire
    When morning came
I looked down at the ashes
and rose and walked out of the world

from a poem in *Ommateum* written about 1951. I found out things about the nature of an event. An event is remarkably unifying. Purpose, time, personality, chance, plan, everything reaches expression in the moment of happening, in event.

Second, an event can have a factual ordinariness about it. That is, it can anchor a poem in a kind of reality. An event has a concreteness equal to that of images, of objects: it externalizes. So, the poem, however fantastic and imaginative, seems credible.

Third, an ordered sequence of events, a plot, produces a level of unity higher than that expressed in a single event.

Event. What happened. The newspaper, the tale, the ballad, the story. We are specially susceptible to belief in the reported fact.

I called this *actionism* because I needed a word. But it's not a limiting as much as a unifying word—that is, it opens out. It comprehends the lyric of image and personal response and adds, as already said, character and all the inscrutable probable and improbable consequences of human engagement.

Event sums up and ties down. It anchors the poem and releases the imagination.[15]

Although he has by now abandoned the unwieldy term "ballyric," the notion of a poetic style that synthesizes the narrative plainness of ballad and the expressive intensity of lyric continues to inform Ammons's account of actionism. By this point *event* has supplanted *action* as his key term; eventually he would take up the even more basic word "motion" to denote all the processes, both physical and mental, that his poetry seeks to encompass and narrate.

Even as Ammons was working to formulate his ideas about the blending of balladic narrative and lyric expression, his own poetry was moving in quite a different direction, away from the mythic sweep of *Ommateum* and toward a more intimate engagement with both the natural world and quotidian experience. In a sense, all these prose statements, up to and including the *Diacritics* interview, represent Ammons's retrospective attempts to understand and justify his early work in light of what followed it. Yet Ammons never entirely abandoned the mythic mode of *Ommateum*, which makes occasional reappearances in his later poetry, most memorably, perhaps, in the dedicatory verses to *Sphere* ("I went to the summit and stood in the high nakedness").[16] As for the ballad, a form that might in its traditional guise seem wholly at odds with his poetics, Ammons invokes it explicitly in a poem from his 1975 book, *Diversifications*, titled simply "Ballad." The speaker of the poem engages in a lively "discussion" with a willow tree and a water oak that are competing for the same space.

I want to know the unity in all things and the difference
between one thing and another
    I said to the willow
and asked what it wanted to know: the willow said it
wanted to know how to get rid of the wateroak
that was throwing it into shade every afternoon at 4 o'clock:[17]

Most readers would be hard-pressed to say what makes this poem a ballad. It displays none of the usual prosodic features associated with the form, and its content is very far from the folktales and historical vignettes typically related by ballads. When we know how closely Ammons identified the ballad with narrative in general, however, the title begins to make more sense. The poem's narrative character only reveals itself in the third line, after an opening statement of the one:many theme that so preoccupied Ammons. Though he deliberately blurs the distinction between reported speech and narration by omitting quotation marks, the line "I said to the willow" definitively shifts the poem into a past tense narrative frame. Yet the substance of that narrative is rather slight, consisting entirely of a conversation between the speaker and the willow. In this respect the poem is closer to a dialogue than a narrative, a quality it shares with traditional ballads like "Lord Randall."

The nearest antecedent for the poem in Ammons's own oeuvre may be "I Went Out to the Sun" in *Ommateum*, in which the speaker acts as mediator in the ancient rivalry between sun and moon. "Ballad" differs from that poem in its strong conceptual core; the conflict between willow and water oak becomes an occasion to ponder "the unity in all things," as well as the differences that breed competition and resentment. Like "Mountain Talk," "Ballad" is essentially a didactic poem recast as a parable. Nothing really happens in the poem beyond the speaker's articulation of a philosophical perspective that neither tree can be expected to embrace. Indeed, there is a touch of self-deprecating humor in his final proposal to approach the water oak with "our powerful concept . . . / and see if he will be moved." A poet may talk to a tree, and under the right circumstances the tree may even talk back, but no poet, however eloquent, can persuade a tree to give up its share of sunlight. The last word underscores the joke; the tree is as likely to be "moved" by the poet's argument as it is to move from its rooted position. The poem's narrative form gives a sharp satiric edge to the perennial conflict between idealism and self-interest, while anchoring its philosophical gestures in the bedrock of act and event.

Procedures

Ammons was fully aware of his own didactic tendencies. Few contemporary poets have been more given to large, abstract statements. Yet it's precisely because he wanted the freedom to include such statements in his poems that Ammons insisted again and again on the fundamentally narrative character of his work. Poems may incorporate discursive statements, but for Ammons, their real interest lies not in the statements themselves but in the emotional arc that connects them. This principle is especially crucial to his long poems, which wander freely among ideas and incidents without claiming any underlying coherence beyond their own movement. While we don't usually think of such associative wandering in terms of narrative, for Ammons this simply marks a limitation in our understanding of the term. In a 1983 interview with Richard Jackson, he says,

> I think we use the word "narrative" in too limited a way. That is, any qualitative progression is also a narrative. I like to have the narrative of the surface, the actions and events that are described, but in reading the poem one should realize that a deeper narrative has taken place. That narrative is made up of the shifts in one's feelings and sensibilities about things.[18]

This kind of deeply internalized narrative forms the basis of Ammons's first book-length poem, *Tape for the Turn of the Year*, marking a radical departure from the mythic narratives of his earlier work. In a key passage Ammons distinguishes his central story from that of another famous wanderer:

> my story is how
> a man comes home
> from haunted
> lands and transformations:[19]

Ammons's version of the great Odyssean story of homecoming does not assume a sequential, linear form but "stands still" while manifesting a continual inner turbulence. Ammons was not the first modern writer to adapt the Homeric epic to a more internalized medium, yet despite its unprecedented exploration of consciousness, Joyce's *Ulysses* retains the traditional novelistic accoutrements of character and event. Though Ammons offers teasing bits of narrative along the way—anticipations of a job offer from Cornell, reports of a plane crash over Delaware, reminiscences of his North Carolina boyhood—the primary substance of the poem is a tissue of haphazard reflections and observations held together merely by contiguity in time and a profound commitment to an idea of home, not as a geographic destination but as a condition to be constantly renewed.[20]

Yet if the poem's narrative content is essentially internal, a variable flux of thought, feeling, and perception, *Tape for the Turn of the Year* does possess an external "plot" of sorts as well. That plot involves the passage of the spool of adding machine tape on which it's being written through the poet's typewriter and into the wastebasket at his feet:

> but the story, tho
> > contained,
> unwinds on this roll
> with time & event: grows
> like a tapeworm, segment
> by
> segment: turns
> > stream corners: issues
> in low
> silence
> > like a snake
> > from its burrow: but
> unwinding and unwound, it
> coils again on
> the floor
> into the unity of its
> > conflicts:[21]

The process or procedure of composition lends a kind of narrative body to the deeper story of homecoming, acceptance, and restoration that pulses beneath every line of the poem. In the same interview with the *Manhattan Review* in which Ammons explains why he can't write fiction, he suggests that "procedure could come to be the essential narrative."[22] *Tape for the Turn of the Year* establishes the procedural basis for all of Ammons's long poems, from *Sphere* and *The Snow Poems* to *Garbage* and *Glare*, each of which tells the story of its own unwinding through turns, segmentations, and silences, and each of which ends by coiling back into itself, its various conflicts and tensions not resolved but merely gathered up into the totality of the completed work.

A few years after the publication of *Tape for the Turn of the Year*, Ammons reflected on its narrative form in a letter to his friend and critical champion Harold Bloom (who had not been especially taken with the poem):

> I made the narrative a matter of getting to the other end—so that the arbitrary cut-off point became absolutely functional, organic to the narrative. I hoped that this narrative of achieving a goal, getting to the other end, would be a criticism of goals in novel and in life, that we kid ourselves that we are reaching goals when, indeed, all we are reaching is the other end of our lives.[23]

In this account the fulfillment of the plan to reach the end of the tape becomes a reductio ad absurdum of all teleological designs, a laying bare of the arbitrary closure on which stories depend. The poem's progress from one end of the tape to the other at once satisfies and parodies the basic human hunger for what Frank Kermode calls "the sense of an ending." Yet such is the power of narrative even when reduced to its most basic elements—beginning, middle, and end, or expectation, movement, and completion—that the conclusion of *Tape for the Turn of the Year* is surprisingly moving:

> I've given
> you my
> emptiness: it may
> not be unlike
>> your emptiness:
>> in voyages, there
>> are wide reaches
>> of water
>> with no islands:
> [. . .]
> the roll has lifted
> from the floor &
> our journey is done:
> thank you

for coming: thank
you for coming along:

the sun's bright:
the wind rocks the
    naked trees:
    so long:[24]

In an essay composed shortly after *Tape for the Turn of the Year*, Ammons
wrote, "The walk magnified is the journey, and probably no figure has
been used more often than the journey for both the structure and concern
of an interior seeking."[25] Both walk and journey figure in this closing passage less as emblems of purposeful movement than as embodiments of
the experiential continuum Ammons sets out to transcribe in all its fluid
interplay of vacancy and meaning.

Ammons continued to write on rolls of tape for the rest of his career,
though he didn't always make them an explicit element of the poem's design.
His last book-length poem, *Glare*, consists of two parts, "Strip" and "Scat
Scan," the second of which was composed on a significantly wider tape than
the first. That physical difference fosters distinct perspectives on language
and mortality; the first part is punctuated by complaints about the cramped
space in which the poet must work, while the second manifests a looser,
more playful sense of possibility. The movement from one tape to another
itself constitutes a kind of procedural narrative, one that seems designed
to counter the inexorable constriction of age, another major theme in the
poem. Ammons introduces a further hedge against the tyranny of linear
time in the poem's first part, "Strip." Like *Tape for the Turn of the Year*, "Strip"
was composed in daily sections, but rather than presenting them consecutively, Ammons arranged them according to a chiastic scheme, interleaving
sections from the first half with sections from the second half in reverse
order; he hoped in this way to simulate the form of a Möbius strip, a recurrent figure in the poem. This deliberate fragmentation and scrambling of
what was originally a continuous sequence might seem to be an inherently
antinarrative strategy, yet under Ammons's expanded definition it too may
be taken as a procedural narrative, one that extends the story of the poem's
creation well beyond its initial scene of composition.[26]

In his tape poems, the spatial medium of the paper roll provides a concrete
measure of temporal movement while establishing fixed parameters that

take the place of a more conventional narrative plot. In some of his other long poems, Ammons relies on weather for the same purpose, to delineate a segment of time that the poem sets out to transcribe or "fill." "Essay on Poetics," "Hibernaculum," and, most spectacularly, *The Snow Poems* are all set during wintry spells ranging in length from a single storm to an entire season (or more—*The Snow Poems* begins with the first flakes in late fall and ends with the last in late spring). One might say that the snowy landscapes in these poems serve as external counterparts to the daunting expanse of blank paper demanding to be filled in *Tape for the Turn of the Year*. Here too "plot" becomes a matter of marking time and space, an artificial frame within which deeper narratives of feeling and sensibility can unfold. By contrast, Ammons's most celebrated long poems, *Sphere* (which won the Bollingen Prize in 1974) and *Garbage* (National Book Award winner, 1993), employ more thematic procedures to create narrative continuity and closure. Each takes a single image—the earth viewed from space, a massive garbage heap seen from I-95—as its point of departure, freely wandering along paths of digression and rumination while periodically circling back to its central trope. But while the presence of a governing symbol makes these poems feel more conventionally unified (which may in turn help explain their enthusiastic reception), they too are essentially procedural works, shaped not by external events but by their own compositional acts.

In "Hibernaculum," Ammons offers a key statement of the principle underlying all his long poems: "procedure's the only procedure: if things don't add / up, they must interest at every moment."[27] In the absence of plot and character, the poem must find other ways to hold the reader's attention; for Ammons, these ways may include verbal wit, descriptive precision, lyrical flights, rhetorical gestures, and provocations of all kinds. An unpublished prose fragment from 1984 explores an athletic analogue to this kind of extended performance:

> The gymnast's routine is his narrative, a story told over and over. But it is an almost totally empty narrative, the subject matter no more than the windings in and out of the major moves between mounting and dismounting. The content becomes the manner of execution, not a programmatics. The gymnast's tension, flow, grace, and mastery are subsumed within a power and force, a largeness, that converts exercises and routines into spontaneous expressions of free will.[28]

In the course of writing his long poems, Ammons develops a remarkably varied repertoire of moves that together can be said to define a largeness. Winding in and out, leaping and tumbling, mounting and dismounting, they chronicle a mind wholly engaged in its own procedures, telling over and over the story of its own motions.

Anecdotes

Ammons's shift from myth to procedure as his preferred narrative mode carried him still further from the realm of the interpersonal and deeper into the solitude that he felt was his fated condition. Where his early mythic poems record conversations with mountains and the wind, his long procedural poems commune primarily with paper and typewriter, inanimate objects that rarely talk back to the poet. (To be fair, Ammons's long poems also contain moving reminiscences of childhood, as well as other stories and vignettes not directly bound to the scene of composition, yet these local narratives remain subordinate to the poem's broader procedural design.) In the last two decades of Ammons's career he began to feel less alienated from other people, and as a result his poems increasingly engage with social landscapes: farmer's markets, malls, fast-food restaurants, hospitals. A new narrative style emerges in the late work that might be described as anecdotal. The speaker in these poems is typically an observer rather than a protagonist, encountering small instances of behavior that provide glimpses into a shared wellspring of feeling and desire. Ammons does not presume to paint fully rounded portraits of other human beings; his temperamental doubt still forbids such imaginative license. But other minds no longer seem radically inaccessible to him. He's particularly drawn to older people, in part because he identifies with them, but also because extreme age often simplifies character and motivation, making them more easily legible.

Ammons's 1981 collection, *A Coast of Trees*, contains two superb poems that tell complementary stories about married couples faced with physical and mental deterioration. As its title suggests, "Sweetened Change" is essentially cheerful in its emphasis on adaptation and accommodation:

The small white-headed man pops out
his side and begins the ten-minute

procedure of getting her out of the car:
he unloads the wheelchair first:
the wife, snow white, gets turned
around, the toes so carefully tender
and tended, till she sits looking as
if headed sideways:[29]

Ammons's interest in the narrative possibilities of procedure remains in evidence, but here the "procedure" being limned is the purely physical one of "getting her out of the car," a complicated series of maneuvers that quietly advertises the couple's profound intimacy. Characteristically, Ammons focuses on the sheer mechanics of the process and lets its emotional meaning emerge in the interstices, helped along by small touches of metaphor. "Parting" offers a much more tragic picture of a marriage burdened by the effects of age:

She was already lean when
a stroke or two slapped
her face like drawn
claw prints: akilter, she
ate less and

sat too much on the edge
of beds looking a width too
wide out of windows:
she lessened: getting
out for a good day, she sat

on the bench still and
thin as a porch post:
the children are all
off, she would think, but a
minute later,

startle, where are the children,
as if school had let
out: her husband watched
her till loosened away himself
for care: then,

seeming to know but never
quite sure, she was put in
a slightly less hopeful
setting: she watched her
husband tremble in to call

and shoot up high head-bent
eyes: her mind
flashed clear through, she was
sure of it, she had seen
that one before: her husband

longed to say goodbye or else
hello, but the room stiffened
as if two lovers had just caught
on sight, every move rigid
misfire in that perilous fire.[30]

Here the affliction at hand is mental rather than physical, and so precludes
the cheerful absorption in procedure that keeps the couple in "Sweetened
Change" connected. Much of the poem's narrative energy comes from a series
of charged words—"akilter," "lessened," "startle," "loosened," "tremble,"
"stiffened," "misfire"—that act like small verbal bombs, hastening the story
toward its unbearably poignant conclusion, as husband and wife face each
other for the last time with all the intensity and apprehension of new lovers.
Even in this bleak scenario, Ammons is moved by the fragile intimacy of
the couple's encounter; ironically, the Alzheimer's-afflicted wife's shattered
memory fosters a renewal of their love, if one more bitter than sweet.

One of Ammons's very last poems, "Right Call," written just a few months
before the stroke that ended his writing life, focuses on an elderly couple
whose situation is considerably less dire:

This old man, a lump with a hat on it,
red nose, ugly cane, lounges on one of
Wal-Mart's inside wooden benches: a

blonde old woman, wife or near wife, comes
up to him and tells him about something
she wants, I couldn't hear what: "how

much do you need," he says, leaning over
to the right to get his backpocket wallet
out: "I don't know," she says—what

appealing uncertainty! opening up rooms
for truth and trust: "five or ten dollars,"
she says, and he gives her a ten: I bet

if she'd asked for a ten he'd have questioned
her beyond a five: the little stories!
where hardly anything happens except the world.[31]

The poem savors the small nuances and undercurrents of a seemingly
inconsequential exchange, finding in it a synecdoche for nothing less than
the world itself. Disarmingly straightforward in manner, it nevertheless
manages some deft maneuvers, beginning with its opening phrase, at once
an echo of a children's song ("*this* old *man*"), an act of deictic specification
("*this* old man"), and a bit of idiomatic narration ("this *old man*"). Initially
described in grotesquely physical terms, the man takes on a quiet dignity
by giving his wife the larger of the two sums she names. That small excess,
a homely manifestation of marital love drained of all romance, is presum-
ably the "right call" of the title, though one that might easily have gone the
other way had the wife not played her part. Ammons sees in this little dance
of request and fulfillment a moving example of human connection in its
barest form. Yet he also recognizes that this is just one of the myriad "little
stories" that make up the world.

Metanarratives

We might detect in Ammons's late turn to "little stories," after the "great
story" invoked in *Tape for the Turn of the Year* and other long poems, a version of the gesture that closes "Mountain Talk": "so I went on / counting my
numberless fingers." Counting and recounting such endlessly particular
stories becomes a way for Ammons to come down from the mountain, to
rejoin the world of other people that had once seemed so foreign and inscrutable. Which leads me to the fourth kind of narrative that Ammons's
poetry encompasses. This is what we might call the metanarrative formed
by his poetry as a whole, the story of the poet's development from the be-

ginning to the end of his career. It's a story I have a particular interest in, since I'm currently writing a biography of Ammons. It's also a story that Ammons himself deliberately chose to foreground in assembling his *Collected Poems*. Unlike most such collections, the volume is not an omnibus of Ammons's individual books as originally published but instead arranges poems in their order of composition. For Ammons, the lived movement from poem to poem has a narrative interest that transcends more artificial schemes.[32] That narrative is simply a larger version of the kind of narrative form he claims for his individual poems, a narrative made up of "shifts in one's feelings and sensibilities about things."

I hope in this essay to have hinted at the broad story of Ammons's career, which is the story of a lonely man traveling from the haunted lands of myth through the transformations of procedure, finally coming home to the shared world of human attachment.

Notes

1. Philip Fried, "'A Place You Can Live In': An Interview with A.R. Ammons," in *Critical Essays on A. R. Ammons*, ed. Robert Kirschten (New York: G. K. Hall, 1997), 110.

2. A sampling of Ammons's unpublished short fiction can be found in Roger Gilbert, ed., "This Is Just a Place: The Life and Work of A. R. Ammons," special issue, *Epoch* 52.3 (2004).

3. Fried, "'A Place You Can Live In,'" 110–111.

4. A. R. Ammons, *Ommateum, with Doxology*, new ed. (New York: W. W. Norton, 2006), 36.

5. Ibid., 38.

6. Jonathan Culler, *The Pursuit of Signs: Semiotics, Literature, Deconstruction*, rev. ed. (Ithaca, NY: Cornell University Press, 2001), 152.

7. David I. Grossvogel, "Interview / A. R. Ammons," *Diacritics* 3 (Winter 1973): 47.

8. A. R. Ammons, "Mountain Talk," in *Collected Poems 1951–1971* (New York: W. W. Norton, 1972), 182.

9. Grossvogel, "Interview," 47.

10. Ibid., 47–48.

11. Kevin McGuirk, "Selected Letters, Journals, and Papers (1954-1974)," in Gilbert, "This Is Just a Place," 598.

12. Ammons, "Actionism," "Actionism and the Ballyric" (two versions), three

unpaginated typescripts, Journal 33, A. R. Ammons Papers, Cornell University, Ithaca, NY.

13. Ammons, "Actionism and the Ballyric."

14. Ibid.

15. A. R. Ammons, "Actionism," unpaginated typescript, A. R. Ammons Papers, East Carolina University, Greenville, NC.

16. A. R. Ammons, *Sphere* (New York: W. W. Norton, 1973), front matter.

17. A. R. Ammons, "Ballad," in *Diversifications* (New York: W. W. Norton, 1975), 40–41.

18. Richard Jackson, "Event: Corrective: Cure (A. R. Ammons)," in *Acts of Mind: Conversations with Contemporary Poets* (Tuscaloosa: University of Alabama Press, 1983), 34.

19. A. R. Ammons, *Tape for the Turn of the Year* (Ithaca, NY: Cornell University Press, 1965), 9.

20. In an important essay on the poem, "'How Does One Come Home': A. R. Ammons's *Tape for the Turn of the Year*" (Kirschten, *Critical Essays on A. R. Ammons*, 150–173), William Harmon calls attention to the lack of any explicit reference in the text to the assassination of President Kennedy, which occurred just two weeks before the poem's first dated entry. Harmon suggests that despite its absence, the assassination is a palpable force in the poem, a "hollow core of shock" (152) around which Ammons gathers his materials. My own suspicion is that Ammons chose to exclude the event from the poem because it would have established too singular an external narrative focus and so distracted from both the internal and procedural narratives he wished to emphasize.

21. Ammons, *Tape for the Turn of the Year*, 10.

22. Fried, "'A Place You Can Live In,'" 109.

23. McGuirk, "Selected Letters, Journals, and Papers (1954-1974)," 631.

24. Ammons, *Tape for the Turn of the Year*, 204–205.

25. A. R. Ammons, "The Poem Is a Walk," in *Set in Motion: Essays and Interviews* (Ann Arbor: University of Michigan Press, 1996), 16.

26. For a fuller discussion of the procedural basis of *Glare*, see my "Mobius Meets Satchmo: Form as Vision in *Glare*," in *Complexities of Motion: New Essays on A. R. Ammons's Long Poems*, ed. Steven P. Schneider (Madison, NJ: Fairleigh Dickinson University Press, 1999), 183–213.

27. Ammons, "Hibernaculum," in *Collected Poems 1951–1971*, 110.

28. A. R. Ammons, untitled, unpaginated typescript, Journal 63, A. R. Ammons Papers, Cornell University, Ithaca, NY.

29. A. R. Ammons, "Sweetened Change," in *A Coast of Trees* (New York: W. W. Norton, 1981), 41.

30. Ammons, "Parting," in *A Coast of Trees*, 42–43.

31. "Right Call," in Gilbert, "This Is Just a Place," 322.

32. For one example of an interpoetic metanarrative, see my discussion of the relationship between "Corsons Inlet" and "Saliences" in "A. R. Ammons and John Ashbery: The Walk as Thinking," in *Walks in the World: Representation and Experience in Modern American Poetry* (Princeton, NJ: Princeton University Press, 1991), 225–250. The two poems were originally published in separate collections; only when they appeared in the *Collected Poems* was it clear that they had been composed consecutively and formed a kind of diptych.

JOHN ASHBERY
AND NARRATOLOGY
The Story Is the Telling

STEPHEN PAUL MILLER

John Ashbery's poetry provides excellent opportunities for studying how a poem's "story" can interact with its "telling." Ashbery's poems often reverse the customary roles in this relationship. We usually assume how a story is told, or the story's telling, embellishes the story, and thus is secondary to the story itself. However, a story in an Ashbery poem often seems like a by-product of some undefined yet significant literary vitality concerning how stories are told. And yet if this significant if contingent vitality can be said to be something like the subject of the poem's story, it only manifests in the poem's telling or narrative.

Early in his career, Ashbery alluded to a similar kind of interactivity between poetic story and poetic telling. In a 1957 review of Gertrude Stein's *Stanzas in Meditation*, Ashbery might be describing his own poetry when he notes that "it is usually not events which interest Miss Stein, rather it is their 'way of happening.'" Stein's *Stanzas in Meditation*, he writes, "gives one the feeling of time passing, of things happening, of a 'plot,' though it would be difficult to say what is going on. Sometimes the story has the logic of a dream."[1] Perhaps to an even greater extent than Stein's poetry, Ashbery's poems consist of loosely related threads of thought and reason that balance relatedness and nonrelatedness, creating narratives of easeful exploration alongside sudden lyrical surprises.

The interweaving of these threads often serves as something like an Ashbery poem's overarching story. However, the Ashberian core "story" is perhaps more aptly described as the poem's *narrative* technique, the form of its telling. One might say the typical Ashbery poem's narrative form becomes that poem's content. Therefore, the poem's telling, its narrative, its narrative shaping, or its generative narratology is often primary and paradoxically the true story of a John Ashbery poem. Any overt story in an Ashbery poem, then, tends to be illustrative and somewhat secondary.

This is not to say that Ashbery's poems do not present stories that are critical in both senses of the word to their poetic workings. Indeed, stories often fuel his poems. However, Ashberian stories can be quite minimal, resembling the narrative lines of writers like Robbe-Grillet and Samuel Beckett by elaborating on seemingly inconsequential details and then elaborating on those elaborations.

This is evident in the narrative thrusts and turns comprising the sense of story concerning time and its movement in "View of Delft," a short poem by Ashbery and published in his collection *Chinese Whispers* (2002). *View of Delft* is also the title of Vermeer's cloud-strewn painting of his quiet-looking Dutch hometown. Ashbery often adopts the title of a painting to title a poem, setting up a tension between the painting as a subject of the poem and the notion that the poem will somehow be a verbal exegesis on the painting. However, there is irony in the title "View of Delft" because "Delft" also refers to a type of earthenware characterized by a round shape, and a "view" within it would tend not to be a singular isolated view completely separate from the ongoing series. It also reminds us that seeing the everyday world means seeing three-dimensional objects such as pots and other pottery, which means our views are necessarily limited because we can't see the backs of those objects. The poem also suggests the small city of Delft, Minnesota, which, like Vermeer's Delft and pottery, also implies a relatively limited or at least down-to-earth view. Connotations suggesting a limited perspective implicit in the title "View of Delft" are duplicated in the poem's opening lines:

> The afternoon is slow, slower and slower
> until a full stop is reached
> before anyone realized it.[2]

The poem's first line suggests a series of differing speeds or "slownesses." However, the second line suggests the more limited number of possibilities of a binary opposition between moving and stopping. Ashbery uses narrative connotations to begin to shape a story that equally describes the "full stop" of a spinning pottery wheel or coming to a rest in a small Dutch or Minnesota town.

The story of "View of Delft" is exceedingly slight. Put simply, as the poem goes on to say, "time is passing," and an imperative seems to flow from this condition:

> Go stack those bricks over there.
> See what the house is doing.
> Everything around you is waiting.

Seemingly ad hoc examples of larger concerns function as narrative markers, or what we might call "tools of telling," to develop a "story" of narrative impasse, and, therefore, "Everything . . . is waiting." Hence, the narrative—in this case, the narrative impasse, or the telling—is in a sense the story.

The major narrative turn of "View from Delft" is the major statement of its theme and the immediately subsequent, quasi-rhetorical questioning of it: "It's all about standing still, / isn't it?" This narrative thesis, in the sense of it being not so much a meaning of the poem or comment on any reality so much as a summation or articulation of the various narrative threads constitutive of the poem's story, is problematized by questioning the very possibility of any kind of definitive thesis or simple story:

> It's all about standing still,
> isn't it? That and remaining in touch with
> a loose-fitting impression of oneself:
> oneself at fifteen, out at night
> or at a party in the daytime.
> Oh sure, I knew it was me all along.
>
> Then the sneezes got up to go.

The poem's speaker remains perhaps "me all along," but this is paradoxically accomplished by "remaining in touch" with a version "of oneself." Time and narrative are contained in something like an intrinsic "story" or "impression," but, significantly, only as the sense that a narrative constitutes the story. What might be termed the poem's enabling narrative tropology, the poem's story, is trumped and problematized, broken up to clear new space for thought, analysis, and conceptualization so that something new can be perceived within the poem's wide Ashberian field of open narrative possibilities. Fittingly, something happens "outside the box," so to speak, and, with little literal context or warning, "the sneezes got up to go," the concluding words of "View of Delft."

"View of Delft" illustrates a layered, multitracked aspect of Ashbery's poetry that is propelled by surprises that only afterward seem appropriate and meaningful/John Ashbery has said he cannot write a word without realizing he could have used another one. This statement poignantly implies a kind of mourning for the loss of a good poetic possibility. And yet the statement also implies a sense of possible equivalence among choices that Ashbery describes is likely reflected in his poetic texts.

Ashbery's best-known poem, "Self-Portrait in Convex Mirror," cites the critic Sydney Freedberg as saying about Parmigianino's painting *Self-Portrait in a Convex Mirror* that "The surprise, the tension are in the concept / Rather than its realization."[3] This account applies as well to Ashbery's poetry, which dodges resolution in favor of a perpetual abeyance that can be experienced as exhilarating because the reader's grasp of the concepts animating Ashbery's poetry is always in flux.

This emulsive quality of narrative and linguistic components existing together recalls Saussure's notions of linguistic stock and utterance, that language exists as all its rules and possibilities in still moments as mediated by a sequence of individual utterances. However, in an Ashbery poem utterances do not cancel or rule out other utterances. In Ashbery's most characteristic poems, the telling—or narration, or narrative commentary— tends ultimately to flatten the stories so they become a part of the poetry's narrative flow, and the primary materials of the poetry—their linguistic and rhetorical flows, their identities as language—are immersed in Ashbery's techniques of poetic narrative and his own peculiar brand of storytelling.

Since the story of an Ashbery poem has so much to do with its narrative techniques, an Ashbery poem's story and its telling are therefore interactive. In an Ashbery poem, story and narrative telling need one another. This is not to say that telling does not supersede story. However, even if story is not dominant over telling, story is still necessary to telling, and a necessary element in Ashbery's poetry. Narrative telling comments on story, and stories concern the reliability of speakers and narrators. Here we may note the first stanza of Ashbery's poem "The Double Dream of Spring." The poem's speaker begins to doubt what he has been told, but calls this "the story," colloquially likening truth to a narrative telling:

Mixed days, the mindless years, perceived
With half-parted lips
The way the breath of spring creeps up on you and floors you.
I had thought of all this years before
But now it was making no sense. And the song had finished:
This was the story.[4]

The poem's first two lines speak of a nebulous sense of time that seems to "perceive," as does Jasper Johns's sculpture *The Critic Sees* (1967), through "half-parted lips." As in the Johns sculpture, in which the lips are framed by eyeglasses, this implies that criticism and language are more disposed to generate their objects of criticism and description than the reverse situation, in which phenomena incite comment. It is in this way that we might think of description, commentary, and storytelling as secondary to the stories they help tell.

The opening stanza's third line equates the generative quality of meaning-making to an insidious yet fresh springlike "breath" that ironically undoes and "floors" the poem's addressee. In the poem's story, meaning-making can be said to supersede what is necessary for meaning. The breath of the poem itself runs past how we expect a poem and a story to work, and in a sense it short-circuits the process of meaning-making through a Pygmalion-like creative power. The next line shifts from a sense of the generative and future-oriented to the past: "I had thought of all this years before."

Perhaps most significant in terms of this essay is how the stanza ends: "But now it was making no sense. And the song had finished / This was the story." The story is mentioned when a song replete with narrative resources ends, as if the story were an unsatisfying replacement for a narrative technique akin to singing. However, in "The Double Dream of Spring," narrative elements continue flowing. According to the poem, "the design is complete" and one "can't have the tune that way," yet one takes "the furthest step one might find" and "little poles pushed away from the small waves in the water / And so outward." In the poem, narrative "locomotives" "chur" and "move." The poem ends with an " 'end of the journey' mentality" "beetling into" a vision-generating "forehead [. . .] As day comes up."[5]

Ashberian poetry's apparently seamless impression of the interfacing of narrative and linguistic elements contributes to the ongoing and flat tone and feeling of his work. Paradoxically, however, this flat quality provides a rich "base of operation" that seems to contain fictive and nonfictive worlds. Like Whitman, Ashbery has developed a subtle medium that "contains multitudes." This method has much to do with interactions between narrative and story. As Whitman opens possibilities of play between content and form that future poets develop, Ashbery similarly opens up plays of possibility between the story and its telling that new generations of poets can explore.

In short, the poetry's telling is somewhat equivalent to narration and commentary about the poetry's stories. In this way Ashbery's poetry is dynamically reflexive, and the reflexivity often coincides with the primary material of the poetry. The flow of language becomes one with the telling, and the narrative telling doubles as the poetry's larger story. A poem's story and its telling interact through a relentless calling of attention to language and its workings.

A story and its telling interact through language. Ashbery is a virtuoso at playing with this three-way interaction. His poetry is first and foremost about itself, in that its subject and its story are both about language play. However, this does not mean that it is not also about other things, for the subject of its word play often alloys or allies itself with the play of other extratextual subjects. For instance, in *The Seventies Now: Culture as Surveillance* (1999), I demonstrate how the subject of Parmigianino trapping himself in a convex mirror of his own making doubles for President Richard M. Nixon setting himself up to be caught through the White House and Oval Office surveillance systems he installs, which in turn doubles for American culture decoding itself after its seeming "breaks from reality" (breaks, that is, from accepted and acceptable realities—the previously accepted mores of society as concerns, for example, informal dress) in the sixties and early seventies. This decoding eventually facilitates a return to a seeming reality under the Reagan presidency that is actually based on the reinterpretation of several sixties-style breaks from reality, breaks derived for very different reasons than in the sixties and put to very different uses. For instance, Reagan adapts an easygoing reluctance to trust government in favor of relying on a "letting things take their natural course" attitude. However, in the late seventies and eighties, this distrust of government empowers corporations.

Unlike in *The Seventies Now*, I here discuss "Self-Portrait in a Convex Mirror" to show how a poem's story and its narration interrelate through language and poetic play. This playfulness calls attention to language as language. Hence, we should not be surprised that these concerns spill over into the subjects and plots of Ashbery's poetry.

If there is a template for an Ashbery poem's story and narrative, that Ashberian model involves a speaker positing an idea, an image, or a situation that is undermined, causing a severe disruption in the speaker's perspectives and indeed an undermining of faith in the significance of his ("his" most of the time in that we perhaps mistakenly tend to associate the gender of the speaker and the author) individualized perspectives, and a revelatory if disillusioned assimilative reaction. For example, "Self-Portrait in a Convex Mirror" begins with an image of completeness—the description of the Mannerist painter Francesco Parmigianino caught within his own rendering of his likeness. In the poem, the painting seems to say "That the soul is a captive."[6] Nevertheless, at the end of the poem this seeming repression is replaced by a new kind of sadness—a sadness that there can be no completeness or any absolutely compelling frame of reference. Therefore, the poem ends with an odd sense of hope established by and within hopelessness:

[. . .] each part of the whole falls off
And cannot know it knew, except
Here and there, in cold pockets
Of remembrance, whispers out of time.[7]

Since the foregrounded story retreats into the seeming background of the narrative telling, its time or plot-line as a hard and fast entity is lost as a ruling master or an arbiter for grasping and understanding the poem. No "part" can "know it knew." And yet the poem's story is still crucially embedded in the poem and becomes intertwined in a kind of "time out of time." Hence, one hears a kind of "remembrance" that "whispers out of time."

"Self-Portrait in a Convex Mirror" can be interpreted as both a failed and a successful search for meaning. Near the start of the poem, "the soul is a captive" held by significance imputed to Parmigianino's painting. At the poem's conclusion, meaning is seen as something that only can be achieved fleetingly and therefore the story of the poem is in a sense a story of failure. However, the poem concerns success because something is achieved and that something is somewhat positive in that the kind of meaning with which the poem begins is relatively negative and the poem's questioning of it is therefore relatively positive. Nonetheless, arching over these positive and negative charges is a grounding of poetry, subject, and story into language, linguistic play, and narrative telling. The poem is a "success story" because it establishes poetry in the conditions and grounds in which it can work. Although it can work on the level of a story, its quality as a story contains huge warehouses of narrative and linguistic play, and it would take us away from a full appreciation of the poem to consider it only as a story. Hence, the story is inevitably one of a sad and poignant form of sacrifice.

Near the end of the poem, this sacrifice is uncannily broached:

> Francesco:
> There is room for one bullet in the chamber:
> Our looking through the wrong end
> Of the telescope as you fall back at a speed
> Faster than that of light to flatten ultimately
> Among the features of the room, an invitation
> Never mailed[8]

Francesco Parmigianino "fall[s] back at a speed / Faster than that of light" because it is as if the narrative of the poem never happens, becoming "an invitation / Never mailed." The self-sacrificing "bullet" Parmigianino takes in the painting's "chamber," which contains Parmigianino's self-image, puns on a pistol's chamber. As in "Forties Flick," there is art and wisdom in recognizing Williams's dictum there are no ideas but in things.

"Looking through the wrong end / Of the telescope" suggests looking for small details in limited contexts. It is not unusual therefore for Ashbery poems to "get off the tracks" of expected timelines that respect a normal progression through time. Playing with this progression also presents interesting linguistic possibilities. For example, another long Ashbery poem, "The Skaters," ends with a paradoxically apt cosmic skewing:

> The constellations are rising
> In perfect order: Taurus, Leo, Gemini.[9]

Similarly, "Self-Portrait in a Convex Mirror" ends with "each" unable "to know it knew" and with a sense of never occurring.

The story of "Self-Portrait in a Convex Mirror" therefore primarily focuses on an embellishment of perspectives on the "story." This changeable focus is a "telling" since the plethora of story data concerns narrative and narration that involves a search for meaning on various levels. A poem such as Frank O'Hara's "The Day Lady Died" demonstrates the informative narrative power that can be embedded in the mere suggestion of a story. O'Hara's poem essentially exists as one digressive story of the speaker seemingly passing time through shopping, eating, browsing, and expressing taste and opinion. However, all the data noted in most of the poem becomes a kind of shrine when it is framed near the end of the poem by the speaker's story of discovering that Billie Holiday had died and then remembering details centered around hearing Holiday sing in a club. In other words, a small story frames, valorizes, and in a sense drives and fuels the poem's many details that in turn support the bulk of the poem. Without these details and data, the last concluding story would perhaps not even be possible since the poem might then lack any kind of an effective poetic field.

When we think of narrative we tend to think of the story as a primary consideration. One might argue that the story *as* story is in fact primary to the workings of Ashbery's "Self-Portrait in a Convex Mirror," especially if one considers the story of Parmigianino and his painting as the poem's primary story. This essay demonstrates why it would be more accurate to consider the primary story as the narrative telling.

A discussion of the narrative of "Self-Portrait in a Convex Mirror" will give us a more concrete idea of what an Ashberian narrative is, in addition to supplying a specific example from which to compare other Ashbery poems and the contexts in which they are written. What then are the story and the narrative of "Self-Portrait in a Convex Mirror"? The poem begins with a relatively conventional story that informs its readers of how Parmigianino's "Self-Portrait in a Convex Mirror" is painted. Nonetheless, the first lines of Ashbery's poem are somewhat enigmatic:

> As Parmigianino did it, the right hand
> Bigger than the head, thrust at the viewer
> And swerving easily away, as though to protect
> What it advertises.[10]

Interestingly, the poem begins with a sentence fragment. What can the "as" with which the poem starts refer to? What is like the way Parmigianino paints his small convex self-portrait? Since the poem's opening sentence fragment examines how "Parmigianino did it" by describing the evidence made available by the painting itself, the poem begins in an atmosphere of self-reflexivity. It therefore makes sense to consider the opening simile as a likening of Parmigianino's painterly process to the poem's compositional process. That "the right hand [is] bigger than the head" indicates a distortion created by the mirror's convexity that is similar to Ashbery's narrative method because the seeming margins of the narrative become larger than the apparent center of the story. Nonetheless, Parmigianino's hand is blurry because although it is bigger in the painting, it is also less focused. There is a kind of equivalence in Ashbery's poetry because his progression through qualification, though verbally fine and sharp in its congregate, is diverse and multifocused. The import of the valuing of the movement and play of language over fixed meaning is reflected by the poem's first line being an incomplete sentence that raises a question within the strong sentiment it advocates in favor of doing something like Parmigianino.

Parmigianino's hand seems to thrust out partially because it is larger in the painting than is Parmigianino's head. It "protects" the subject of Parmigianino, a subject it also "advertises." Certainly this is true in terms of Parmigianino's position within art history since *Self-Portrait in a Convex Mirror* is probably Parmigianino's prime "logo." Similarly, the "hand" of Ashbery's writing—his narrative and poetic craft—"protects" the poetic workings that the poem implicitly "advertises." Ashbery's poem "swerv[es] easily away" centripetally. However, the poem counters these implications by rendering a kind of "bottom-line" description of the contents of the painting around Parmigianino that is a springboard for much of the poem:

> A few leaded panes, old beams,
> Fur, pleated muslin, a coral ring run together
> In a movement supporting the face, which swims
> Toward and away like the hand
> Except that it is in repose.[11]

The apparent quotidian itemization of the circumference background contents surrounding Parmigianino's self-portrait is punctuated by an apparent contradiction.

How can "the face . . . like the hand" "swim toward and away" and yet also be in repose? We should note that this is not in fact a contradiction. One can after all be "in repose" while also be traveling in an automobile, an airplane, or a railroad train. To be in repose implies that one is at rest: however, the word "repose" also suggests that someone or thing is supporting the one who is in repose and at rest. It is therefore not unlikely and is in keeping with the meaning of the word "repose" that one might be at rest yet also moving, while also being supported by someone or something else.

Indeed, when we are in repose on the earth we are always speeding through space. This certainly concerns Ashbery's "Self-Portrait in a Convex Mirror." The subject of the poem, Parmigianino, is a contemporary of Copernicus, who posited that the earth is in a secondary position to the sun and revolves around it, which in terms of Ashbery's poem parallels the "story's" secondary position to the otherwise seemingly primary positions of the narrative "telling" and the language of the poem itself. In a similar sense, in Ashbery's poem what is seemingly in repose can actually be moving of its own volition.

In terms of the relevance of science to Ashbery's poem, the painting *Self-Portrait in a Convex Mirror* concerns glass in a manner that anticipates Galileo, since telescopes require both convex and concave lenses. Indeed, Galileo himself talks of how one can feel in repose while the earth is moving and rotating. How can we stand while upside down?

The image of finding oneself reflected in glass metaphorically suggests Ashbery's method of seemingly talking straight to the poem's audience even if in a slightly mannered fashion. As regards the particular passage under discussion, however, there is a hint of an even greater formulation of the fleeting, if powerfully frozen, quality of content, subject, and story. The poem's quick rundown of the objects that constitute the background of the painting's content becomes a "movement." This movement eventually yields a poem that dwarfs this simple description in a manner that can be likened to how Einstein is able to demonstrate that matter has no substance distinct from the unbelievably massive amounts of energy that "freeze" into small bits of mass yet, as the atomic bomb and nuclear energy prove, can also be returned to the realm of energy, like ice turning to water and vice versa. In a similar fashion, a little bit of Ashberian description yields a plethora of discourse that in due course resolves itself in another image or description.

Physicists have shown that small amounts of matter contain huge reservoirs of energy. Similarly, Ashbery's poetry demonstrates that a seemingly anecdotal story or reference contains vast potential when opened up through the fissure of analysis or, for that matter, when broken down by a kind of fusion method of bombarding that small story or reference with other small bits of story and reference so that a resulting overload causes an energy-producing breakdown of the smallest narratological—in the sense of incorporating both narrative telling and story—elements. This way of thinking about linguistic production has something in common with Einstein's usual method of starting from a relatively simple thought experiment.

Subject matter also causes us to consider Einstein when studying Ashbery. "Self-Portrait in a Convex Mirror," like Einstein's work, has much to do with light. Light, after all, is essential to mirror play.

Ashbery introduces a narrative mode that is true to the world as we increasingly know and experience it. Therefore, even though Ashbery might not have been thinking as a scientist when he wrote "Self-Portrait in a Convex Mirror," it is not surprising that his poetry should relate to these scientific works in various ways. As I have already said, "Self-Portrait in a Convex Mirror" concerns mirror play and the workings of light, and light is central to Einstein's work. Einstein himself pondered the absurdities of a light ray looking at itself in a mirror. The light ray would see itself as invisible because the light would have a constant speed and could not stand still. Light would move at the same speed as the workings of the mirror. This informal thought experiment helped Einstein to conceive of light as both a wave and a particle. In a sense, the mirror would—and from light's perspective does—move around light in its broader aspect. This very much relates to Ashbery because, as we shall see, objects and subjects often exchange positions in "Self-Portrait in a Convex Mirror," exemplifying how referents constantly convert into plays of language and vice versa in something like the manner in which, as Einstein showed, matter and energy are convertible into one another.

From a narratological perspective, we might liken this to conversion of an emphasis on story to an emphasis on its telling, although paradoxically, an Ashbery poem's telling tends to be closest to something like the most direct aspect of the story. The Ashbery poem's narrative telling, in a manner of speaking, is here the energy producing the narrative telling that is the poem.

It might seem like a joke to say that narrative equals story times the flow of the language squared except that there might be some truth in it. Essentially, the narrative is the story interfaced with the play of language *squared*—squared in the sense that it is language interfaced with itself, or, that is, language that is constructed to call attention to itself. It is unlikely that it can be proved, but perhaps $N = SL^2$ describes how a work is poetically effective. Of course, poems signify many things, but it is possible that $N = SL^2$ explains how a poem works as a poem.

Einstein's general theory of relativity posits a curved time-space in which time rides through space more than space rides through time. Since the now classic painting *Self-Portrait in a Convex Mirror* is more or less a constant through time, it is time that moves around it, metaphorically matching Einstein's theory. Perhaps the background of Parmigianino's painting in Ashbery's poem can move yet also be in repose because it indicates a moving limit and something like time as a mere component of light in that we experience time in relation to the speed of light as its square and mass and energy negotiate it. The closer we get to traveling at the speed of light, the heavier we get, and the slower times passes.

And yet Parmigianino's painting is time-specific: "A few leaded panes, old beams, / Fur, pleated muslin, a coral ring." Parmigianino is dressed in a certain mannered style of a particular time, and he is in a room that also indicates a style and a time. The painting can stay in repose within these time markers as it flies through time-space along with the museum in Vienna in which it is displayed.

Following these lines of analysis, the poem describes the contents of the painting as "It is what is / Sequestered." The poem does not merely characterize the contents of the painting as sequestered but rather categorically calls the painting and its contents *what is* sequestered: the part of the painting we have, though perhaps not the living part of the painting that entirely tells what is so artistically or historically valuable about all the experiences and thoughts related to Parmigianino's painting as a work of art and historical artifact. Instead, what is sequestered is saved with some degree of sadness because the present physical version of the painting cannot adequately take the place of all the painting's experiential value.

Nonetheless, the "sequestered" painting is what is available and, economic considerations aside, is quite valuable. Therefore, Parmigianino's painting is sequestered so that it is not, in a manner of speaking, contaminated and destroyed in and by the other eras "Self-Portrait in a Convex Mirror" moves through. That the work is sequestered may neutralize it in a manner not entirely in consonance with its "true" value, but this is in a sense the point: the classic painting is shielded and sequestered from the effects and prejudices of particular times, even its own time.

The poem's speaker then quotes Giorgio Vasari's *Lives of the Painters, Sculptors and Architects* (1550), often considered the founding text of modern art criticism, at length about the painting:

Vasari says, "Francesco one day set himself
To take his own portrait, looking at himself for that purpose
In a convex mirror, such as is used by barbers . . .
He accordingly caused a ball of wood to be made
By a turner, and having divided it in half and
Brought it to the size of the mirror, he set himself
With great art to copy all that he saw in the glass,"[12]

Simply put, "Self-Portrait in a Convex Mirror" concerns and is generated by what is literally and poetically "sequestered."[13] Near the start of the poem:

The soul establishes itself.
But how far can it swim out through the eyes
And still return safely to its nest? The surface
Of the mirror being convex, the distance increases
Significantly; that is, enough to make the point
That the soul is a captive, treated humanely, kept
In suspension, unable to advance much farther
Than your look as it intercepts the picture.[14]

Initially, the convexity serves to limit possibility. However, near the end of the poem, "One feels too confined," and "All things happen / On its balcony and are resumed within" in a "syrupy flow / Of a pageant."[15] The interactions within the purview of the convex mirror, though indeed organized within a purview, nonetheless take on their own lives and interactions.

I would argue that "Self-Portrait in a Convex Mirror" is John Ashbery's most successful poem because of its topos—an all-encompassing focus that necessarily intermeshes all available subjects and plays of phenomena and process, or, in the words of the poem, "the chaos / Of your round mirror which organizes everything."[16] Indeed, in the paradox of the organized chaos of the interactions that ensue, the most vital interaction is between story and narrative telling.

Notes

1. John Ashbery, "The Impossible: Gertrude Stein," in *Selected Prose*, ed. Eugene Richie (Ann Arbor: University of Michigan Press, 2004), 12.
2. John Ashbery, "View of Delft," in *Chinese Whispers* (New York: Farrar, Straus,

and Giroux, 2002), 18.

3. John Ashbery, "Self-Portrait in a Convex Mirror," in *Selected Poems* (New York: Penguin, 1986), 194.

4. John Ashbery, "The Double Dream of Spring," in *The Mooring of Starting Out* (Hopewell, NJ: Ecco Press, 1986), 254.

5. Ibid., 255.

6. Ashbery, "Self-Portrait in a Convex Mirror," 188.

7. Ibid., 204.

8. Ibid., 203.

9. Ashbery, "The Skaters," in *The Mooring of Starting Out*, 223.

10. Ashbery, "Self-Portrait in a Convex Mirror," 188.

11. Ibid.

12. Ibid.

13. Ibid.

14. Ibid.

15. Ibid., 204.

16. Ibid., 191.

SPLAYED TEXTS, BODILY WORDS

Handwriting and Seriality in Feminist Poetics

ELISABETH A. FROST

For Leslie Scalapino, in memory

While the linkage of poetry to art and art to poetry has often embodied a narrative impulse—to tell a story within or about the work of art—the visuality that surfaces in many recent avant-garde works resists narrative in favor of what I will argue is an embodied continual present, an immersion in the moment that the materiality of the poetic text makes possible. The poets I discuss explore not only the materiality of the work of art but also the corporeal itself—how bodies are known and represented. Such works ask us not only to read but to "see" text—to experience what Liz Kotz calls "words to be looked at."[1] During the mid-1980s through the mid-1990s, Kathleen Fraser, Rachel Blau DuPlessis, and Leslie Scalapino all experimented with the serial poem, combining typeset text, handwriting, and image to explore language not for its symbolic function alone but also as material. These poets highlight the concrete aspects of words so that words might function as objects within the poetic text, as traces of the bodies that made them.[2]

Why go to the trouble to include handwriting in a traditionally typeset book? The handwritten performs important functions in each of these poems. First, in these instances, writers, who traffic in language as symbolic, embrace the visual awareness that all words are always already "drawing"—a material part of a distinctive page space. In this respect, these poets remain cognizant of what Johanna Drucker has termed "material words." As Drucker puts it, "writing's visual forms possess an irresolvably dual identity in their material existence as images and their function as elements of language."[3] In Fraser's "Etruscan Pages" (1993), the marks of a vanished language become signs of loss and of the difficulty of witness, as well as a means of exploring the materiality of texts and bodies alike. Recording the illegible signs found at Etruscan tomb sites, Fraser confronts the inability to decipher (let alone understand) the traces of a now disappeared culture. The lack of symbolic function for this language—its very materiality—parallels a collapse or erasure of story and narrative. By contrast, DuPlessis' "Writing" (1987), in particular its handwritten portions, directly renders bodily experiences, all of which are linked in the poem not only with the creation of both human life and art but also with language-making as such. The form and language of "Writing" reflect the speaker's maternal (material) daily life, disrupting the linearity of traditional narrative in favor of an embodied, necessarily fragmented, experience of both mothering and writing. Finally, in *Crowd and not evening or light* (1992), Scalapino uses serial form in a phenomenological approach to observing and documenting ordinary events. The poem depicts human and animal bodies in various states of motion and rest; the page space combines snapshots with handwritten phrases, plunging the reader into a moment-by-moment immersion in word and image, a perpetual present tense performed by the fragmented visual-verbal textures of the poem. All three poets reveal the inadequacy of linearity to the lived experience of fragmentation, challenging us to rethink sign and image, body and text.

There is, of course, a lengthy modernist (and much earlier) tradition of visual poetics. I raise here just one aspect of that history. The poets I discuss employ not just any image but handwriting itself, and they do so not merely as an aesthetic device. More significant, anything handwritten supplies a link to the body—a human, even biological presence that dramatically offsets the *absence* that language necessarily conveys. For many conceptual artists of the 1960s and 1970s, words became a means to *de*materialize art. Proposing that language alone might constitute a work by symbolically representing actions, ideas, or objects, Lawrence Weiner obviated the concrete, eliminating not only the artist's materials but also any physical product. Gone is visual art's power as fetish, a purveyor of what Walter Benjamin in "The Work of Art in the Age of Mechanical Reproduction" called the "aura" of the irreplaceable art object.[4] Weiner's 1968 "Declaration of Intent" transforms that object to concept via language: "(1) The artist may construct the piece. (2) The piece may be fabricated. (3) The piece need not be built. Each being equal and consistent with the intent of artist, the decision as to condition rests with the receiver upon the occasion of receivership." As Anne Rorimer notes, these assertions "sweep away the vestiges of authorial presence. . . . Because of language's unique capacity to be the very substance of the message it delivers, works by these artists are congruent with that of which they speak, since what they *are* and what they are *of* coincide."[5] As a corollary, "what they are of" can no longer be sold as a one-of-a-kind object. Radically noncommercial, conceptual artists like Weiner often resisted the pressures of the market by refusing, quite simply, to make things.

By contrast, for many poets, the exact inverse of this transformation offers a different kind of refusal. Embracing language not only for its symbolic function but also as material, they highlight the concrete aspects of writing to allow words to work as objects. Specifically, handwriting is a means of retrieving the very authorial presence Rorimer identifies as the root to be plucked out of the artist's garden. Handwriting is a trace of the artist-as-person, a trace of the body. In engaged, feminist poetics, Fraser, DuPlessis, and Scalapino explore this notion in works published in book form between 1987 and 1993, preceding the explosion of digital media but falling squarely in the midst of the popular availability of the personal computer. These poems can be seen as rebellions against the advent of the "processed" word, since they engage print technologies irreverently, with the ultimate in low-tech method: pen and ink. Developing divergent idioms, Fraser, DuPlessis, and Scalapino mix signifying systems and modes of representation. As the signifier takes on increasing materiality, it draws us performatively to the poet's body. It also individualizes the work: handwriting personalizes the page, serving (in Derridean terms) as an inscription, as inimitable as a signature. For many women poets, bodies (often, though not always, female) are a central concern, and for these writers, material words become marks of the bodies that made them.

In Fraser's "Etruscan Pages," the remains of a vanished language spark a poetic meditation on loss and the difficulty of witness. In this fragmentary poem, Fraser confronts the gendered nature of historical and cultural erasure, as well as the resulting challenges the poet faces in attempting to explore how art can render the realities of such vanishings. In recording impressions of the lost, largely unknowable Etruscan culture, Fraser turns to multiple modes of address, registers of diction, and visual forms within a fluid page-space, ranging from the epistolary to the diaristic, from lyric fragment to descriptive prose. Ironically, and poignantly, Fraser's handwritten passages comprise symbols whose content has been emptied by history—that is, by the effects of war, imperialism, and cultural obliteration.

The poem that emerges is both visually and textually layered, including mysterious symbols rendered by the hand of the poet. As a serial poem, "Etruscan Pages" furthers Fraser's long-standing explorations of nonlinear poetics. As Linda Kinnahan points out, as early as Fraser's 1980 volume *Each Next*, Fraser "confronts . . . 'dis-ease' with traditions of language, literature, and authority." In the work that emerges, Fraser's " 'narratives' break from sequential, conventional forms and rely instead on discrete units of thought, perception, and experience." Exploring "movement by process," rather than conventional story, Fraser eschews not only predetermined forms but all linearity, since "process, accident, and betweenness alter the sense of language order" in Fraser's practice.[6] Similarly, Fraser's interest in French feminist theory manifests in her work throughout the 1980s, including meditations on the relationships among bodies, language, and gender constructs—subjects that surface in "Etruscan Pages" as well.

The sequence opens with a "Prologo" that recounts the difficulty of even locating Norchia, one of three Etruscan tomb sites explored in the poem, since no paths seem to lead there: "Same wrong direction, again," "blur each side of several white roads." This elusive place suggests not only the sanctity of a burial ground but also the disorienting awareness that its history has been overshadowed, as the poet and her fellow travelers are left "Feeling around for something lost."[7] That loss underlies the engagement with, and resistance to, narrative throughout the poem: the absence of historical record spurs a search for ways not to tell a story but rather to represent its absence in poetic form. In two personal letters included in the poem (one, Fraser notes, is fictional), Fraser takes the opportunity to "tell" what she can. She describes her trips to Norchia and Tarquinia as tourist expeditions complete with "maps and a mostly useless little guidebook" (18), and she describes the landscape, the unmarked roads, even her party's debates about how to locate a place for lunch and what each person wants to eat. As Fraser points out, she decided to include the letters as "an interesting narrative device," one that offers "an almost intentionally flat, low-key register, but the detail is very precise, selective." Indeed, the letters "gave me a chance to speak narratively, as a more relaxed counterpoint to the extremely compressed poetic language" in the rest of the poem.[8] The letters encapsulate the story of Fraser's visit, but they serve more as foils to a profoundly "untellable" experience. The expedition to the tomb sites yields a desire to record what Fraser discovers in dense, lyrical form—to document what she sees and to transform it imaginatively in a way that conventional narrative cannot.

The focus is the tombs themselves, where the only evidence of the Etruscan language survives (save in urn paintings, which Fraser also details in the poem). At these sites Fraser studies "downhill writing / carved with metal object // or red and black brushed with finger / into soft stone recess // above the place they lay the dead one" (11). Early on in the series, renditions of texts found at the tomb sites appear. The resulting handwriting is, literally, drawing: the poet's marks function as visual images that allow Fraser to meditate on the word-as-material-thing, as found art. Yet, just as the letters bear witness to a lost civilization, they also evoke overwhelming emotion: the experience of tomb sites such as Norchia *defies* words. Fraser describes the experience as profoundly nonverbal—so much so that she was uncertain she would be able to write about it at all.[9] In one of the two letters to friends, Fraser notes: "I wanted to write about the trip but I couldn't find words for those places at once so peaceful & full of what was & wasn't there."[10] Elsewhere, Fraser describes the impact of the places seen, "their absence informed by presence."[11]

That jarring absence is coupled with the extraordinary intimacy of the poet's hand at work. Of course, as a technological issue, we can surmise that no type could be set for the letters Fraser reproduces from this now mysterious alphabet; hence, the hand of the writer is pulled into the work, to provide—to draw—the language that cannot be translated, or indeed represented, in any other way. But the impulse goes deeper: "My page wanted to be inscribed as if it were a canvas," Fraser explains, "my own linguistic motion and visual notation appropriating the Etruscan lexicon and alphabet as subject and object."[12] Paradoxically, the intimacy of the handwriting in Fraser's text takes us further from rather than closer to meaning, at least in the straightforward sense of denotation. Some of the letters tantalize with their familiar-looking shapes—an O, an A, reversed forms of our letters S and N—but any similarity may have little relevance to their function in the lost Etruscan tongue. Although the poet's imagination bears witness to Etruscan culture in suggesting the forms of letters and words, the writing finally comprises only traces for which we have no referent. We are left, like the poet, "wanting messages," while in fact "we know what each mark is equal to / but not, in retrospect, what was intended" (11).

Although it is crucial, then, that these marks be *seen*, in the same manner as those Drucker calls "material words," it is even more critical that they be recognized not only for their abstract qualities as drawing but also for their lost symbolic function. The poet can approach this language only by association or figuration in response to visual cues. One line drawing included in the poem resembles one of the many Etruscan letters handwritten elsewhere, but this drawing represents the doorlike entrance to a tomb site: two slightly angled vertical lines are connected at the top by a horizontal line (fig. 1). The image prompts a compact metaphorical linkage of place, shape, and symbol: "lintel of their own Alpha," Fraser muses, but the entryway (lintel) to the start of this alphabet (its "alpha") has long vanished. In another sequence, a suggestive alliterative word game appears: "alpha. aslant. appal. answer. anodic. A. // stooping. struggle. squeeze of light. sling. slate. shut. scrutiny. S" (21). Fraser explains that this "miniature lexicon" consists of words used elsewhere in the poem.[13] In the list form, though, these lines also suggest a search for association, as well as a meditation on shape and disposition. Even as the writing is in one sense playful, a ludic exercise, it is also inescapably elegiac: the poet can never read these signs. Any quest for denotation will be disappointed. Rather, the images lead back to fantasies of meaning, as in the musing that "The Letter A is a plow / (mare pulling into *mare*)" (20).

Fraser's fascination with the Etruscans recalls D. H. Lawrence's 1932 travelogue *Etruscan Places*, yet even this direct reference (evoked in an epigraph) becomes a sign of Fraser's attention to the materiality of art and language, in her choice of the word "pages" as a substitute for Lawrence's "places."[14] By the same token, the poem extends not only Fraser's dialogue with Charles Olson and field composition but also Ezra Pound's and Olson's attraction to non-Western writing systems as "poetic" material, whose meanings are mimicked in their appearance, supposedly defying the arbitrary relation of signifier to signified (a fantasy Ernest Fenollosa, among others, mistakenly indulged). But Fraser's text differs profoundly

1. A piece of the "Norchia" section of "Etruscan Pages," by Kathleen Fraser. Kathleen Fraser, *when new time folds up* (Minneapolis, MN: Chax Press, 1993): 21.

from these forays into visual poetics via non-Western alphabets. Pound, in particular, focused primarily on the aesthetics of the character-as-image, useful for his theorization of poetic language; similarly, both Pound and Olson tended to romanticize and exoticize the languages they found so fascinating. Despite mentioning that she employs Etruscan letters in her poem, rendering them intimately with her own "pen," Fraser resists any appropriation of the "other" language. Rather, her poem testifies to an irreparable loss of culture and meaning alike. The illegibility of these symbols is echoed in the observation that the Etruscans "built everything from their vast and cultivated forests" and "wrote most of their texts on wood." Made of such ephemeral material, this evidence (let alone an understanding of it) has long since disappeared.

Like H.D., a major influence on Fraser's poetics and on her sense of words as both numinous and concrete, Fraser sees the world and its survivals in terms of palimpsest, including the layered histories of words themselves. Fraser, and several critics, have connected both the influence of H.D.'s poetics in general, and the concept of palimpsest specifically, to *Etruscan Pages*.[15] In particular, etymological play recurs, often parenthetically: "(Fibula fabula, blood fable)," runs one passage; accordingly, "*Fibula:* pin; clasp. *The bone in man is a clasp*" (28). Another offers "mulberry *mare, mar Tirreno*" (10). Such moments reveal the search for elusive origins or connections that a layered object—a word—might reveal. For H.D., all words are palimpsests of cultural and linguistic histories; picking up on this notion, Fraser engages in wordplay reminiscent of H.D.'s *Trilogy* in hopes of uncovering hidden meanings.

Often, though, the presence not only of signs but also of bodies—especially female bodies—links word and flesh. Exploring the tomb site of

Tarquinia, the speaker is keenly aware "of the places we longed for / where the dead lived under us" (12). In particular, Fraser bears witness to what she calls the "erotic and celebratory culture" of the Etruscans.[16] At the same time, she also responds to the disturbing knowledge that the female body was as vulnerable in Etruria as in any other period of history: "Rome sends young men to Etruscan women / for wisdom // In war propaganda / they called her audacious." (17). In depicting the distinctive Etruscan urns, Fraser describes the sex scenes in which "unreservedly" (16) men take their pleasure. While resisting any metaphorical gendering of Etruria in sweeping terms (as, for example, a symbol of a "disappeared" feminine or matriarchal culture), Fraser links the fragility of the historical record, especially for women, whose lives are relegated to the private sphere, to the vulnerability of female bodies.[17]

In one central passage, the poet describes an important discovery, the so-called Zagreb Mummy. A female body is found wrapped in linen, each piece "written on through centuries . . . used as 'pages' for new writing whenever the old text had faded. Her family had wrapped her in this cloth, this writing, because it was available" (27). Through a chance discovery, then, a palimpsest of words unites language and flesh: corporeal remnant and material word are at last, fittingly, conflated. Both the image of the mummy and the notion of the palimpsestic text clearly recall H.D., her immersion in Egyptian culture and her search for the feminine principle in the ancient world. Here, Fraser summons the archaeological finding to serve as bodily witness to a vanished culture whose signs are, sadly, unreadable.

In responding to such a context, then, "Etruscan Pages" seeks not only to meditate on the materiality of words—specifically, those of a language whose symbolic function has long been lost—but also to render the resulting collapse of narrative itself. With little surviving evidence to recover, the "story" of Etruscan lives remains not merely hidden but obliterated. As a poet, Fraser can capture this absence only in a work whose materiality and whose fragmentary visual form mimic the loss of historical and cultural record. Like such contemporaries as Susan Howe, whose work explores silenced voices—particularly those of women ignored in the historical record—Fraser employs a visual page to depict absence. Specifically, handwriting in "Etruscan Pages" renders vividly the inadequacy of traditional narrative as a means of witness.

Published in DuPlessis' transitional volume *Tabula Rosa*, "Writing" was the point of departure for "Drafts," DuPlessis' ongoing serial poem (now approaching one hundred in number, each a long poem of its own). As the inception for "Drafts," "Writing" marked a new direction for DuPlessis, through its focus on process and the continual interplay between margin and center, as well as its play with field composition and elements of collage—concerns that continue to surface in DuPlessis' work.[18] Further, "Writing" engages deeply with the relationships between gendered experience and writing itself. DuPlessis creates a dialogue between bodily realities and the social experience of mothering. Even as the limits of narrative closure confront the poet's embrace of open form, the materiality of the poet's life, especially the role of parent, bumps up against symbolic language. In response, DuPlessis reminds us (and indeed herself) that the words we traffic in are also matter. They are wrestled with, graphically, and they are reveled in.

In an endpiece to the poem called "writing on 'Writing' "—notes whose form parallels the processual nature of the poem—DuPlessis lists what we might think of as her numerous preoccupations in this sui generis piece. They are social, personal, and formal: "Writing from the center of, the centers of, otherness," "Making otherness central," "Understanding formal marginality," "Part of the debate . . . between literature and writing."[19] DuPlessis' concept of the marginal brings to bear theories of poetic process, poetic form, subject position, and gender identity. Marked by the theoretical milieu of the mid-1980s, "Writing" creates a dialogue with newly translated feminist texts by Hélène Cixous, Luce Irigaray, and Julia Kristeva. Invoking the concept of écriture feminine, DuPlessis notes that a visual pun on menstruation characterizes all of the poem's pages: each of its twenty-eight sections begins with a period. This play on the menstrual cycle complements DuPlessis' use of color motifs: "there is inscription, writings of all sorts to be read and gleaned. Usually black and white. Intermittently, there is an almost unfollowable flash of (flesh of) red or a related color. Red is the trace or signal of otherness"—a "red flag," as DuPlessis playfully puts it, that marks the site of a female body. DuPlessis also engages with related psychoanalytic feminist theories, especially through the idea that the semiotic chora, the presymbolic, might harbor a disruptive source for "revolution" realized in poetic language, to use Kristeva's formulation. In her list of concerns for "Writing," DuPlessis mentions "Creating chora," along with the subversion of linearity: "Beginning-middle-end, ha." At several points in the poem, she evokes the infant's glossolalia that precedes symbolic language: ".One word one / "word" kkhkkhgggh / Koré la la / [. . .] Conventionally, 'goo gah.' " In this way, DuPlessis borrows the metaphors used in a radical text like "The Laugh of the Medusa," as well as its psychoanalytic frame, to explore maternal experience as a disruption of the linearity of phallogocentric discourse: "Narrative: the oedipal plot? ends by revealing the hidden / father. Pre-oedipal plot? the mother, hidden" (77).[20]

Yet DuPlessis also makes standpoint crucial to her project: "Taking myself as central, yet in all my otherness" (84). This "otherness" does not emerge from any universal "female identity." To the contrary, DuPlessis challenges essentialist ideas by exploring her experience as a nonbiological mother: "As to subject [for the poem]: a first or really second month of a baby who comes as otherness, as difference, which cannot necessarily be understood easily, but demands to, needs to be felt, understood" (84). This is an infant who "comes" (or arrives) rather than being "birthed" by her mother. Even as the poet engages one of the central feminist metaphors for female difference (proposed by Kristeva, among others), she does so with skepticism: "a menstrual cycle, the very core of female difference (they say. Sometimes we say) over centuries of our culture. Getting that into writing." Who exactly is the arbiter, the authority, who wields the power to "say" what constitutes "female difference"? How does the metaphor (or the reality) of menstruation resonate for a woman whose experience of "failed pregnancy" has been repeatedly signaled by its arrival? DuPlessis' way of "getting that into writing" will avoid assumptions about universal motherhood, let alone "female identity." Nor will her evocation of parenting include pregnancy or birth, the subjects of so many 1970s feminist poems about female bodies. As her notes make apparent, DuPlessis does evoke in "Writing" corporeal experiences common to most women (menstruation, for example). But she primarily explores a non-normative role—as an adoptive mother, she confronts the ultimate otherness of an infant.

To render the experience of the maternal as non-biological, DuPlessis makes "Writing" into a highly literary and self-conscious text. As DuPlessis indicates, it constitutes "Part of the debate, or a contribution to the debate, between literature and writing," or between the codified, canonized (or that which simply aspires to being "finished") and the processual. This agenda engages directly DuPlessis' theoretical explorations in her essay "Language

Acquisition," in which DuPlessis describes a poetics of palimpsest: "Can see both writings. Can see them as interactive. . . . place them together in the situation of writing."[21] Her formal enterprise is to remind us both that various forms of writing are everywhere and that all printed matter is indeed material: ".Letters: a readable staining / inked jelly floats loosely / lacking pectin. / Paper: thick rags, even, sometimes / flowers leaf bits" (67). As a writer, she will loosen language, restore an awareness of its origins in a fundamental, corporeal fluidity. DuPlessis renders this corporeality in a dialogue between typeset and handwritten words. Technologies of textual reproduction (off-set printing, pen and ink) become tropes for the corporeal. As she explains, "Making poetry and writing be in the same page-space" allows for polysemy, "marks: pen, smudge, letters, things that make marks or take impressions (Baby wipes). Handwriting (inc. in text)" (85). The hand of the poet is a material presence, almost as visceral as her Baby Wipes, and the dialogue between typeset and handwritten words creates an oscillating movement between immanence and abstraction, the bodily and the symbolic.

In one such dialogic page (fig. 2), the typeset portion is lyric, elliptical, a meditation on letters seen in various metaphorical guises ("A wri- / ting" as "wet carlight" through "mist"; "Letters are canal- / ized as white foams / zagging, a fissure on the / sheet"). A typeset list (probably a shopping list) appears on the right-hand portion of the page, humorously mixing the synthetic and the bodily, the writerly and the maternal, in an assortment of items that it would be disastrous to run out of: "film / fine tip flairs / baby wipes / khaki thread / nipples" (57). Finally, handwritten notes almost overlap with the last series of typeset lines on this page: "tangle of branches unorganized without the leaves," "outtakes, can imagine conversations? / conversions?" Here yet another discourse enters in notations about the writer's thought process, her "imaginings" that constitute an "unorganized" field (a page-space, a scene), a "tangle of branches" that echoes the lyric imagery in the typeset lines and provides a self-referential gloss.

In this and other pages, the handwriting that appears in "Writing" attests to a Derridean awareness. It exemplifies the concept of *différance*, since the handwritten segments cannot be heard, only seen—thus, they reject a notion of speech in favor of multiple conceptions of the written and multiple technologies for the "dissemination" of written culture. Indeed, because DuPlessis' page space contains blocks of text and multiple margins, there

.A wri-
ting marks the
patch of void
foggy reflecting
mist catches wet carlight

that everything tests   film
condenses   fine tip flairs
refracted silence   baby wipes
The cold rush up   khaki thread
the dark dark trees   nipples
Somnulent spots of travel

Letters are canal-
ized as white foams
zagging, a fissure on the
sheet,
tangle of branches unorganized without the leaves
cock-eyed underbelly of
plenitude of

mark. *outtakes, can imagine conversations?*
conversions?
Long passages of satisfaction swallowed up
in darkness.

[. . .]

2. Two pages from "Writing," by Rachel Blau DuPlessis. Rachel Blau DuPlessis, *Tabula Rosa* (Elmwood, CT: Potes and Poets Press, 1987): 81.

is no one way to read or to sequence the poem. DuPlessis notes that the handwriting emphasizes this quality: "in this poem—because of having two poems, handwritten and typeset, in some of the page space—things became marginal to each other. There was no real core. Everything was happening on the side!"[22] At times the handwritten marginalia explicitly evoke the idea of women's social marginality, in literary and cultural history; thus, one page queries, in handwriting, "what were the women like? / Evidence he wrote in *The Vita Nuova*: they / travelled together / and commented incessantly on Dante's / red blotches / his leaning weakly against a wall / for love" (81). The search for the material realities of women's lives (in opposition to their

.The torso fleurie *wanting to have her book virtually nameless*
flying vagini under full sail
twirl out a leaf print *what is the most transperent name?*
the point, sweet business,
treads water   *is everything, or enough — so that*

                           we are where
charging janus penis janus
thick right at the cusp

                     we are.
slowly cover the space
bright disc harken

               what were the women like?
down down down *Evidence he wrote in The Vita Nuova: They*
by the orbiting ocean.
          travelled together
          and commented incessantly on Dante's
          red blotches

          his leaning weakly against a wall
          for love.

idealized image in courtly love poetry) resonates with DuPlessis' project,
just as her multiple forms of writing on this page suggest simultaneous
avenues of thought, feeling, and utterance.

In undermining the conventions of poetic progress—the process of moving through a text as a function of order and of time—DuPlessis seeks to
raise awareness of a far less abstract idea. "Writing" suggests that such
multiplicity has another connotation: for a new mother (or parent) whose
primary daily experiences are not the margins of philosophy but the disposal
of diapers, DuPlessis shapes a text that, like those of Irigaray and other
feminist theorists, both critiques and amplifies Derridean and Lacanian
models of language. At the same time, DuPlessis' method intervenes in
the dominant style of second-wave feminist poetry—largely transparent,
"accessible," voice-based, and narrative:

"Writing" was also talking about women's experiences in a kind of
splay—as fragmented and as serial. . . . The . . . "seeing I" in the poem,
is fragmented and fissured in a positive way. It doesn't seek wholeness,

healing, all of the ideologies of closure that we are very familiar with from another mode of feminist poetry.[23]

As DuPlessis describes it, "Writing" bears witness to lived experience not in the misleadingly neat capsule of narrative but rather as "splay"—as fragmented, material transactions.

But being true to lived experience poses difficulties: "Impossible maybe to write / the techne of dailiness," whose objects provide ironic reminders of the "feminine" nature of conventional women's work: "the coupon torn or cut, saved / as a lacy proof of thriftiness." At the other extreme lies the sensory onslaught of daily life as a child-rearer, the "in- / undation of contexts" for mother and child alike: "little wails cringing," "props. shitskies. / phone. no. ba-ba. / what; was wet" (65). The question of how to show the "splay" of home life must make its way into the writing, in order to be true to the process itself, which is banal and sublime, enervating and energizing: "how / to assimilate   how to discuss   to represent / the pulses of pleasure and heartlessness to ascertain / fairly the moon small cadences" (65). The notational form of "Writing," with its interplay of lines and phrases in indeterminate relation to one another, evokes multi-tasking (before that term was coined). Along the way, we confront a mix of linguistic registers. One section presents, at the left-hand margin, a series of heady questions: ".Undesired acts. Could code. / or the novel? // [. . .] Acts of attention?" At the same time, in a column located in the center of the same page, commercial language erupts onto the poetic page:

I have removed the finance
charge of $2.11 and you
may look for this adjust-
ment on your next, that
is, your May, statement. (71)

Broken into lines, rendered "poetic," this found language, flat and functional, testifies to the challenge the poet sets herself: to represent dailiness in all its fragmentary, but demanding, blandness. Throughout "Writing," the reader experiences the formality of the typeset page, even as we encounter sheer spontaneity—lists, notes—suggesting the continually unfinished state that is more "real" than literary conventions, paralleling the speaker's plunge into caring for another.

The "other"—in this case the infant—is and isn't linked to the speaker's body; indeed, the mix of printed and handwritten passages de-essentializes female bodies.[24] While DuPlessis describes the "period" as the operative bodily pun in the poem, she also points out its abstract and diacritical role: "besides menstruation, a period also marks the end of a sentence. Every single section is written as if after the end of conventional statements, so that the whole poem is in a certain sense conceptualized as existing on the other side of a period."[25] That "other side" comprises at once a reference to a biological commonplace (that what follows a "period" is a so-called lack of fertility) and its reversal (that for DuPlessis, her own maternal body was no longer the determinant of that typical narrative). "The end of conventional statements"—or the end of conventional stories of pregnancy and birth—marks the instant where DuPlessis' experience as a mother begins. It also marks the beginning of a new poetic process. DuPlessis' early critical book *Writing beyond the Ending* explored another kind of continual restarting—the revision of the traditional marriage plot in novels by women. In "Writing," DuPlessis explains, she similarly defies conventional plots. A trope familiar from the ancients through Simone de Beauvoir assumes division between biological fertility (the female function) and creative production (a male prerogative). To the contrary, DuPlessis makes poetry *from* the experience of raising her daughter, refusing to choose between mothering and art. She notes, "For me, motherhood was very generative, and that was a great gift. The poem 'Writing' came out of that experience."[26] Further, DuPlessis makes explicit her resistance to conventional endings: "People worry the ends of novels, / marry. Sonnets like novels." To the contrary, as in her work, "lives encode bounty," a plenitude in which "the end (ends up) every / where" (68). In this way, "Writing" bears witness both to the material action of language and to the bodily realities that cannot be neatly captured in traditional narratives.

Like DuPlessis' "Writing," Scalapino's *Crowd and not evening or light* (1992) uses handwriting to challenge both conventional narrative and conceptions of bodies. A mixed-media work combining photographs with handwriting, *Crowd and not evening or light* performs Scalapino's assertion that internal and external states (minds and bodies) are not distinct, they are simultaneous and mutually constitutive.[27] As Laura Hinton argues, Scalapino "rejects a perception of motion based on linear or chronological time" in favor of simultaneity.[28] Here, that disregard for chronology leads to an immersion in the continual present of the work, in its deliberately non-narrative scenes. The text collapses distinctions between the material and the symbolic, flesh and word, in an exploration of what it means to inhabit bodies and societies alike. Scalapino does more than contemplate the surface of her. She writes of *Goya's L.A.:* "I want the play to be, to reduce to, one's inner apprehension *as* action," and in "Note, 1996," she argues that "One's physical motions are the same thing as their conception." Externality is in the mind of the beholder; there is Cartesian split. As *New Time* affirms, "the mind is action literally."[29]

But what happens to bodies—which are everywhere in Scalapino's writing—in a text devoid of Cartesian assumptions? Unlike modernist writers and artists who tended to assert the immanence of spirit in the material world, Scalapino, like many recent conceptual artists, inquires into the very nature of cultural identities and corporeal existence. On the one hand, she inherits a full generation of feminist work in which identities are often unproblematically embodied, even essentialized, and in which political commitment means putting one's body on the line, often literally. On the other hand, she inherits as well recent theories that destabilize this sense of subjectivity, exploring how identities exist as simulacra, social fictions, linguistic constructs. Perhaps most to the point, long before either of these discourses, Scalapino had inherited from an early introduction to Japanese and Zen philosophy a deeply non-Cartesian sense: as in the concept of *qi*, often translated as body / self (therefore implying the social body as well). Scalapino notes that "In Zen practice 'appearances' which *are* the world are the same as mind."[30] This alternative to Western divisions between the conceptual and the experiential is fundamental to Scalapino's search for new poetic idioms. Finding closure in poems "completely stifling," Scalapino avoids both fixed forms and the short lyric, preferring instead serial form.[31] Discrete units of text, potentially infinite in number, subvert the linearity of a beginning, middle, and end, unfolding intricate permutations that continually defy distinctions between external and internal event. Scalapino summarizes her project: "I am concerned in my work with the sense that phenomena appear to unfold. (What is it or) how is it that the viewer sees the impression of history created, created by oneself though it's occurring outside?" How individual perception creates historical narrative preoccupies Scalapino, along with what Gertrude Stein defined as the "continuous present," a textual enactment of the immediate moment, which Stein describes in "Composition as Explanation" as a form of constant immersion.[32]

One of her most experimental serial works, and the first of several mixed-media series, *Crowd and not evening or light* consists of black-and-white snapshots capturing beach scenes with bathers in small groups, half-immersed in the water.[33] Scalapino combines these images with handwritten phrases. Many are repeated, and they often allude to injustice or economic inequity ("man who's suffering / pushed out"; "drunks who were homeless"; "floating on those who have—nothing"; "people who've always been / wealthy not knowing suffering"). Scalapino's page space is like that of an eccentric photo album, labels askew, or a scratch pad covered with rushed notes scrawled in all directions. The juxtapositions create tension between the rhetoric of the images and that of the highly elliptical text, in both subject and tonal register.

In their very ordinariness, the pictures in *Crowd and not evening or light* defy traditional standards for the art photograph. Neither posed nor produced, the photographs are deliberately amateurish—grainy and flawed. Scalapino described the process of taking pictures of the "crowd" she became fascinated by:

> I was using a cheap camera that focused automatically, and I'd not taken many pictures before. . . . I was trying to photograph people standing in the ocean—something that fascinated me was watching them as herds, a crowd of people, just standing and chatting with each other. I simply stood in one place and kept snapping the camera and didn't do anything to organize it. . . . The terrain is completely flat, and so are the photographs. They give the impression that everything's flat, that there's no inside to them. It was as if they give the inside of something else. I also wanted the photos to be a nonverbal surface that cannot be separated from the writing.[34]

Despite the materiality of Scalapino's subject matter (human bodies), the images reduce to surfaces with little suggestion of physical presence. Rather, as Scalapino points out, these "nonverbal surfaces" become one with the writing on the page. As the semiexposed bodies in the photographs veer toward flatness, language takes on increasing materiality—indeed, bodily presence. The highly immanent text consists of handwritten marks, immediate and permanently unfinished. In this way, the writing exists materially on the page, recording the activities of the poet's body, even as, ironically, the images of the beachgoers approach the disembodied purity of abstraction.

On one level, the photographs—unstaged, the subjects unaware of being shot—evoke submerged stories; they suggest the narrative tradition of
documentary. Susan Sontag reminds us that photographs "do not seem to
be statements about the world so much as pieces of it, miniatures of reality";
further, photographs are evidence, whether legal or clinical.[35] On their face,
Scalapino's prints seem to share this registry of a historical place and time,
an instant of reality that implies, however obliquely, a hidden narrative. But
the most noticeable aspect of Scalapino's composition is that her bits of text
resist describing the grainy, black-and-white shots. In fact, the proximity on
each page of the photographs to the text serves to subvert any impression of
a caption, illustration, or narrative sequence by means of which the text and
the image would reinforce one another. In the text that appears alongside the
photographs, indeterminate reference and open-ended deictic statements
belie the seeming transparency of the captured scenes: "That is that," "not
quite that," "not like anything," "on this" all appear, like refrains, pointing
only to themselves as language, offering no guidance about the subjects of
the photographs. Engaging simultaneously in reading and viewing—neither subordinate to the other—we experience the opposite of what Roland
Barthes describes as the stabilizing function of the textual caption in the
advertising image. Here, disorientation is a repeated experience.

While the complex connections between word and image shift continually,
the visual motifs are fairly consistent. Most of the pictures show beach scenes,
especially human bodies in the ocean; with its repetitions and permutations
of key phrases (often including puns on bodily parts), the text might read,
for example, "stretched out hams up wading on / grass" (50). In the first image in the series, a couple (man and woman) appear to be conversing while
standing knee-deep in the water, which stretches out toward the horizon.
The text reads, "wading in the grass—it is like an elephant / trunk extended
/ on the trunk" (fig. 3). Scalapino has noted that, wading in the water, these
human bodies resemble tree trunks rooted in the ground. At the same time,
mentioned throughout the text, men's "trunks" stand for social convention
(swimming trunks). In still another allusion, "trunks" suggest that these
male humans stretch out proboscises that look rather like elephant trunks;
similarly, these men also possess vaguely sexual "stems" (both phallic and
plantlike, perhaps aroused, or perhaps altogether nonsentient). The viewer
is struck by the flatness of the field, by an equivalence between foreground
and background, despite the presence of a horizon line and the sailboats

Wading in the grass - it is like an elephant trunk extended on the trunk

3. An image from "Crowd and not evening or light," by Leslie Scalapino. Leslie Scalapino, *Crowd and not evening or light* (Oakland, CA: O Books, 1992): 49.

in the distance. Rather than creating depth, these details bleed into shades of gray, blending into the page space and its handwritten notes. Rather than contextualizing or illuminating the image (as they appear to at first glance, given their placement beneath the photograph), the unpunctuated phrases assert a link between bathers in water and elephants in grass. Similarly, another series of photographs shows trees whose shapely trunks in proximity to one another echo the formal arrangement of the bathers—a relationship much of the text underscores as well: "conversing / trunks / on each other." Exploring the dual surfaces of text and image, Scalapino also blurs established boundaries between humans and other beings.[36]

Perhaps the most surreal photographs in the series show fields of cattle with words that suggest social privilege, as in the piece that supplies the book's cover image: "floating on those who have—nothing" (76). Deliberate ambiguities of reference invite us to consider what it means to be human, or, more pointedly relevant to contemporary American culture, to "have—nothing." Certainly the phrase evokes both social exploitation—of an underclass, for example—and the "nothing" of Zen practice, the "emptiness" of mind that is a kind of serenity.[37] Scalapino's slippery construction makes both—or either—likely references. The conjoining of photograph and text puns not just on the beach imagery elsewhere in the series but also on the floating referents that surface throughout Scalapino's handwritten markings. Several appear sideways or upside down, afloat on the page. Further, floating is a condition of the corporeal and a condition of cognition, as in the circular "that is that," or the abstract assertion "it's the same."

The idea of floating supplies one link between the ocean imagery in the photographs and the linguistic fluidity Scalapino explores. An even more concrete example of a verbal-visual pun likewise evokes bodily experience. The phrase "scratch on it" recurs frequently, apparently referring to the accompanying pictures (87, 90, 91). There are indeed scratches, vertical and horizontal, on several of the photographs. They appear as bleached-out lines on the images, folds dividing a glossy surface. But just in case we miss these reminders of the material nature of these seemingly transparent images, these miniatures of reality, a mark outside the frame of the photographs extends the trajectory of the scratch in a strong, straight line. Scalapino explains that a scratch on the photograph appeared during the printing process; the printer offered to try to minimize or correct the scratch, but Scalapino chose instead to highlight it not just within the photograph (making it more apparent visually as a vertical flow on the picture) but outside it; hence the heavy black lines that extend *outside* the photograph's frame. As Scalapino indicates, she chose to make the artificiality of the construct more rather than less evident, and she took the same attitude toward the quality of the images, declining the printer's offers to correct levels of contrast, for example. In this way, Scalapino renders the images *less* legible than they would be otherwise.

It seems fitting, then, that the word "scratch" evokes so many possibilities, appearing next to a picture of a figure swinging on a pair of rings, captured with body suspended midair, upside down, defying earthly rules. Of course, the phrase evokes the photograph's physical surface as well, drawing attention to the medium and its imperfect reproduction, but it also suggests a bodily urge (an itch) or a wound, and it can serve as an imperative, a verb, or a noun. Evocative language appears below the image in one of these instances ("the nudity of poverty / and calm" [87]): while poverty too often results in a form of gross nudity—exposure to extreme conditions, physical (and emotional) distress—the word "calm" suggests serenity. The body here is located in a pure instant, one that in its reproduced state might suggest to us a "fall"—into something like poverty, perhaps—or a more Zen-like ability to be "present" in an immediate and irreplaceable moment, the now. Through the chance occurrence of a printer's error, Scalapino creates an opportunity to reflect on the materiality of her composition, evoking a body suspended in space, weightless, to suggest the purity of a moment in its fluid state, a resistance to the passage of time or to the prepackaged structures of narrative.

In this highly concrete, non-narrative text, Scalapino asks us to consider ourselves as bodies. Even as humans in *Crowd and not evening or light* are pictured as quintessentially social animals (we move in herds, groom and play in groups), Scalapino also uses the singularity of her own hand to establish complex corporeal presence. Both representing and defamiliarizing human figures, Scalapino employs image and text alike to remind us of the animal presence that is our humanness. In this respect, Scalapino, like Fraser and DuPlessis, anticipates the *post*-poststructuralist question: how to understand not only social construction but also embodiment itself. For these poets, traditional means of representation—especially conventional narrative modes—simply won't provide such new understanding. Their works help us move toward a layered awareness of bodies and texts alike.

Notes

1. Liz Kotz, *Words to Be Looked At: Language in 1960s Art* (Cambridge, MA: MIT Press, 2007.

2. My focus is on shared formal and political concerns, but as social history, there is an asymmetry among the writers. DuPlessis and Fraser have been close colleagues since the early 1980s, when DuPlessis was a contributing editor for the journal *HOW(ever)*, launched by Fraser in 1983; they also share connections to the objectivists and to Charles Olson that have made for close artistic ties. Fraser read DuPlessis' "For the Etruscans," and DuPlessis' "Draft 44: Stretto" is dedicated to Fraser; the poem describes DuPlessis' encounter with Etruscan burial sites, forging "a deliberate connection to Kathleen Fraser's 'Etruscan Pages'" (*Drafts 39–57, Pledge* [Cambridge: Salt, 2004], 225). By contrast, neither DuPlessis nor Fraser had ties to Scalapino, whose writing emerged from quite different influences. It is all the more striking that all three writers share formal and ideological preoccupations.

3. Johanna Drucker, *Figuring the Word: Essays on Books, Writing, and Visual Poetics* (New York: Granary Books, 1998), 57.

4. Walter Benjamin, *Illuminations*, ed. Hannah Arendt, trans. Harry Zohn (New York: Schocken Books, 1968), 221.

5. Lawrence Weiner, "Declaration of Intent," http://artiststatements.wordpress
.com/2010/12/08/declaration-of-intent-1968/; Anne Rorimer, *New Art in the 60s
and 70s: Redefining Reality* (London: Thames and Hudson, 2001), 76.

6. Kinnahan, *Poetics of the Feminine: Authority and Literary Tradition in William
Carlos Williams, Mina Loy, Denise Levertov, and Kathleen Fraser* (New York: Cambridge,
1994), 193, 194–195. Kinnahan's "'An Incremental Shaping': Kathleen Fraser and a
Visual Poetics," *Contemporary Women's Writing* 4.1 (2010): 2–23, discusses Fraser's
visual poetics. Fraser's mid-1980s work "Bresson Project" (reprinted in *il cuore*
[Hanover, NH: Wesleyan University Press, 1997]) includes drawing, and Fraser has
worked with collage, both in her own works and in collaborations.

7. Kathleen Fraser, "Etruscan Pages," in *when new time folds up* (Minneapolis,
MN: Chax Press, 1993), 9–10.

8. Cynthia Hogue, "An Interview with Kathleen Fraser," *Contemporary Literature*
39.1 (1998): 7.

9. Hogue, "Interview," 6–7.

10. Fraser, "Etruscan Pages," *when new time folds up*, 26.

11. Kathleen Fraser, *Translating the Unspeakable: Poetry and the Innovative Necessity*
(Tuscaloosa: University of Alabama Press, 1999), 56.

12. Ibid., 57.

13. Ibid., 57.

14. Fraser discusses the dialogue with Lawrence's "Etruscan Places" in *Translating
the Unspeakable*, 58.

15. See Fraser, *Translating the Unspeakable*, 55ff, and Hogue, "Interview," 5–10,
for Fraser's discussions of H.D. and palimpsest in the poem.

16. Hogue, "Interview," 6.

17. Fraser notes that she had read DuPlessis' essay "For the Etruscans" but did
not have it in mind when writing the poem, although she responded to DuPlessis' metaphoric (gendered) associations between the Etruscans and silencing. See
Hogue, "Interview," 9.

18. See Rachel Blau DuPlessis, *The Collage Poems of Drafts* (Cambridge: Salt,
2011).

19. Rachel Blau DuPlessis, "Writing," in *Tabula Rosa* (Elmwood, CT: Potes and
Poets Press, 1987), 84.

20. "In 1984, our baby daughter arrived after a lot of *Sturm und Drang* around
children. That was very liberating, and then I wrote the poem called 'Writing.' That
poem . . . tipped me into Drafts. By then, at the age of 42, I was a late early mother
and a somewhat late early poet" (Jeanne Heuving, "An Interview with Rachel Blau
DuPlessis," *Contemporary Literature* 45.3 [2004]: 411).

21. Rachel Blau DuPlessis, *The Pink Guitar: Writing as Feminist Practice* (New

York: Routledge, 1990), 86. DuPlessis' focus here is on how the maternal chora is continually in dialogue with "the signs of the 'father.'" In reply to Kristeva's strict sexual divisions (and her privileging of male writers), DuPlessis also suggests, "If [the chora] represents the mother, it is a mother visualized as a font of linguality" (85).

22. Heuving, "Interview," 401.

23. Ibid., 401–402.

24. Anti-essentialism has been important to DuPlessis throughout her career. "Reader I married me: Becoming a Feminist Critic" responds to critiques that "For the Etruscans" was essentialist in exploring what was called the "female aesthetic." DuPlessis argues that the essay showed how "'feminine' writing tactics . . . can be chosen by any nondominant group. The rhetorics and strategies are situational." See *Blue Studios: Poetry and Its Cultural Work* (Tuscaloosa: University of Alabama Press, 2006), 28.

25. Heuving, "Interview," 401.

26. Ibid., 401. DuPlessis mentions the influence of Mary Kelly's "Post-Partum Document" (1973–1979) on "Writing."

27. See Scalapino's "Disbelief," *Jacket* 40 (July 2010), n.p. (http://jacketmagazine .com/40/scalapino-essay.shtml), among her last published works, for her meditations on this question. She also discusses the issue in my interview with her: Elisabeth A. Frost, "An Interview with Leslie Scalapino," *Contemporary Literature* 37.1 (1996): 10.

28. Laura Hinton, "Formalism, Feminism, and Genre Slipping in the Poetic Writings of Leslie Scalapino," in *Women Poets of the Americas: Toward a Pan-American Gathering*, ed. Jacqueline Vaught Brogan and Cordelia Chávez Candelaria (Notre Dame, IN: University of Notre Dame Press, 1999), 135.

29. Scalapino, *Goya's L.A.: A Play* (Elmwood, CT: Potes and Poets, 1994), 6; Scalapino, *Green and Black: Selected Writings* (Jersey City, NJ: Talisman House, 1996), 70, 78.

30. Scalapino, *Objects in the Terrifying Tense Longing from Taking Place* (New York: Roof, 1993), 9.

31. Frost, "An Interview with Leslie Scalapino," 10.

32. Scalapino, *How Phenomena Appear to Unfold* (Elmwood, CT: Potes and Poets Press, 1989), 119; see Stein, "Composition as Explanation," in *Selected Writings of Gertrude Stein*, ed. Carl Van Vechten (New York: Random House, 1962), 511–523.

33. Scalapino, *Crowd and not evening or light* (Oakland, CA: O Books, 1992). *The Tango* is among Scalapino's explorations of the genre I have called the "photo-text." Like several of her late works, including *The Dihedrons Gazelle-Dihedrals Zoom* (Sausalito, CA: Post-Apollo Press, 2010), *The Tango* involved collaboration (in this book with the artist Marina Adams). See Elisabeth A. Frost, "How Bodies Act: Leslie Scalapino's Still Performance," *How2: A Journal of Innovative Writing by Women*,

2004, n.p. (http://www.departments.bucknell.edu/stadler _center/how2), for my discussion of Scalapino's photo-texts.

34. Frost, "Interview," 9.

35. Susan Sontag, *On Photography* (New York: Picador, 2001), 4–5.

36. Here, Scalapino returns to a less erotic version of motifs from *that they were at the beach* (1985), in which the words "trunk" and "elephant" recur in conjunction with pictures of people, referring to the human body. But here the motif is more deeply engaged through visual images as well as text. Scalapino discusses these issues in relation to carnality in "Disbelief."

37. See Jason Lagapa, "Something from Nothing: The Disontological Poetics of Leslie Scalapino," *Contemporary Literature* 47.1 (2006): 30–61, for a discussion of Zen influence on Scalapino. Also see Elisabeth A. Frost, "Signifyin(g) on Stein: The Revisionist Poetics of Harryette Mullen and Leslie Scalapino," *Postmodern Culture* 5.3 (1995): n.p. (http://muse.jhu.edu/journals/postmodern_culture/v005/5.3frost.html), and Frost, "How Bodies Act," for discussions of these issues in Scalapino's work.

CONTRIBUTORS

JACQUELINE VAUGHT BROGAN, professor emeritus of English and American literature at the University of Notre Dame, is herself a poet and critic. She has published widely on American writers, including Wallace Stevens, Elizabeth Bishop, Adrienne Rich, Ernest Hemingway, and Alice Walker. Her most recent books include *"The Violence Within / The Violence Without": Wallace Stevens and the Emergence of "A Revolutionary Poetics,"* a book of original poetry, *Damage,* and a book-length experimental poem, *ta(l)king eyes.*

CHRISTINE CASSON is the author of *After the First World,* a book of poems, and was named Poet of the Month by *PoetryNet.org.* Her work has appeared in the *Cortland Review, Agenda* (England), *Stand* (England), the *Dalhousie Review, DoubleTake,* and *Natural Bridge,* among others, and in the anthologies *Conversation Pieces, Never Before,* and *Fashioned Pleasures.* She has also published critical essays on the work of Leslie Marmon Silko and Linda Hogan. She is Writer in Residence at Emerson College.

GREGORY DOWLING is associate professor of American literature at Ca' Foscari University of Venice. He is the author of *Someone's Road Home: Questions of Home and Exile in American Narrative Poetry.* He is the nonfiction editor for the online journal *Able Muse* and the author of numerous articles and essays on British and American poetry. He writes for and regularly updates the *Time Out Guide to Venice* and is the author of four thrillers. His most recent book is a guide to Byron's Venice.

ELISABETH A. FROST is the author of a critical study, *The Feminist Avant-Garde in American Poetry,* and a poetry collection, *All of Us.* She is also coeditor of *Innovative Women Poets: An Anthology of Contemporary Poetry and Interviews*. She is associate professor of English and women's studies at Fordham University, where she edits the Poets Out Loud Prize series from Fordham University Press.

ROGER GILBERT is professor of English at Cornell University, specializing in modern and contemporary American poetry. He is the author of *Walks in the World: Representation and Experience in Modern American Poetry* and coeditor of *Considering the Radiance: Essays on the Poetry of A. R. Ammons*. His essays and reviews have appeared in *Southwest Review, Michigan Quarterly Review, Salmagundi, Parnassus, Epoch*, and other journals. He is currently writing a critical biography of A. R. Ammons, for which he has been awarded a Guggenheim Fellowship and a National Humanities Center Fellowship.

APRIL LINDNER is the author of *Jane*, a contemporary retelling of *Jane Eyre*. Her poetry collection, *Skin*, received the 2001 Walt McDonald First Book Poetry Prize, and her poems have appeared in the *Hudson Review*, the *Paris Review, Prairie Schooner*, the *Formalist*, and many other journals. She is professor of English at Saint Joseph's University, Philadelphia.

STEPHEN PAUL MILLER is the author of several books, including *Seventies Now*, and several poetry books, including *Being with a Bullet*, and *There's Only One God and You're Not It*. He coedits the online journal *Critiphoria*. His poetry has also appeared in *Best American Poetry, Jacket*, the *Columbia Review, Boundary 2, Another Chicago Magazine*, and elsewhere. He is professor of English at St. John's University, New York, and was a Senior Fulbright Scholar at Jagiellonian University, Krakow, Poland.

ROBERT MILTNER is associate professor of English at Kent State University and on the poetry faculty of the Northeast Ohio MFA program at Kent State University. His *Hotel Utopia*, winner of the New Rivers Press Poetry Prize, was published in 2011, and he is working on a novel. Miltner has published articles and book chapters on Raymond Carver, J. D. Salinger, John Steinbeck, Haniel Long, Rane Arroyo, Russell Edson, Jorie Graham, Virginia Woolf, Albert Goldbarth, Richard Adams, Terry Tempest Williams, and James Joyce. He edits the *Raymond Carver Review*.

ROBERT B. SHAW is Emily Dickinson Professor of English at Mount Holyoke College. His fifth and most recent collection of poetry, *Solving for X,* won the Hollis Summers Prize. His most recent prose work, *Blank Verse: A Guide to Its History and Use,* received the Robert Fitzgerald Award.

DANIEL TOBIN is the author of six books of poems, including *Where the World Is Made, The Narrows,* and *The Net,* as well as the critical studies *Passage to the Center: Imagination and the Sacred in the Poetry of Seamus Heaney* and *Awake in America: On Irish American Poetry.* Among his awards are the "The Discovery/*The Nation* Award," the Robert Penn Warren Award, the *Greensboro Review* Prize, the Robert Frost Fellowship, the Katherine Bakeless Nason Prize, the Massachusetts Book Award in Poetry, and a creative writing fellowship from the National Endowment for the Arts. He is also a recent recipient of a Guggenheim Fellowship. His work has been anthologized in *The Bread Loaf Anthology of New American Poets* and *The Norton Introduction to Poetry,* among other anthologies. He is interim dean of the College of the Arts at Emerson College in Boston.

literary traditions, 10–20

literary travelogues, 64

Lives of the Painters, Sculptors and Architects (Vasari), 218–19

Logan, William, 27, 51n4, 189–90

logo, 215

long poems: and Ammons, 194, 195–99, 202; and audience, 30, 103–4; and lyric, 102–5; and postmodernism, 77; sequence form in, 98; vs. sequence, 98

"The Lord of the Castle of Indolence" (Thomson), 38

"Lord Randall" (Ammons), 193

"The Lotos-Eaters" (Tennyson), 38

The Lotus Flowers (Voight), 180

Louis XVI, 126

"Love and Knowledge" (Warren), 141

Lowell, Robert, 84

luminous detail, 98

lyricism and lyric poetry: and Ammons, 185; and *Audubon: A Vision,* 125–26, 125–27, 139, 141; and the ballyric, 189–94; and biographical narrative, 102–5; and broken narrative, 137–38; and *Carver,* 106–10; and emplotment, 133–37; and long poems, 102–5; lyric compression, 98–99; lyric mode, 110–11; lyric moment, 120; lyric-narrative poems, 61; and New Narrative, 103–5, 106, 110, 120; and plot, 153–54; and poetic sequence, 123–25, 141; and *The Red Virgin,* 110–11; and tension with narrative, 3–4, 7–8, 104–5; and *Thomas and Beulah,* 114–20; and time/temporality, 133, 135–38; and vision, 127

MacArthur Foundation, 56

MacNeice, Louis, 31, 35, 41, 51–52n7

Magritte, René, 23

Manhattan Review, 195

Maniero, Tony, 175

"A Map of Dodge County, Wisconsin" (McGrath), 69–70, 71

"March 10 (Barbarians): In Flight, Chicago to Miami" (McGrath), 67, 71

"March Moon" (Gilbert), 22

Marie Antoinette, 126

Marlowe, Christopher, 37

"The Marshes of Glynn" (Lanier), 94

Martin, Charles, 51–52n7

Marvel, Andrew, 14

Masefield, John, 31

Mason, David, xiv, xvii, 29, 85, 93, 103–5

mass/energy equivalency, 216–18

materiality, 221–23, 225–28, 229, 231–35, 236–41

The Maximus Poems (Olson), 162–63

Maxwell, Glyn, 51–52n7

McDowell, Robert, xiv, 103, 104

McGinn, Colin, 156–57

McGrath, Campbell: Halpern on, 56; and historical narratives, xvii; and James Wright, 63; and prose poetry, 57–59; and travelogue prose poems, 63–69; and the West Chester seminars, xv

McGrath, Campbell, works of: *American Noise,* 58; "The Bob Hope Poem," 56, 58; "Campbell McGrath," 67; *Capitalism,* 56, 57–58, 65; *Florida Poems,* 58; *Heart of Anthracite,* 56, 58; "A Letter to James Wright," 63; "A Map of Dodge County, Wisconsin," 69–70,

71; "March 10 (Barbarians): In Flight, Chicago to Miami," 67, 71; *Pax Atomica,* 58; "Plums," 58; "The Prose Poem," 65, 71; "Rifle, Colorado," 66, 71; *Road Atlas: Prose & Other Poems,* 58, 65–67; *Seven Notebooks,* 58, 65, 67–68; "Silt, Colorado," 66–67, 71; *Spring Comes to Chicago,* 56; "Sunset, Route 90, Brewster County, Texas," 70, 71

McMurtry, Larry, 27

medias res, 4–6, 167, 175

meditative mode, 110

memoirs, 67

memory, 9

menstruation, 229–30, 235

Meriam, Mary, 53n27

Merrill, Christopher, 61, 62

Merrill, James, 51–52n7

metanarratives, 202–3

metaphoric means, principle of, 173

metaphysics, 15–16, 19

meter, 28, 30, 51n4, 103, 160

mid-century poets and poetry, 82, 83

"Middle Passage" (Hayden), 175

"Millennium Letter" (Waterman), 39–40

Miller, Stephen Paul, xiv, xviii–xix

Millet, Edna St. Vincent, 14–15

Milne, A. A., 31

Miłosz, Cresław, 67

Miltner, Robert, xv, xvii

Milton, John, xv, 162

mimesis, 133–34, 152, 155

minimalism, 207

mise en abyme, 9–10, 24n16

modernism and modernist poetry: and accessibility of poetry, 99; and Ashbery, 176; and chronology of narratives, 80; and *Death's Door,* 21,

25n23; and dogma of the image, 189–90; and the epic impulse, 161–62; and Gilbert's "Belongings," 18; and narrative continuity, 104; and narrative style, 166; and plot, 151; and Romantic subjectivity, 85; and subjectivist aesthetic, 169

moment of vision, 140, 141

"The Moose" (Bishop), 174

Morris, Daniel, xiv

Morris, William, 31

Mortola, Angela Maria Incoronata Caruso, 3–6, 7–10, 11–20, 22, 23n3, 25n37

motherhood, 230, 235

"Moton Field" (Nelson), 109

"Mountain Talk" (Ammons), 187–88, 193–94, 202

Mullin, Rick, 53n27

Murphy, Margueritte, 57

music, 124, 143n16

muthos: and *The Bridge,* 163; and *The Lost War,* 167; and lyrics dimensions of narrative, 154; and mimesis, 134; and nonlinear narrative, 171–72; and "Over 2,000 Illustrations and a Complete Concordance," 173; and plot, 151, 156, 179; and Ricoeur's narrative, 144n51; and *Saturday Night Fever,* 150; and "states of becoming," 161; and temporal order, 160; and *The Waste Land,* 153

"My *Not* Burns" (Strickland), 113–14

"My People" (Nelson), 96

The Mysterious Flame (McGinn), 156–57

mysticism, 127–28

myths and mythology: and Ammons,

184–89, 192, 194, 199, 203; and an-
ecdotes, 199; and *Audubon,* 127–28;
and biblical narratives, 179–80; and
The Bridge, 163; creation myths, 87;
myth of modern death, 11; mythic
mode, 192; mythopoetic style,
187–88; and temporal order, 161.
See also muthos

Nabokov, Vladimir, 42
"Names/Ugliness" (Strickland), 111–12
narrative conventions, 185
narrative history, 10–20
narrative mode, 110
narrative prose poems, 60
"Narrative Secrets, Lyric Openings"
(Bishop), 10–11
narrative sequence, 114–15
narrative structure, 162
narrative theory, 7–10
narrative voice, 93
narratology, 207, 217
narrators, 8, 28–29
National Endowment for the Arts, xiv
Native Americans, 86–89, 89–91
"Nature" (Emerson), 169
Nelson, Marilyn: and audience of
works, 99; *Carver,* xiv, xvii, 86,
95–97, 105, 106–10; and historical
narratives, xvii, 29; and narrative/
lyric tension, 120; and the West
Chester seminars, xiv
Nelson, Melvin Moton, 109
New England Review, 125
New Expansive poetry, 180
New Formalism, xv, xvi, 50, 106, 172,
180
New Narrative movement: and *Carver,*
106; and fallacy of imitative form,

172; and lyric poems, 103–5, 106,
110, 120; and narrative theory,
7; and *The Red Virgin,* 110; and
Romantic subjectivity, 85; and subjectivity, 93; and the West Chester
seminars, xiv
New Republic, 130
Newbery Medal of Honor, 106
Nixon, Richard M., 211
"No thank you, I don't care for artichokes" (Gilbert), 8
nonlinear poetics, 222, 224, 230, 235,
236
Norchia, 224–25, 227
"The Novel of Consciousness" (Woolf),
150–51
novelistic approaches, 91–92
numerology (Christian and Jewish),
15, 22

objectivism, 190
"Occasionem Cognosce" (Berryman),
84
octave stanza, 31
"Ode on a Grecian Urn" (Keats), 18–19
odes, 67
The Odyssey (Homer), 161–62, 194
"Of Pied Beauty" (Hopkins), 13, 18
O'Hara, Frank, 178, 214
old age, 200–202
Olson, Charles, xv, 162–63, 190,
226–27, 241n2
Ommateum (Ammons), 185–87,
191–93
On the Road (Kerouac), 64
"One Song" (Crane), 163
Onegin stanza, 29, 40–49, 53n32
Orlando Furioso (Ariosto), 34
Osceola, 91

Ostriker, Alicia, 21
"Other Lives: On Shorter Narrative Poems" (Mason), 85
"Other Voices, Other Lives" (Mason), xvii
ottava rima, 29, 31, 32–37, 49, 52n12, 53n27
"Out for the Elements" (Waterman), 39–40, 41–44
"Out of 'Slave's Ransom'" (Nelson), 106
"Over 2,000 Illustrations and a Complete Concordance" (Bishop), 173–75
"The Owl in the Sarcophagus" (Stevens), 25n23

palimpsest, 92, 227–28, 231
panegyric, 4, 6
Paradiso (Dante), 160, 161
pararhyme, 30
Paris Review, 130
Paris Spleen (Le splen de Paris) (Baudelaire), 57
Parlement of Foules (Chaucer), 30
Parmigianino, Francesco, 209, 211, 212, 214, 218
Parnassus, 56
The Party Train (Alexander), 57
Paterson (Williams), 77, 79–80, 162–63
Patroclus, 6
Pax Atomica (McGrath), 58
A Peaceable Kingdom (Hicks), 86
"The Pearl" (The Pearl Poet), 11, 14–15, 18
Peich, Michael, xiv
Penn, William, 86–89
Penn's Treaty with the Indians (West), 86
Pennsylvania, 86–89

Pequots, 91
"The Perceiving Self" (Nelson), 108
Perloff, Marjorie, 172
Petrarch, 14
Phelan, James, 8
philosophical perspectives, 193–94
photography, 235–40, 239
physics, 216–18
place prose poems, 59
Plath, Sylvia, 14, 17, 21
plot and emplotment: and Ammons, 195, 198; and archetypal plots, 153; and ateleological narrative, 171–72; and causality, 157–58; and epics, 160–64; and human consciousness, 156–57; and literary traditions, 12; and mimesis, 152; and movement, 177; and narrative structure, 150–58; and polyphony and configuration, 158–68; and schema, 170–81; and self-understanding, 152; and sentence sound, 168–70; and teleology, 160, 162–63; and temporal order, 133–37, 152, 160
"Plums" (McGrath), 58
Poe, Edgar Allan, 79, 165, 168
"Poem of the Year" (James), 53n27
"The Poet in an Age of Prose" (Gioia), xiv, xvi
poetic sequence, 123, 143n16
Poetics (Aristotle), 134, 154, 161
"The Poet's Zodiac" (Meriam), 53n27
political critique in historical poetry, 81, 85
polyphony, 158–68
polytropic principle, 161–62, 171
pop culture, 64, 70
Pope, Alexander, 44
postmodernism and postmodern

poetry: and Aristotelian plot structure, 171; and Ashbery, 176–77; and cultural context, 170; and the epic impulse, 162; and the long poem, 77; and narrative style, 166; and Onegin stanza, 47–48; and plot, 157; and subjectivist aesthetic, 169

poststructuralism, 241

Pound, Ezra: and the epic impulse, 162; and Expansive Poetry movement, 85; and Gilbert's "Belongings," 14; and handwriting, 226, 227; and historical narratives, xvii; and imagism, 190; and "luminous detail," 98; and McGrath, 68; and plot, 153

Pound, Ezra, works of: *The Cantos,* 68, 77–78, 153, 162; "I Gather the Limbs of Osiris," 78

"The Power of the Meta-Genre" (Huang-Tiller), 14

"Powhatan's Daughter" (Crane), 163, 164, 165

"The Prayer of Miss Budd" (Nelson), 107

pregnancy, 230, 235

Pre-Oedipal plot, 230

presencing, 140

present intention, 132, 134

principle of metaphoric means, 173

Prior, Matthew, 44–45

procedure, 194–99, 199–201, 203

"Proem: To Brooklyn Bridge" (Crane), 164–65, 165–66

profluence, 139

progression of effects, 124

projectivism, 190

Prophecy of Dante (Byron), 51–52n7

prose and prose poems: catalogue travelogue prose poems, 69–70; history of, 57; and McGrath's works, 57–59, 63–69; prose paired with poetry, 26n54; travelogue prose poems, 56–57, 59–63, 63–69, 71

"The Prose Poem" (McGrath), 65, 71

"Prose/Poetry" (Alexander), 57

Pulitzer Prize for Poetry, 114

Pushkin, Alexander, 40–41, 46

qi, 236

Quakers, 86, 88

Questions of Possibility (Caplan), 30

Rabinowitz, Peter, 7–10

racism, 109

The Rape of Lucrece (Shakespeare), 31

The Rape of the Lock (Pope), 44

Rather, Dan, 27

"Reader's Life" (Dobyns), 102

Reagan, Ronald, 211–12

realism, 151

The Reaper, xiv, 103

Rebel Angels, 50

recursive reading, 115

recursive symmetries, 168–69

The Red Virgin (Strickland), xvii, 105, 110–14

"The Red Wheelbarrow" (Williams), 58–59

relativity theory, 217–18

"Resolution and Independence" (Wordsworth), 31

resurgence of narrative poetry, xiii

"Revolution: Simone at 27" (Strickland), 112

rhyme: and *The Alamo,* 27–30; artifice of rhyme and meter, 51n4; and contemporary poetry, 49–51; half-

and plot, 150–57, 161; and schema, 170–71; and subjectivist aesthetic, 169; and Tobin, xviii

Wordsworth, William, 31

World Enough and Time (Warren), 125

World War II, 110

Wright, Annie, 62

Wright, C. D., xvii

Wright, James, 59, 61–62, 71

Wrongful Death (Gilbert), 20, 21–22

"Yahrzeit" (Gilbert), 22

"A Year and a Day" (Gilbert), 22

Yeats, William Butler, 14, 20, 31–32

Young, David, 59

Young, Kevin, xvii

"Your Death: What Is Said" (Strickland), 112

Zagreb Mummy, 228

"Zealot in a Zoo" (Strickland), 113

Zeitlichkeit, 135–36

Zen philosophy, 236, 239, 240–41

Zeno, 168

Zukofsky, Louis, 190